DISCARDED

The Unrecognized Precursors of Montemayor's *Diana*

THE UNRECOGNIZED PRECURSORS OF MONTEMAYOR'S *DIANA*

ELIZABETH RHODES

UNIVERSITY OF MISSOURI PRESS
COLUMBIA AND LONDON

Copyright © 1992 by
The Curators of the University of Missouri
University of Missouri Press, Columbia, Missouri 65201
Printed and bound in the United States of America
All rights reserved
5 4 3 2 1   96 95 94 93 92

Library of Congress Cataloging-in-Publication Data

Rhodes, Elizabeth, 1955–
   The unrecognized precursors of Montemayor's Diana / Elizabeth Rhodes
     p. cm.
   Includes bibliographical references and index.
   ISBN 0-8262-0818-5 (alk. paper)
   1. Montemayor, Jorge de, 1520?–1561. Diana. 2. Pastoral literature, Spanish—History and criticism. 3. Montemayor, Jorge de, 1520?–1561—Religion. I. Title.
PQ6414.A2R46   1992
863'.3—dc20   92-9798
                                                              CIP

∞™ This paper meets the requirements of the
American National Standard for Permanence of Paper
for Printed Library Materials, Z39.48, 1984.

This work is brought to publication with the assistance
of The Program for Cultural Cooperation Between Spain's
Ministry of Culture and United States Universities.

Designer: Rhonda Miller
Typesetter: Connell-Zeko Type & Graphics
Printer and Binder: Thomson-Shore, Inc.
Typeface: Clearface

per a l'Enric
ut signaculum super cor meum

Contents

Preface ix

Acknowledgments xiii

Abbreviations xv

Reforming the Canon: *An Introduction* 1

1. Before the *Diana*: *Jorge de Montemayor and Catholic Reformism* 20

2. Formal Vehicles of Ideology: *Character Typology and Narrative Structure in Spanish Pastoral Narrations* 108

3. *Los siete libros de la Diana*: *Ideological Love and Human Experience* 139

Conclusion 215

Works Cited 233

Index 255

Preface

In this book I relate Golden Age Spanish religious culture with what is generally considered to be secular literature. My central subject is a writer whose life and works still pose mysteries to the literary critic and historian alike; this is not so much an attempt to unravel the mysteries as to appreciate them. Because this topic involves the intricacies of religious history and devotional literature, I have made an effort to provide what background information is necessary to appreciate the influence of that history and literature on Golden Age culture as a whole. Such an enterprise should rightly constitute a book in itself; what follows is but one step in that direction, taken largely because the nature of Montemayor's works makes that step necessary. Mine is a synthetic approach, then, that culls from studies in theology and religious history per se elements of special importance for literary studies. I attempt to introduce readers to the spiritual environment in which Montemayor lived and wrote, in sufficient detail so that they can appreciate its most fundamental complexities.

Because so little is known about Montemayor himself, there remains but one approach to his works: the texts themselves. In modern literary history, however, virtually none of Montemayor's writings except the *Diana* are typically considered as his contribution to European literature. These two circumstances, central use of material related to religious studies and the same fundamental reference to Montemayor's works other than the *Diana*, have necessitated extensive documentation and citation, particularly in chapter 1.

The book is divided into three units which, although constituting an interwoven whole, function independently for the reader interested in one or two of them. In each chapter, the Introduction, and the Conclusion, source titles are cited completely the first time they are used, in their original languages followed by parenthetical translations into English. Subsequent references to those titles in the main body of the text use only the English versions, except when translations would be inadequate. All references are shortened when appropriate. In the notes, they are quoted in their original languages only, again using shortened versions after the first, complete citation. Abbreviations are used to simplify references to the major primary texts used, as well as some secondary sources that are cited frequently. When identification of a biblical verse cited in a quotation aids in the comprehension of that quotation, the reference is included parenthetically; the numbering of the Psalms used is that of the Vulgate. Similarly, first publication dates of sixteenth-century works that are not well known are included parenthetically, when that information is helpful.

Part of the critical design of this book is to make its thesis and sources accessible to those who study other literatures. Quotations of primary sources, for the most part works by Montemayor, Luis de Granada, and Leone Hebreo, are cited in English translation, followed by the original Spanish or Italian and an indication of the source. Also cited in translation and in their original languages are a few important, often dramatic, quotations (the raging fury of the Inquisitor General, for example) and cases in which I am trying to establish a lexical similarity between Montemayor and another author, a similarity which does not always emerge in translation. All other materials are cited in English only.

Although political titles, such as "queen" or "duke," are translated, religious titles, such as "fray" and "santa," and proper names are not. Common Latin phrases (*locus amoenus*) and titles of well-known works in Latin (such as Erasmus's *Enchiridion*), as well as common words and phrases in other languages (*hidalgo*), are not translated. Uncommon foreign terms cited regularly that resist translation, such as *recogimiento* and *converso*, are explained the first time they are used and appear in their original language thereafter.

All translations are mine. Following sixteenth-century usage, in texts from that century, references to the divinity are translated as masculine and are not capitalized. Likewise, "*el hombre*" is always translated as "man," and "*uno*" is rendered only masculine in English. In the Preface to his English translation of the *Diana* published in 1598, Bartholomew Yong rightly refers to Montemayor's language as a "hard and strange kinde of Spanish"; the Portuguese author's style is often obtuse, and my translations grant priority to accuracy over elegance. That is, they often reflect the author's "strange kinde of Spanish."

In his book *Los libros de pastores en la literatura española*, Francisco López Estrada recommends the sixteenth-century term *libros de pastores* for books like the *Diana*, a phrase that translates problematically into English as "pastoral books." Critics have traditionally opted for "pastoral novel" and, more recently, "pastoral romance," which are less awkward but also less accurate. This type of prose fiction consisted of numerous chapters or sections, each called a *libro* (literally, 'book'), which, put together, constituted an entity called *libros de pastores*, just as the books of chivalry were called *libros de caballería*. Thus, in Spanish the word *libro* is used for 'chapter' and also, in plural, for a collection of the same, the *libros de pastores*. To avoid this redundancy, I use "pastoral narration" here to mean the whole, and "book" to mean each part thereof.

This study deals with sixteenth-century pastoral narrations that were written in Spanish. Although he spent most of his adult life in Spain, Montemayor was born in Portugal, and there are passages in Portuguese in the *Diana*. Because his book is traditionally considered part of Spain's literary heritage, I refer to it as Spanish. Also, although the term has an archaic ring, I use the word *religiousness* to refer to the whole of Montemayor's pious beliefs as reflected in his writings. The alternative, *religiosity*, although more popular, has negative connotations that are inappropriate in this context.

Quotation of Montemayor's works is a complicated business. The González Palencia edition of his poetry, published in 1932, was based on the 1554 *Obras* (including the *Obras de devoción*) and the 1562 *Cancionero*, passing over the 1558 twin *Segundo cancionero* and *Segundo cancionero spiritual* volumes, the most significant of Montemayor's career. González Palencia's edition, which presents an enormous corpus of verse, is incomplete and often inaccurate; nonetheless, it is the only one currently available to the reader for consultation. Therefore, direct quotation of Montemayor's verse herein is from the *Segundo cancionero* and the *Segundo cancionero spiritual*, followed by reference to the appropriate page in the González Palencia edition when the poem is indeed in it; indirect references cite the González Palencia edition only, and the poems cited that are not in that edition are so indicated. For works that appeared only in the *Obras*, I cite the González Palencia edition, but correct any mistakes in it using the 1554 text. To facilitate reading, I have modernized spelling and punctuation in passages from Montemayor's unedited works and all of his poetry. On the other hand, I respect the texts of those edited by others than González Palencia because these editions are linguistically rigorous; these include editions of Montemayor's single works such as the "Exposición moral" and the "Epístola a Sâ de Miranda." The editorial criteria used by their editors, however, differ from the ones I use when citing from Montemayor's poetry collections and unedited prose. The López Estrada edition of the *Diana* remains the best one; although several new editions have appeared in the last two years, they are inferior to his. I refer my readers to Juan Montero's forthcoming edition in Crítica. Likewise I cite Juan Bautista Avalle-Arce's 1961 edition of the *Galatea* as superior to his 1987 edition of the same.

I greet my readers, then, as Montemayor greeted his: "In this book will be found some pleasing things to one who brings good will to them, whose correction I remit to the readers, because anyone who reads them is a better judge of them than I" (En este libro creo se hallarán algunas cosas que agradarán al que con buenos ojos las mirare, la enmienda de las cuales remito a los lectores, porque nadie las puede leer que no tenga en ellas mejor voto que yo, SC "Al lector").

ACKNOWLEDGMENTS

I thank Bruce Wardropper for his careful readings of early drafts of this book, helpful suggestions for its preparation, and generous spirit. Francisco Márquez Villanueva provided guidance and inspiration at a crucial point during the difficult task of relating Montemayor's religious works to the proper currents of sixteenth-century Spanish piety. Ronald Surtz offered valuable assistance in the same area, related to Montemayor's "Diálogo spiritual." Isabel Cid of the Biblioteca Pública in Évora, Portugal, provided personal assistance with the riddle of the same dialogue.

For her reading of the final version of the manuscript, valuable ideas, and moral support, I thank Dian Fox. To Willard King goes my continued affectionate appreciation for years of inspiration and assistance, both of which have taken many forms. Time away from my position at Boston College and other support were made possible by generosity on the parts of William Neenan and Betty Rahv.

The author seeking to publish a work of scholarship that is at odds with long-accepted critical interpretations of any given material catches herself daydreaming of prepublication evaluators with the curiosity and special verve necessary to accept a challenge to the familiar. I was fortunate to have two such readers, Edward Friedman and Catherine Swietlicki, whose lively engagement with the manuscript made possible its improvement and its publication. I am grateful to Sara Fefer, my editor at Missouri, for her patience and careful attention.

Time and funds to pursue research for this book were made possible by generous support from the National Endowment for the Humanities, in the form of a Fellowship for College Teachers during the academic year, beginning in September of 1986. Funds for research on Montemayor's "Diálogo spiritual" and his secular poetry were received first as a grant from the American Philosophical Society in 1983 and then, in 1985, in the form of a nine-month fellowship from the Joint Committee for Cultural Cooperation between North America and Spain; a great deal of that work figures into this study.

Finally, special and personal thanks to some teachers: Betty Sedwick Brimm, Graham Brimm, Alice Mae Rhodes Brimm, John Brimm, and Sarah Clarissa Bou-Rhodes.

ABBREVIATIONS

Works by Montemayor:

DS	"Diálogo spiritual"
LD	*Los siete libros de la Diana*, ed. López Estrada
GP	*El cancionero del poeta Jorge de Montemayor*, ed. González Palencia
O	*Obras*, 1554
SC	*Segundo cancionero*, 1558
SCS	*Segundo cancionero spiritual*, 1558

Works by Others:

AG	*Amadís de Gaula* by Garci Rodríguez de Montalvo, ed. Place
Audi	*Avisos y reglas cristianas sobre aquel verso de David: Audi, filia* by Juan de Ávila, ed. Sala Balust
CC	*Comentarios sobre el Catechismo christiano* by Bartolomé Carranza de Miranda, ed. Tellechea Idígoras
DA	*Dialoghi d'amore* by Leone Hebreo [1535]
DQ	*El ingenioso hidalgo Don Quijote de la Mancha* by Miguel de Cervantes Saavedra, ed. Murillo
E&E	*Erasmo y España: Estudios sobre la historia espiritual del siglo 16* by Marcel Bataillon
Guía	*Guía de pecadores* by Fray Luis de Granada, ed. Balcells
IC	*Il libro del cortegiano* by Baldassarre Castiglione, ed. Bonora
LG	*La Galatea* by Miguel de Cervantes Saavedra, ed. Avalle-Arce
LdO	*Libro de la oración y meditación* by Fray Luis de Granada, ed. Cuervo
LdP	*Los libros de pastores en la literatura española* by Francisco López Estrada
LR	*Los recogidos: Nueva visión de la mística española (1500–1700)* by Melquíades Andrés Martín
NPE	*La novela pastoril española* by Juan Bautista Avalle-Arce

The Unrecognized
Precursors of Montemayor's *Diana*

REFORMING THE CANON
An Introduction

"Setting aside Cervantes, there is no writer in the Spanish language born in the sixteenth century who has enjoyed such a profound and durable success as Jorge de Montemayor. The fortune of the Diana *was extraordinary."*
(*Michel Darbord*, Poésie religieuse espagnole)

What follows is an attempt to redirect critical approaches to the works of sixteenth-century author Jorge de Montemayor to better align modern appreciation of them with the period in which they were created; by synecdoche, the same process is implied for Golden Age literature in general. This examination of currents of spirituality, and the ways in which they are represented in Montemayor's religious and secular works, culminates in a new reading of his well-known pastoral narration, *Los siete libros de la Diana* (*The Seven Books of the Diana*). For its focus on my interest in the recovery of a particular historical and cultural context, this book is in some ways what Robert Scholes calls a "centripetal reading," which "conceives of a text in terms of an original intention located at the center of that text." For the same reason, it employs Scholes's "reactionary theory" of reading texts, one that emphasizes a direction toward the source and the original context of the signs in the text. I do not attempt herein to capture Montemayor's literary intentions, long lost, which would in any case probably be less meaningful to us than what his books themselves offer us. I do, however, propose to illuminate certain facets of his texts and their contexts for what they can tell us about those intentions, recognizing with Scholes that "as readers, we cannot ignore the intentions of writers without an act of textual violence that threatens our own existence as textual beings."[1]

Importantly, as Scholes further indicates, this approach inevitably transforms itself into its counterpart, which he calls the face of reading that

1. *Protocols of Reading*, 7–8, 51.

looks forward, oriented toward the textual situation of the reader. This is "centrifugal reading," devoted to explorations of the text's meaning at its circumference, expanding its limits. Through the resulting interplay between these two methods, I propose to bring Montemayor's texts and those ideologically similar to them closer to the modern reader, so that they become more meaningful and pertinent to our own lives than previous scholarship, by imposing an inappropriate paradigm of reading upon them, has allowed them to be. I believe Scholes is right in saying that "we should, in fact, read so as to get the most out of each experience of reading," and that "what we get from every text is precisely balanced by what we give."[2] This book constitutes an offering, then, to modern readers of old books from a particular period and place, of something to bring to their readings, of something to give.

To accomplish these objectives, I follow two basic procedures: First, Montemayor's writings are presented as a fundamentally coherent whole in which his religious and secular writings complement each other, in contrast to scholarly work to date, which has tended to divorce the two in reference to both Montemayor and to literature in general. Second, Montemayor's works are presented within the context of an ideology specific to the Iberian Peninsula's spiritual history, a religious movement called *recogimiento*, which loosely translates as "withdrawal" or "the recollection of the self into itself." This school of piety has not been studied in relation to literature before, although it was probably the most representative form of Spanish religious devotion during Montemayor's day and, as such, perhaps the most influential on Spanish Golden Age culture. However straightforward these two procedures may seem, they are based on delicate premises that have complex ramifications in the critical field, and merit some amplification.

Interpretation of the *Diana* and Montemayor's secular poetry departs dramatically from the traditional scholarly approach to them when the author's religious works, their sources, and their history, are taken into account. Reconsideration of those works, particularly the *Diana*, in the context of sixteenth-century Spanish piety is meant to illustrate how the ideological foundation upon which scholars have long based their studies of Golden Age Spanish literature would itself benefit from a reformation,

2. *Protocols*, 19. Scholes defines centripetal versus centrifugal reading on pages 7–8.

meaning a reassessment of the literary canon as it now stands, as well as the nature of its representativeness. In this context, I recommend that works such as Montemayor's be removed from the shadow of the classical and humanistic tradition under which they have been studied to date. Evidence for this assertion emerges from a study of the complex relationship between what the modern reader understands to be "secular literature," such as the *Diana*, and the literature of the Spanish Reformation, works written in attempts to alter the orthodox religious canon during the first half of the sixteenth century in Spain. Thus the phrase "reforming the canon," with which this book is introduced, refers to its contents and to its critical intentions as well.

As an alternative to the aegis of humanism, I contend that the religious environment in which Montemayor's devout works were written, and prohibited by the Inquisition, not only bore heavily and positively on him as he wrote the *Diana*, but also conditioned the cultural milieu in which his book became an international success. Scholars have not yet clearly associated this environment with sixteenth-century literary history, and consequently Montemayor's pastoral narration still constitutes something of an enigma. Whereas the fundamental tenets of Spanish Golden Age religious ideology waned with the Golden Age itself, the premises of Renaissance humanism are still thriving today. Therefore, modern comprehension of, and engagement with, those texts encompassed by humanism is relatively facile. On the other hand, encounters with texts representative of other ideologies, which confound modern notions such as the inherent dignity of the human race, are systematically avoided, as a glance at the contents of any modern literary history of the sixteenth and seventeenth centuries will prove. More specifically, although the best of studies treating the *Diana* do indeed carefully list Montemayor's many religious writings, they refer only in broad terms to his "interest in spirituality" and consider only the stylistic similarities between the two fields of his writing, such as his combination of prose and poetry in the same work. Likewise, the few studies of his religious writings do not refer in any systematic way to the *Diana*. Thus, a relationship has yet to be established.

Montemayor's secular and religious writings are indeed related and compatible, although not in the context in which either is typically considered. That reconciliation is important, for in the *Diana* Montemayor produced a book that was immensely popular with its original readership, yet one that is difficult for the modern reader to appreciate. The purpose of this study is to reveal how Montemayor's religious vision can be seen to illuminate not only his pastoral book but the spiritual ambiance in which the *Diana* was so popular; hence the potential application of this material to Golden Age literature beyond the works of this one author. The most fundamental tenets of that religious vision, such as the belief in an unresolvable chasm between humanity and divinity, must be considered with care since they are well removed from both modern religious experience and the type of spirituality typically mined in sixteenth-century texts.[3] A view widely held in modern literary studies has been that Montemayor's ideas about such important themes as human potential and the nature of God's presence on earth are minority opinions, for he expresses a vision of life quite distinct from the humanistic optimism that scholarship enthusiastically and consistently seeks in books such as the *Diana*. Recent studies in religious history and quantitative analyses of what the presses were printing, however, reveal that in his own day, Montemayor's attitudes were not minority at all.

The respectable bibliography on the matter of canonical representativeness has received cursory attention, when any at all. Primary among the works in that bibliography are such important studies as Keith Whinnom's article, "The Problem of the 'Best-seller' in Spanish Golden-Age Literature," which challenges the priorities of the traditional literary canon by revealing the relatively few editions attained during the sixteenth and seventeenth centuries by what is now held to be "masterpiece" literature. Those books that did indeed merit repeated reprinting are precisely those to which Montemayor's works are most directly related. In his book *Los recogidos* (*The Withdrawn Ones*), the Dominican religious historian Melquíades Andrés Martín contends that what he calls recogido spirituality, the type practiced by Montemayor's most important religious sources, was indeed the mainstream form of devotion in sixteenth- and seventeenth-century Spain. Luis Sala Balust's excellent synthesis of the period under consideration, "La espiritualidad española en la primera mitad del siglo 16," likewise allots priority to the Catholic reformists with whom Montemayor was intimately associated.

---

3. R. V. Young, *Richard Crashaw and the Spanish Golden Age*, points out that the works of Crashaw (ca. 1613–1649) share the same distance from modern experience and mainstream scholarship and have suffered a similar fate. Young proposes the influence of Spanish Catholic literature on Crashaw as a primary reason for critical misinterpretation of the English poet's works.

Chapter 1 indicates how Montemayor's religiousness can be unquestionably allied with the spirituality on which Sala Balust focuses, a piety considered orthodox until the 1559 *Index*. This approach challenges interpretations of the same material to date, but supports an idea casually presented by Marcel Bataillon in *Erasmo y España* (*Erasmus and Spain*). In order to make the reasons for that identification clear, I devote considerable attention to descriptive material about currents of piety during the years immediately preceding and coincident with the publication of Montemayor's religious works. This is an ideological environment that has yet to be factored into literary studies, which favor instead the works of the Christian humanists, particularly the Erasmists, and movements that were more spectacular, and less generally representative in Spain, such as Illuminism and Protestantism.

Chapter 2 is a theoretical exposition that singles out the particular traits of the characters and the structure of Montemayor's pastoral narration that were likely influenced by the religious climate of the Peninsula during the period, and are therefore particular to the pastoral narrations of sixteenth-century Spain. This material is meant to counterbalance the inevitable references to Theocritus, Plato, Virgil, and Sannazaro which generally, and I believe erroneously, dominate studies of the *Diana*. Presenting a definition of pastoral based on modal theory, it shows how the bucolic impulse itself could have channeled Montemayor's particular sensitivities and talents into pastoral literature without implicating him in the deepest complexities of humanistic classicism.

Chapter 3 is an in-depth interpretation of the *Diana* in light of the material developed in the first two chapters; it explores Montemayor's book in the manner described above, removed from the shadow of classical humanism. Therein, I call attention to important elements of the text that critics have generally chosen to avoid, and focus instead on nonhumanistic material such as romance and themes from Montemayor's other works. Careful examination of the *Diana*, particularly the exposition on love in book four, reveals that it is not at all the Neoplatonic book that scholars have long declared it to be. Instead, the vision of life it presents, one that supports melancholy and unchallenging acceptance of the established order of things, corresponds directly to predominant themes of Montemayor's spirituality, which, in turn, are echoed in the most printed literature of his day, religious and secular alike. Those themes differ fundamentally from the ideology that informs texts more directly allied with

Renaissance humanism, for attention in them is decidedly fixed on noble human desire subjected to powers greater than individual will. This vision, which typifies Montemayor's writings and is most characteristic of the *Diana*, was surely made possible by the pervasive influence of Spanish religious ideals on his ideological beliefs as a whole.

Such a study of Montemayor's works immediately presents three problems, all of which fall within the realm of literary history as it has been written to date. The first is the broadest, and encompasses the other two. It is the question of what sort of literature has traditionally been considered "representative" of Golden Age Spain, or indeed of any period in literary history. In its interpretations, modern literary scholarship has not only tended to mirror its own divorce of the secular and religious realms, but also to project its own enthusiasm for premodern visions of modernity onto literature of all eras, thereby reproducing itself anachronistically. This problem is especially acute in Renaissance studies, those related to the period in which the concept of *modernity* and anthropocentric culture is typically thought to originate. Scholarship about the Renaissance and the ages immediately following it often finds whatever does not represent such concepts to be expendable. Exceptions exist to this established pattern of critical approaches to texts; the essays in *Literature Among Discourses: The Spanish Golden Age*, edited by Wlad Godzich and Nicholas Spadaccini, all propose innovative, alternative approaches to the same period by considering non-traditional materials (oral texts, for example), and ways to read them (via non-literary themes such as patterns of economic expansion and decline). Such work is still, however, marginal scholarship that is judged by traditional criteria rather than providing the criteria against which more orthodox scholarship is judged itself. Within the traditional, restrictive interpretative scheme, Montemayor's works and others like them will be considered oddities at best.

Several contemporary scholars describe the nature of that traditional interpretative scheme, saying,

> Burckhardt's account of the Renaissance as an era of splendid achievements in art and science—achievements made possible by the early humanists' rediscovery of the "freedom and dignity of man"—illustrates the ideologically significant skewing of perspective that occurs when cultural historians focus their

attention chiefly on the beliefs and productions of a small elite group. The humanists constituted such a group.[4]

In a study of this type, which interprets spiritual issues in a spectrum broader than that of religion, difficulties with background materials immediately surface because of the lack of pertinent literary studies and critical editions available to support such research, a function of the "skewing" described by Ferguson and her colleagues. The large amount of scholarship devoted to politically elite writers or to those whose works reflect the humanist vision is quite curious when compared to the negligible amount of attention scholars devote to other types of literature, literature which statistics nonetheless indicate was the most read during the period. Scholarly acknowledgment of books like Fray Luis de Granada's is all but nonexistent in the field of literature, in spite of their tremendously high publication rate compared with what are generally considered to be "classic" literary works, not all of which are purely literary. Contrary to what the histories of literature would have us believe, Granada's *Libro de la oración y meditación* (*Book of Prayer and Meditation*) was by far the most printed book of its century in Spain. Nonetheless, in the canonical volumes that purport to represent Spain's sixteenth- and seventeenth-century literature to the modern reader, Granada is almost invisible. In the volume of the *Historia y crítica de la literatura española* (*History and Criticism of Spanish Literature*) edited by Francisco López Estrada, two and one-half pages are devoted to the Dominican. (This tome, the first of two about the Golden Age, is 748 pages long.) The Royston Jones volume on the Golden Age in the earlier *A Literary History of Spain*, translated into Spanish as the popular *Historia de la literatura española*, gives the same amount of attention to Granada and does not mention the *Book of Prayer* at all.[5]

On the other hand, attention to religious authors who fall within the

---

4. Margaret Ferguson, Maureen Quinlan, and Nancy Vickers, "Introduction," *Rewriting the Renaissance: The Discourses of Sexual Difference in Early Modern Europe*, xv–xvi.

5. *Historia y crítica de la literatura española*, 506–9; *Historia de la literatura española*, 129–32. For further details, see Elizabeth Rhodes, "Spain's Misfired Canon: The Case of Fray Luis de Granada's *Libro de la oración*."

humanistic intellectual tradition, such as Fray Luis de León, or to authors whose works are conveniently labelled as "exceptional," such as San Juan de la Cruz and Santa Teresa de Jesús, is high. This peculiar selectivity displays scholarly prejudice toward currents of thought that misrepresent sixteenth-century culture, and even those critics who address such issues tread lightly on the heart of the matter. In his article on the best-seller cited above, Keith Whinnom silences one of the largest questions raised by his own argument, that of what constitutes literary worth, thereby validating the evaluative criteria that suppressed the very books he so effectively defends: "Since we are trained to recognize and appreciate *literary merit*, we tend to assume that the works we study have gained a place in the history of Spanish literature by virtue of their literary value. But the best-seller leads us instantly into much deeper waters. *Literary excellence*—even when it exists—is a manifestly inadequate explanation [of these books' popularity]."[6] (emphasis added)

As Whinnom himself implies, it is worth reconsidering who and what it is that determines "literary excellence," when those determinations are made, and to what period they can rightly be applied; the current state of affairs implicitly contends that the vast majority of sixteenth-century readers, an elite class in themselves, were wrong. This is not to imply that there is an automatic relationship between the books most printed and those determined to be worthy of perpetuation. But, the problem, complex and thorny, deserves further consideration, and a thorough study of Montemayor's works necessarily confronts it, exposing the hidden agenda of the literary canon as it now stands. As mentioned above, the Portuguese author, an avid and famous writer of religious prose and poetry, is still known merely as the author of the *Diana*. Consequently, that book has always been read in light of classical and humanistic themes or as the inevitable precursor of the modern novel, in defiance of everything known about Montemayor himself (who was neither a classicist, a humanist, nor a novelist).

The second difficulty of the three mentioned above is one encountered in any study that attempts to account for the whole of Montemayor's works with as little distortion as possible. In the best of his prose and poetry, secular and religious alike, Montemayor is an emotional writer. In his works, a constant battle wages between dogmatism, or ideological pre-

6. Keith Whinnom, "The Problem of the 'Best-seller,'" 189.

scriptivism, and personal experience, with its evidence of dogma's failure to produce the expected and deserved happy results. Never able to abandon the expression through literature of his staunch belief in the importance of spiritual and behavioral standards by which to live, Montemayor never failed either to lament those standards' inability to stabilize the ups and downs of human emotional experience. Thus, his poetry and prose belong to a mode of literature that has long been disdained, the sentimental.

Sentimentality is at the core of Montemayor's religious writings, influenced deeply by a piety in which emotional immersion in religious practice was highly commended. With regard to secular literature, pastoral's unhappy history in this context need not be reviewed again. Hugo Rennert's dictum suffices as an illustration of the point beyond which studies in pastoral, overwhelmingly dedicated to the recovery of classical themes in all pastoral literature, have still to progress: "Many of the incidents in the *Diana* are quite improbable, and its beauty is often marred by an excessive sentimentality, at times bordering on the ridiculous."[7] Although scholarly preference for strictly realistic verisimilitude has diminished since Rennert's day, perhaps due in part to the influence of Latin American boom fiction, alternative paths around the block against sentimental literature are only beginning to form. Feminist literary theory has not only made readers aware of the problem, but has taken steps to overcome it. Recent studies in the mode of romance also offer important alternatives to standards of empirical realism in literary scholarship.[8]

This book is based on the understanding that sentimental approaches to the representation of certain human experiences, such as love and faith, are as valid and as worthy as any others. Thus, the sentimentality at the core of Montemayor's style and that of his sources is here exposed without comment, and certainly without apology. Although the reasons for this may be self-evident, they are worth reviewing, especially in the context of pastoral literature, which in the post-classical era has often been devoted to the representation of emotional experience.

---

7. *The Spanish Pastoral Romances*, 37.
8. See Lillian S. Robinson, "Treason Our Text: Feminist Challenges to the Literary Canon"; Jane P. Tompkins, "Sentimental Power: *Uncle Tom's Cabin* and the Politics of Literary History." Ruth El Saffar's fine study, "The Truth of the Matter: The Place of Romance in the Works of Cervantes," provides bibliography on the issue of romance.

The *Diana* is undeniably a book about love, meaning affectionate devotion, or secular spirituality. For this, it poses special problems to traditional approaches to literature, since modern literary scholarship tends to side-step issues of spiritual experience in literature by transforming them into philosophical themes, on one hand, and eroticism, on the other. Prominent scholars of Spanish literature most often account for love as it is represented in literature in terms of three categories: "chaste love," meaning desire not physically fulfilled; "erotic love," meaning a celebration of physical sexual experience; and "religious love," meaning desire for union with that which is beyond the limits of human experience confined within the flesh. Among these three categories, the body and physical sensations as "love" provide the central evaluative criteria, to the detriment of spiritual desires and needs, most notably those which are not of a philosophical nature. Thus, beyond the *Diana*, debate wages over the relative importance of these interpretive possibilities in *cancionero* (songbook) lyrics and mystical poetry, in which readers are encouraged to enjoy particularly delightful ambiguities in poems centered on the concept of passion.[9]

Montemayor's works, many of which are similar in tone and theme to traditional cancionero verse, throb to the pulse of sentiment, an experiential category not accounted for in the "chastity-sex-God" triangle. Religious ecstasy, long plagued with labels of "misguided" or "sublimated" sexuality, has suffered the same fate and constitutes an experience similar to sentimental love. Both types of affection exist beyond the realm of reason and the intellect, both are archetypically feminine experiences, and both have long been disdained in literary studies. Certainly, the attempt to circumvent affectionate devotion has produced a wide variety of philosophical and stylistic acrobatics in studies of the *Diana*. Unwilling to recognize that sentimentality successfully dominates a "classical" text, yet simultaneously unable to disavow the importance of Montemayor's book, critics have constructed a wide variety of interpretative devices to explain the obsessive interest in the emotion of love, meaning the non-empirical reality of human affection, which Montemayor's characters display. For

---

9. See Ian Macpherson, "Secret Language in the *Cancioneros:* Some Courtly Codes"; Alexander A. Parker, *The Philosophy of Love in Spanish Literature, 1480–1680;* Jane Tillier, "Passion Poetry in the *Cancioneros*"; and Keith Whinnom, *La poesía amatoria de la época de los Reyes Católicos*.

example, Bryant L. Creel insists that "the *Diana* is a powerful contribution to a sophisticated erotic-sentimental literature," yet immediately thereafter admits that it reflects "a cult of chaste innocence." Is eroticism chaste or innocent?[10]

All such approaches have left either Montemayor's artistic reputation tarnished, by supposing that his book is inconsistent and therefore flawed, or that of the critic, who must distort Montemayor's supposed sources, such as Ficino or Hebreo, to the point of misleading so they will be applicable to the book. Philosophically incorrect, relatively unconcerned with sexual fulfillment, and stubbornly refusing to acknowledge love's transcendence to anything beyond the realm of the human, the best of Montemayor's poetry and prose, basically sentimental in nature, focuses on those moments in life when concerns of the heart, not the mind, the body, or the immortal soul, override all others. The *Diana* is an outstanding piece of sentimental fiction, whose attractiveness to women readers was no coincidence.[11]

Montemayor's literary lovers, particularly his pastoral characters and the first-person voice of his poetry, practice chaste love because it comes naturally to them as part of the nobility Montemayor bestowed on them all. In these circumstances, the significance of physical experience fades drastically when compared to the more eloquent and personal attention he constantly allots to the fallen spirit, not the fallen flesh, to the disappointed heart, not the disappointed body. It may well be that literary scholarship's reluctance to account for sentimental experience as the fundamental issue of representing love itself, whether divine or human, is directly related to the difficulties involved in finding a spot for Montemayor, and the best of his imitators, within traditional literary categories.

The sentimentality that dominates Montemayor's pastoral narration also becomes more poignant in his later poetry, the central theme of which is the effect of emotional disillusion on the individual. During the last years of his life, he devoted pages of poetry and the entire *Diana* to describing how the lover feels and behaves when betrayed by the beloved. Love, as represented by Montemayor, allows for the establishment of a mutually

---

10. "Aesthetics of Change in a Renaissance Pastoral: New Ideals of Moral Culture in Montemayor's *La Diana*," 8.
11. On women as readers of pastoral narrations, see Elizabeth Rhodes, "Skirting the Men: Gender Roles in Sixteenth-century Pastoral Books."

satisfying relationship between two virtuous individuals, neither one of whom is perceived as inordinately superior to the other, and then tells of that relationship's unravelling due to the fallibility of one of the partners, time, and fortune. This is an unusual perspective in the love literature of Montemayor's day, which typically has as one of its fundamental tenets the extreme idealization of the beloved and of love itself. I will suggest that this perspective was made possible by his religious ideas, which exclude God and divine qualities such as timelessness, from the immediacies of human emotions. Montemayor's literary world, circumscribed by the dominion of sentiment over all other facets of existence, perches restlessly atop canonical culture and its steady foundation on the classics. It was in the context of sixteenth-century affective religiousness that what was perhaps Montemayor's innate propensity toward this type of expression was nurtured.

The third problem in discussing Montemayor's works involves the paucity of studies that directly relate sixteenth-century religious and secular literature to each other. Montemayor's approach to devout expression is fundamentally identical to his approach to secular topics—combining dogmatic exposition with sentiment—and thus the third problem is compounded by the second, and both ultimately derive from the first. Literary scholarship still has the considerable task ahead of bridging the gap between sixteenth-century culture and its modern secular counterpart. As a result, the modern reader of books like Montemayor's is still relatively unfamiliar with Golden Age religiousness and its discreet presence in Golden Age culture. Much research still retroactively and anachronistically imposes the modern distinction between secular and religious culture on pre-modern periods by studying either one or the other, without specifically considering the profound alliance between the two that existed for centuries. Although the question has been beautifully formulated, the answers have not been as well attended: "To what extent have possible formal innovations and new inner forms been produced in lyric expression by its contact with ascetic literature and, above all, through the crystallization in poetry of different methods and attitudes about prayer, meditation, spiritual exercise, etc.?"[12]

The "either/or" approach does not address that alliance and may not do justice to the interrelationships between the arenas of divine and secu-

---

12. Eberhard Müller-Bochat, "Técnicas literarias y métodos de meditación en la poesía sagrada del siglo de oro," 613.

lar spirituality as they were experienced in the sixteenth century. Alexander Parker exemplifies this pattern of critical thought: "When religious faith grows weak or disappears," he writes, "a man must normally find something to take its place as a goal of worthy endeavour and the source of happiness; love and sex will naturally be among the many alternatives to religious faith and experience." In the same spirit, Anjelo J. DiSalvo assumes an antagonism between such ascetic meditative treatises and sixteenth-century secular fiction, positing the former as alternatives to the latter, although they have much in common. Studies of the reading patterns of the lay population during those years, the most recent of which may radically alter critical approaches to Golden Age literary history, indicate a complementary, not exclusive, relationship between the two.[13] Montemayor was a devout Catholic, and self-consciously so; he was also a devoted chronicler of human love, and wrote comfortably about both fields of experience until the Inquisition "discouraged" him from continuing with the former in 1559. By that date, the *Diana* had been written. There is nothing in his works that suggests conflict between the religious and the secular. On the contrary, the works themselves written during those years (1548–1558) are conceptually and ideologically identical.

It is important that those members of Montemayor's reading public with the time and money to devote to literature were avid consumers of religious works as well as, or more than, secular fiction. López Estrada evokes the harmony between divine and profane spirituality in sixteenth-century Spain when he observes:

> It is true that pastoral books, for their status as imaginative literature, were looked upon critically by the moralists, especially by authors of devotional treatises and their secular supporters, but one might suppose that in a signifi-

---

13. Parker, *The Philosophy of Love*, 36; DiSalvo, "The Ascetical Meditative Literature of Renaissance Spain: An Alternative to Amadís, Elisa and Diana." Sara T. Nalle's article uses Inquisitorial documents to reveal unexpected readers and readings as well: "Literacy and Culture in Early Modern Castile." See also Pedro M. Cátedra, "La biblioteca del caballero cristiano don Antonio de Rojas, ayo del príncipe don Carlos (1556)"; Maxime Chevalier, "'La Diana' de Montemayor y su público en la España del siglo 16" and *Lectura y lectores en la España del siglo 16 y 17;* D. W. Cruickshank, "Literature and the Book Trade"; Edward Glaser, "Nuevos datos sobre la crítica de los libros de caballerías en los siglos 16 y 17"; and J. N. H. Lawrance, "The Spread of Lay Literacy in Late Medieval Castile."

cant number of cases the same person would read religious books and secular ones at the same time or in close sequence; this was especially the case with educated people of lively imagination who enjoyed printed literature, particularly women. The social class of the gentleman tended the most toward what I am talking about. . . . So it was that a religious spirituality and a secular one were created at the same time, both having the same foundation in parallel reading experiences.[14]

The concept of secular spirituality, to which López Estrada refers repeatedly in general terms in his studies of Spanish pastoral and religious literature, is approached here more specifically.

What few studies have been done of secular literature's relationships to issues of religiousness have been extremely helpful in enabling the modern reader to better understand sixteenth-century culture. They are interpretations that provide information specific to sixteenth-century religious spirituality, and deal in varying degrees with the interplay between religious and literary history. Antonio Carreño's study of Lope de Vega's *Pastores de Belén* (*Shepherds of Bethlehem*) as a *risposta* to Lope's own, earlier *Arcadia* illustrates a rich relationship between a single author's religious and secular works. Alberto Blecua's article on Gregorio Silvestre's religious works in relationship to his secular love poetry is another example of how studies in specific areas of spirituality can enhance our readings of texts which are otherwise quite alien to modern taste. These approaches are particularly helpful in the context of pastoral fiction, whose popularity still tends to baffle its contemporary reader.[15]

Marcel Bataillon's monumental work on Erasmism in Spain still stands as the best example of the light to be shed on what we now hold to be secular literature by thorough study of religious culture and history. Indeed, *Erasmus and Spain* is almost biblical itself in its relationship to sixteenth-century literary studies, for scholars too often find Erasmism in works that would be more accurately categorized as other, less magnificently illuminated, brands of piety. Montemayor is the immediate example of a writer classified as Erasmist in important respects by virtually all critics who have dealt with the matter (except Bataillon), through what I suggest is over-zealous application of Erasmist themes. Luis Cortest describes the

---

14. *Notas sobre la espiritualidad española de los siglos de oro. Estudio del Tratado llamado El Deseoso*, 54–55.
15. "La otra *Arcadia* de Lope de Vega: *Pastores de Belén*"; "¿Signos viejos o signos nuevos? (fino amor y religio amoris en Gregorio Silvestre)."

same problem in his defense of Fray Alonso de Madrid saying, "A clear bias has developed among scholars who consider the movement toward interior spirituality in sixteenth-century Spain something entirely new and almost exclusively 'Erasmian.'"[16]

Consideration of how issues of spirituality were shuttled naturally and gracefully between the secular and the religious by Montemayor ultimately reaches beyond Montemayor himself. Many who followed in his path, particularly authors of continuations and imitations of the *Diana*, continued that practice, taking advantage of pastoral's inherently spiritual, contemplative nature, which provided an especially fertile ground for a secular exposition of spiritual concerns. One of this book's objectives is to illuminate the unrecognized ideological foundations of Spain's most influential piece of pastoral literature. Those foundations are not only true to the other works of the author, but they are also common to the original "bestsellers" of sixteenth-century Spain, among which are Montemayor's books and Luis de Granada's as well.

All of the "classics," such as Cervantes's works, deserve a rereading in light of authors such as Luis de Granada, whose influence on Golden Age culture was ubiquitous yet now goes unperceived. Similarly, the recogidos provide indispensable background for any study of sixteenth- and seventeenth-century women's literature, which has yet to be freed from the university-bound intellectual traditions with which women had little to do. Their contact with the recogidos, via the pulpit, the confessional, devotional literature, and cultural currency in general, however, was profound. Applications of what follows may also be appropriate for Britain's literary counterparts of the same period: English readers heartily enjoyed not only Montemayor's *Diana*, but also Spanish treatises such as Granada's on affective piety.[17]

---

16. "Fray Alonso de Madrid, the *Arte para servir a Dios* and Sixteenth-century Religious Literature," 370. Those who have found Erasmist qualities in Montemayor's works include Juan Bautista Avalle-Arce (NPE, 71); Michel Darbord (*La poésie religieuse espagnole des Rois Catholiques à Philippe II*); Creel (*The Religious Poetry of Jorge de Montemayor* and "Reformist Dialectics and Poetic Adaptations of Psalm 137, *Super flumina Babylonis* in the Sixteenth Century"); María Dolores Estevá ("El 'Diálogo spiritual' de Jorge de Montemayor").

17. Judith M. Kennedy's editions of Bartholomew Yong's translation of the *Diana* and Barnabe Googe's use of Montemayor's works in his eclogues are very helpful. Tomas P. Harrison's articles enumerate the more superficial parallels between English texts and Montemayor's. Louis Lohr Martz, *The Poetry of Meditation: A Study in*

Three factors are currently making it possible to resolve the problems described above. First, in recent years, a veritable renaissance in Spanish religious studies has led to publication of religious texts and religious histories, making primary and secondary texts available that previously were quite scarce, particularly those censored by the Inquisition.[18] The editors of such texts are typically erudite members of religious orders whose specifically religious interests do not nullify the importance of their work, which has yet to be tapped by literary scholars and accommodated into the critical vision of sixteenth-century literature as a whole.

Interest in the pastoral mode in literary analysis recently blossomed with a success equal to that of religious studies. Long-standing scholarly opinion about pastoral literature is well known; even Empson's complex study of its relationship to social classes and what he found to be its inherent simplicity did little to alter the critical approach to pastoral that had been taken in classical poetics, wherein it was considered among the most lowly of styles. The new critical evaluation of pastoral literature may be due in part to the fact that some of the critics who have fostered it also witnessed the Peace Movement of the 1960s and early 1970s, a secular spirituality that promoted free love, return to the earth through retreat from bellicose civilization, and lyrical outpouring of protest and emotion—the essential ideals of pastoral. Self-conscious political and moral examination during the 1960s led directly back to eclogues, idylls, and psalms, all testimony of the regularity with which humanity recycles the same mode to represent the human experience. What has yet to happen is the inclusion of Spain's sixteenth-century pastoral literature in the domain of generic studies dedicated to "universal" pastoral, and it is toward

---

English Religious Literature of the Seventeenth Century, attributes the emergence of British metaphysical poetry to the influence of continental piety, to Granada's *Book of Prayer* in particular. See also Anne Ferry's book, *The "Inward" Language: Sonnets of Wyatt, Sidney, Shakespeare, Donne.*

18. In the Juan Flos "Espirituales Españoles" series, of particular interest is the edition of Juan de Ávila's *Audi, filia,* with the Inquisitorial censure of Fray Juan de la Peña of the College of San Gregorio. Montemayor claimed his 1558 religious poetry was reviewed at San Gregorio. Isaías Rodríguez's extensive 1971 catalogue of religious authors who published between 1500 and 1572 in Spain also includes secondary sources that were published before his 1971 article, "Autores espirituales españoles (1500–1572)."

that goal that the following chapters work, to inform those who read Spanish literature and those who do not.[19]

The establishment of cultural studies and feminist literary theory in recent years, and the latter's attention to poetics of gender, have enhanced the study of noncanonical themes and techniques. Feminist theory in particular makes renewed appreciation of the pastoral narrations possible in its insistence on the need to reread history and culture with a willingness to approach themes of subjectivity without deprecating them as unrealistic or irrational, or labelling with sexual clichés. Ettin says that "pastoral society is predominantly male," contending that it is the absence of female characters which allows the male characters to "express a range of emotions not traditionally ascribed to men or publicly expressed by men in literature of society." He continues, saying, "Insofar as the pastoral posits a set of values opposed to such more familiar masculine pursuits as physical competition, the force of arms, stolid devotion to labor, and the accumulation of wealth and wide fame, pastoral literature expresses the conventionally 'feminine' part of the human temperament."[20] More because of this than in spite of it, women figure as importantly as men in most sixteenth-century Spanish pastoral narrations, and in some cases more so, without inhibiting masculine expression within the same range. Their presence contradicts categorizations such as Ettin's and leads to a broader conclusion about the nature of pastoral itself: pastoral characters express an inner voice which has been traditionally ascribed to "the feminine," but which need not be relegated by quality or quantity to biological sexual categories.

Edward William Tayler observes that "pastoral is a form of medita-

---

19. On the history of pastoral criticism, see Paul Alpers's article "Empson on Pastoral." In his book *Literature and the Pastoral*, Andrew Ettin considers the pastoral motifs in Joni Mitchell's song "Woodstock" (164–65). He attends to Luis de Góngora and García Lorca, yet curiously neglects not only Montemayor, but also Garcilaso de la Vega. W. Leonard Grant's book, *Neo-Latin Literature and the Pastoral*, does not mention Spain at all, and neither does Anabel Patterson's recent *Pastoral Ideology: Virgil to Valéry*. Two noteworthy exceptions to this trend are Walter Davis's *A Map of Arcadia: Sidney's Romance in its Tradition* and Myriam Yvonne Jehenson's excellent synthesis *The Golden World of the Pastoral: A Comparative Study of Sidney's New Arcadia and d'Urfé's L'Astrée*.

20. *Literature and the Pastoral*, 146, 149.

tion"[21]; it and religious literature are branches of the same trunk that supersede divisions by gender insofar as they both depict the realm of human subjective experience, the ineffability of which constantly challenges not only the impulse for expression, but also historically predominant literary values and forms. In this context, the fact that sixteenth-century Spanish women were enthusiastic participants in Catholic reformist piety is a logical complement to their fervent reading of pastoral narrations and religious literature. In the same fashion, there is a positive relationship between the fact that Jorge de Montemayor was an avid writer of devotional works that represent that same Catholic reformism, and that his pastoral prose and verse takes up many of the same themes in secular form.

The circumstances described above, renewed intellectual activity in the field of religious studies in Spain, new literary analyses of pastoral literature in general, and the insights afforded by feminist literary theory, make this a propitious moment to consider relationships between the pastoral narrations and religious literature. However, the strongest motivation for pursuing such a parallel is suggested by Montemayor's works themselves. The body of the case for spirituality in the *Diana*, therefore, comes from evidence in Montemayor's religious writings, most of which are only now being edited, and those of his religious sources, almost all of which are unknown in literary studies. Together they provide the justification for this book, and the ultimate proof of its thesis lies within them. His international success as a poet and a prose author justifies consideration of Montemayor as one of the primary sources for the vogue of pastoral literature in the whole of sixteenth- and seventeenth-century Europe. This success derived largely from his sensitive tapping of something held by his readers to be of great consequence, expression of the conflicts between ideology and experience, which in turn reflects the spiritual climate in which those readers lived.

The popularity of pastoral literature in fifteenth- to seventeenth-century Europe is an elaborate problem. The emphasis placed here on relationships between Montemayor's religiousness and his sense of pastoral is intended to complement, not replace, the multiple other sources of the genre and reasons for its original success. It attempts to modify the historical paradigm traditionally invoked for reading books like Montemayor's

---

21. *Nature and Art in Renaissance Literature*, 56.

by renegotiating their basic otherness, providing information that illuminates their meanings which are otherwise unrecognizable to the modern reader. I am motivated by the belief that our ability to understand difference is of crucial importance in the world today and that such ability can be enriched by delving into this otherness. Through such discovery, we may learn to accept and appreciate plurality.

1
BEFORE THE *DIANA*
Jorge de Montemayor and Catholic Reformism

"I am trying to work in an area that lies between traditional literary studies and the historical and social disciplines."
(Robert Scholes, Protocols of Reading)

Biographical Considerations

In 1559 a little book entitled *Los siete libros de la Diana* (*The Seven Books of the Diana*) was published in Valencia, Spain, bringing rapid international fame to its author, Jorge de Montemayor. It was literally a little book: most sixteenth-century editions of it fitted tidily into the reader's palm, making it small enough to be hidden in young ladies' pockets. The *Diana*'s miniature size, as well as its popularity, annoyed moralists such as Fray Malón de Chaide, who complained bitterly that "little girls who could scarcely walk" toddled about with copies in their aprons.[1] Although evidence remains of the book's phenomenal success, its origins are clouded; the one known copy of what is assumed to be the *princeps* edition lacks the date of publication, which has caused some debate about the year it was first printed. However, in the prologue to his religious adaptation of Montemayor's book, the *Clara Diana a lo divino* (*Illustrious Diana Turned Divine*), Fray Bartolomé Ponce claims to have read the original *Diana* in book form in 1559, and there is no reason to doubt his word.[2]

---

1. *La conversión de la Magdalena* (1588), 1:26.
2. On the first edition of the *Diana*, see López Estrada, 57. Ponce refers to having read Montemayor's book on fol. 5r of his own. Ponce's *Clara Diana*, although not published until 1599, was finished by 1561, according to Michel Darbord ("La Clara Diana a lo divino").

A seven-part collection of love stories told by their protagonists, the *Diana* was the first book of its kind, the prototype of Spain's many *libros de pastores*, or pastoral narrations. By 1600, it was the most fashionable Spanish book in England, and it had inaugurated a vogue of pastoral prose fiction in Europe that lasted into the next century. A new style of pastoral fashion followed on the crest of the bucolic wave, inspiring patterns of courtly dress and behavior. In Spain alone, Montemayor's book engendered a multitude of continuations and imitations, influencing Cervantes's first known publication, the *Galatea*. It directly touched English authors such as Sir Philip Sidney, William Shakespeare, Barnabe Googe, Edward Paston, Thomas Wilson, and the anonymous author of *The Troublesome and Hard Adventures in Love*. In France, François de Belleforest and Honoré d'Ufré were among the first to write adaptations of the *Diana*. Now in the Tate Gallery in London, Rembrandt's portrait of his second wife, Saskia Van Ulenborch, dressed as a shepherdess pays a visual tribute to the pastoral style for which Montemayor was largely responsible.[3]

In spite of such international renown, the mystery shrouding the *Diana* and its author continues to this day. Almost nothing is known about Montemayor, neither the date of his birth nor that of his death, not even his real name. "Montemayor" is generally assumed to be a Castilian version of the Portuguese town Montemôr-o-velho, where he was presumably born. Early biographies are now the only sources for dates referent to the Portuguese author's life, and their documentation is difficult to trace. For example, in his 1890 almanac, Baltasar Saldoni says of the author, "Following the musical calendar for 1860 by Roberto, I set the date of his birth as March 19, 1523."[4]

The perfectly kept secret of his name and the repeated references in his works to the importance of nobility of soul rather than of blood make it likely that Montemayor was illegitimate or born of a family of converted

---

3. On the *Diana*'s success in England, see Dale B. J. Randall, "*The Troublesome and Hard Adventures in Love*: an English Addition to the Bibliography of *Diana*." On Montemayor's influence on British pastoral, see Mary Lascelles's "Shakespeare's Pastoral Comedy," and John de Oliveira e Silva's "Recurrent Onomastic Textures in the *Diana* of Jorge de Montemayor and the *Arcadia* of Sir Philip Sidney" and "Sir Philip Sidney and the Castilian Tongue." See Margaret Collins Weitz, "François de Belleforest's *La Pyrénée:* The First French Pastoral Novel."
4. *Diccionario biográfico-bibliográfico de efemérides de músicos españoles*, 2:129. The Roberto to whom he refers is Soriano Roberto, of Barcelona.

Jews, probably with one Spanish and one Portuguese parent; possibly, he was both. A Jewish heritage would have beset him with particular strife. In 1492, all residents of Spain who were not Catholics were ordered to convert to Catholicism or leave the country. Those who converted were subsequently labelled *conversos*, a pejorative term that functioned as a social branding, used to mean not merely "converts" but rather specifically "converts from Judaism" and so implicitly meaning "impure and inferior." (Although there were Moslem converts as well, their lesser economic and political power as a people relative to that of the Jews has always called less attention to their plight in this context; this does not mean their situation was any less unfortunate.) Many Spanish Jews, perhaps including one of Montemayor's parents, fled to Portugal, where their formal conversion to Catholicism was not decreed until 1497.

Throughout the sixteenth century, anticonverso sentiment in the Iberian Peninsula was high. Further, because the Inquisition was eliminating "impurities" from the Catholic population, it was dangerous to be called a converso in Montemayor's day. Several biographical factors, however, make a strong case for his inclusion in this persecuted minority. The name "Montemayor" attracts attention because it was particularly characteristic of Jewish converts to Christianity in the Peninsula to adopt the town of their residence as their last name at baptism. In a poetic diatribe, an anonymous ecclesiastic using the pseudonym "Juan de Alcalá" accused Montemayor's father of being a silversmith, a stigmatized occupation then understood to be pursued by converted Jews. This vituperative exchange between Montemayor and Alcalá was extremely popular in the late sixteenth century; eight different versions of it circulated in a multitude of manuscript *Cancioneros* during that period. In one of them, Alcalá lowered himself to considerable depths by calling the Portuguese poet outright a *"marrano,"* literally "swine" but understood to mean "Jew" with the worst of intentions:

> Being such a good swine
> you tried to label me;
> you'd better shut your mouth
> since neither late nor early
> did anyone ever want to Christianize you.
>
> (Siendo tú tan buen marrano
> me quisiste motejar;

mejor te fuera callar
que a ti tarde ni temprano
te quisieron Cristianar.)[5]

Since his contemporaries evidently knew who he was (had they not, some comment about their doubts probably would have survived), and since by the early sixteenth century "Montemayor" was a less than optimal choice for a man trying to hide his origins, it seems unlikely that he chose it himself. Michel Darbord notes that a silversmith named Montemayor was indeed included repeatedly in the accounts of Queen Isabel la Católica.[6] Such details, combined with the scarcity of historical information about his family and the recurrent theme of marginality throughout his works, make it likely that the author was of a converso heritage.

In his "Epístola a Sâ," a verse letter to the Portuguese poet Francisco de Sâ de Miranda dated around 1552 by Michaëlis de Vasconcelos, Montemayor reveals what little is known of his early years: after enjoying his youth along the Mondego river in Portugal and obtaining a limited education, he was forced to seek out gainful employment, thereby identifying himself as being among those at court who worked for a living (versus those who were able to live off a private income). Whether in reference to his status as a working man or an artist, Montemayor complained to his compatriot of fortune's unwillingness to raise him to the heights he apparently felt he deserved:

> The course of my life I see myself obliged
> To tell you briefly, although more brief
> Fortune proved itself to be in my affairs.
> With me, it became narrow, and does not budge
> To raise me above a certain degree,
> And never dares move me from there.
>
> (De mi vida el discurso io me obligo
> A contar te lo, en breve, aunque mas breve
> Fortuna se mostró para comigo.
> Comigo se estrechó, i no se mueve

---

5. From the untitled sixteenth-century manuscript 98-A-V in the Library of the Castle of Perelada, fol. 186r. (I thank Alberto Blecua for calling this manuscript to my attention.) José López Toro published one version of the exchange in his article "El poeta sevillano Juan de Alcalá."
6. *La poésie religieuse espagnole des Rois Catholiques à Philippe II*, 340.

A me subir a mas que a un cierto grado,
I a me pasar de alli iamas se atreve.)[7]

There were those, however, who held that fortune had been quite generous with him. Miguel Sánchez de Lima praised Montemayor's poetic gifts in *El arte poética en romance castellano* (*The Art of Poetry in Romance Castilian*, 1580). The Portuguese author's case, said Sánchez de Lima, proved the supremacy of natural talent over study in poetic genius, since Montemayor was not learned ("no fue letrado") but was extremely talented ("fue hombre de grandissimo natural").[8]

References in his works indicate that Montemayor traveled within Spain and Portugal and to England, France, the Low Countries, and Italy during his short adult life. His career as a soldier has not been officially documented, though it seems likely that he went to Italy around 1560 with the Duke of Sessa's troops. A sarcastic remark by Pedro Espinosa seems to indicate that he did have a military career: describing what was "old-fashioned poetry" by 1605, Espinosa refers to Montemayor as a "venerable relic of the soldiers in the infantry regiment."[9] Throughout his peripatetic life, Montemayor wrote about love for God or love between women and men, a devotion Fray Ponce captured well in his often-quoted description of the Portuguese writer: "With love he lived and with it he was raised, in love he entangled himself, and upon it he ever contemplated; he extolled love and wrote of it, and for love he died." Of the author's death, the same friar says, "I was told how a very good friend of his killed him over some jealousy or affairs of love." This and similar second-hand accounts have established a traditional understanding that Montemayor was killed in a duel over love in Piedmont, Italy, sometime in 1561. Joaquín Hazañas y la Rua, writing before 1895, specified that Montemayor "died in a duel in Turin in 1561."[10] Surely the air of intrigue about him lent a special attractiveness to his book after his untimely death.

---

7. From Montemayor's "Epístola a Sâ de Miranda" in the edition of Francisco de Sâ de Miranda's poetry by Carolina Michaëlis de Vasconcelos, 654–55.
8. *Arte poética*, 37.
9. "Prologue," *Primera parte de las flores de poetas ilustres de España*, quoted in Antonio Rodríguez-Moñino, *Manual bibliográfico de cancioneros y romanceros impresos durante el siglo 17*, 1:105.
10. Ponce, *Clara Diana*, fol. 6r–v; 6v. Joaquín Hazañas y la Rua, ed., *Obras de Gutierre de Cetina*, 1:173.

Historical documents and his own writings reveal that Montemayor, although not of a noble family himself, worked his entire life in noble or royal circles and had contact with some of the most important literary, political, and religious figures of his day. The men and women with whom he associated exercised a profound influence on his ideas about religion, courtly life, love, and himself; his contact with them probably inspired the noble airs that characterize his writings, presumptuous airs that are dissonant with his clouded origins (or perhaps give the lie to them). He dedicated his prose exposition of Catholic dogma, the "Diálogo spiritual" ("Spiritual Dialogue"), to no less a personage than King João III of Portugal, who ruled from 1521 to 1557. In the prologue to that dialogue, he speaks of his residence with the nobility at the Portuguese court ("resido en palacio entre caballeros y damas"), and of the fact that the "Dialogue" was the first product of some unidentified studies ("lo que estudiando sembré en la flaca tierra de mi ingenio," DS, IIr–v). His first gloss of Jorge Manrique's "Coplas que fizo a la muerte de su padre" ("Verses Written upon the Death of His Father"), which he used to lament the death of Portugal's Princess María in 1545, describes her royal family in intimate terms and leads one to believe that Montemayor was in some way connected with the court in Lisbon in 1543, when the princess left for Spain for her marriage to Felipe II. Since his gloss is dedicated to Juan de Silva, alderman of Portugal, it is quite likely that Montemayor was in Portugal in 1545.[11] More definitive contacts with royalty were made possible by his position in the imperial court as singer in the Spanish royal chapel from 1548–1552. While spending these years immersed in the rituals and music of Spanish Catholicism, he apparently earned a certain renown, according to an eighteenth-century historian: "In his early years he was among the famous singers of the Royal Chapel of Castile, not only for the melody of his voice, but for the singularity of his style."[12]

Montemayor was so favored that Princess Juana, daughter of Charles V, chose him to accompany her to Portugal as her chamberlain during her

---

11. Bryant L. Creel transcribes this first gloss in *The Religious Poetry of Jorge de Montemayor*, 246–56; it is also available in a modern facsimile edition in the *Pliegos poéticos españoles de la Biblioteca Nacional de Lisboa*, 49–60.

12. Diogo Barbosa Machado, *Biblioteca lusitana histórica, crítica e cronológica*, 2:744. Narciso Alonso Cortés describes the documents revealing that Montemayor worked in the chapel in "Sobre Montemayor y 'La Diana,'" 129.

years there as the wife of Prince João IV (1552-1554), and, since the chamberlain's duties involved the princess's most private life, the two were probably close. Montemayor dedicated his first important collection of poetry, the *Obras* (*Works*), published in Antwerp in 1554, to the royal couple. This alliance was important, not only because of the prestige it carried but also because of Juana's well-known staunch Catholic devotion and her support of Catholic reform activists during the very years Montemayor was serving her. Bataillon said of the Princess: "For Juana of Austria, Princess of Portugal, was the friend, the protectress of the Catholic reformers during the period when they were most threatened. She increased their influence, felt their cause somewhat as her own, and this spiritual affinity perhaps helps pierce the mystery of her stern and veiled countenance."[13] Bataillon perceptively sensed something unusual about Juana's demeanor; he apparently did not know about, or chose to respect the secrecy of, Juana's Jesuit vows, vows which made her the only woman ever admitted to that order. After her husband's early death, the princess had planned to join the Franciscans but was probably convinced to pursue entry into the Jesuits by Francisco de Borja around 1554. To this day, she is hidden behind the pseudonym "Mateo Sánchez" throughout the lively correspondence related to her audacious request, which ended in her admission as a scholastic.[14] Juana was an ardent supporter of the Jesuits for the rest of her life, and her court was famous for its devout severity. Montemayor seems to have severed his relationship with the princess during the very years she was formulating her vows with the Society of Jesus. Because of the princess's patronage, it is likely that Montemayor was very familiar with the reformist Francisco de Borja, Juana's dearest spiritual advisor. Importantly, he also probably became intimately acquainted with the details of aristocratic asceticism while in her service.

It is also probable that Montemayor met Fray Luis de Granada while serving the Spanish princess in Portugal, if he had not already encountered Granada during his years there before 1548; Fray Luis had become the chaplain of Cardinal Enrique, Juana's brother-in-law, in 1551. Further, Michaëlis de Vasconcelos indicates that the Portuguese Princess María, then at the Portuguese court as well, granted preference to visits from

13. Marcel Bataillon, "Jeanne d'Autriche, Princesse de Portugal," 260.
14. The letters and other documents are in Hugo Rahner, *Saint Ignatius Loyola: Letters to Women*, 52-67.

doctors of theology and philosophy, Francisco de Borja and Fray Luis de Granada in particular. Fray Miguel Pacheco's 1645 biography of the princess likewise describes intimate contact between María and the Dominican friar.[15]

During the second quarter of the sixteenth century, Granada and Borja were shining stars of the Catholic reform movement whose fates, as well as that of Borja's patroness, indicate well the bewildering pace at which the religious environment was changing during the years Montemayor was writing. After having established herself as an avid supporter of reformist Catholic religion by 1554, on September 7, 1558, Princess Juana presided over the first *auto de fe*, or public sentencing of heretics, in Valladolid, leading a significant step in the Church's attempts to curtail the reform she herself had helped foster. Although Francisco de Borja had been a favorite of Spanish royalty in the early 1550s, in 1559 he fled Seville for fear of being arrested by the Inquisition as a Lutheran. He left Spain, never to return, in 1560 (ironically enough, he was canonized in 1671). Luis de Granada, among Spain's most popular preachers and the most published writer during the same years, saw his works placed on the Valdés *Index of Prohibited Books* in 1559. This happened in spite of his personal appeal to his powerful brother to exclude them.[16]

The case of Constantino Ponce de la Fuente is paradigmatic of the suffering brought about by the closing fist of the conservative Church during the years Montemayor was establishing himself as an author. Ponce, also of converso heritage, was a renowned student at the University of Alcalá and the former preacher of Charles V. By mid-century, he was among the country's most popular religious speakers. According to María Paz Aspe,

---

15. Vasconcelos, *A Infanta D. Maria de Portugal (1521-1577) e as suas damas*, 25. This María was the daughter of Manoel of Portugal and Leonor of Austria and the aunt of the Princess María who died in 1545. María Idalina Resina Rodrígues quotes from Pacheco's biography in *Fray Luis de Granada y la literatura de espiritualidad en Portugal (1554-1632)*, 12.

16. Álvaro Huerga describes the events leading up to Francisco de Borja's flight in *Predicadores, alumbrados e Inquisición en el siglo 16*; Henry Kamen provides a different version in *Inquisition and Society in Spain in the Sixteenth and Seventeenth Centuries*, 82. Rahner considers the saint's problematic relationship with Felipe II as another possible reason for his precipitous departure from the country (*Saint Ignatius*, 62-66). On Granada's trip to Spain to see Valdés about the *Index*, see Huerga, *Fray Luis de Granada: Una vida al servicio de la Iglesia*, 142-46.

he had no time to adapt himself to the antireformist politics of the Inquisitor General Fernando de Valdés, which soon had a stranglehold on the nation. Accused of Lutheranism, Ponce died in the cells of the Inquisition sometime between 1558 and 1559; his remains were disinterred and burned in an auto de fe in 1560.[17] Clearly, it was a dangerous time to be enmeshed in the issues of Catholic doctrine. Montemayor went ahead, apparently undaunted. This reveals a notable facet of his personality, which by all available historical, anecdotal, and literary evidence was characterized by youthful self-assurance bordering on presumption, something that would be softened dramatically by his changing fortune over the years that followed.

Montemayor's early works, dating from 1545 to 1552, are almost all religious. His first poem appears to have been the gloss of Manrique's "Coplas" mentioned above, a work significant for the undeniable alliance it creates between Montemayor's literary taste and Spanish medieval, not Renaissance, ways of expression and themes. In this alliance, he reflects the dominant literary taste of his age, which, contrary to what most scholarship would lead one to believe, favored fifteenth-century authors like Jorge Manrique and Fernando de Rojas much more than sixteenth-century works. Montemayor's very popular gloss of "Dios puso en hombre su nombre" ("God Put His Name upon Man") appeared under his name in Pedro del Pozo's manuscript *Cancionero* (*Songbook*), and then again anonymously in the 1549 *Cancionero espiritual* (*Spiritual Songbook*), believed by Bruce Wardropper to have been written and compiled by a Franciscan, also anonymous.[18]

Sometime before 1548, Montemayor wrote the first version of his "Spiritual Dialogue," a lengthy prose treatise which was never published and of which one manuscript is known to exist. In the dedication to King João III,

---

17. María Paz Aspe, "El cambio de rumbo de la espiritualidad española a mediados del siglo 17."
18. Rodríguez-Moñino found other appearances of Montemayor's poem; see "El cancionero de Pedro del Pozo," 493. See Wardropper's edition of the *Cancionero espiritual (Valladolid 1549),* in which Montemayor's poem apparently lacks verse 8 (210–11). The gloss reappeared in Montemayor's own 1554 *Obras* (140r–164v; GP, 131–32) and, modified, in his 1558 *Segundo cancionero spiritual* (29r–30v). On reading patterns of the lay population, see Keith Whinnom, "The Problem of the 'Bestseller' in Spanish Golden Age Literature," and Sara T. Nalle, "Literacy and Culture in Early Modern Castile."

Montemayor claims this "Dialogue" is his first work, leading critics, few of whom seem to have read the entire manuscript, to assume it was written before his first known publication of 1548. In that dedication, however, he also refers to himself as the servant of Princess Juana, therefore presumably so writing after 1552. This conflict is resolved by the fact that the dialogue is copied in two mid-sixteenth-century hands, revealing the work of two separate periods, and the dedication clearly pertains to the later period of the manuscript's development.[19] The combination of the two writing styles is such that there appears to have been a first version established, upon which a substantial revision was superimposed later. The revision took care to support points of faith that the earlier draft probably did not: good works, ceremony, and conformism to Church authority in particular. This change reflects exactly the transformation effected in Catholic reformist literature during the mid-sixteenth century, which Montemayor probably followed with some anxiety. In 1548, his prose and verse exposition of Psalm 86 was printed on parchment in Alcalá de Henares by Juan de Brocar, and was exquisitely done. The first 110 lines of the same poem had been published already as the introductory verse to Francisco de Trasmiera's 1546 book, *Vida y excelencias de la . . . Virgen* (*Life and Excellencies of the . . . Virgin*). The diffusion and prestige of these early writings may be adduced as evidence that the Portuguese author was a well-known and respected figure years before the publication of the *Diana*.

During the following six years, Montemayor published both secular and religious poetry. Documents exist stating that the religious section of a book of his, the title of which is not given, had been approved by Dominicans for publication in Medina del Campo; Jean Dupont uses a 1552 broadsheet containing some religious poems of Montemayor's to put forth his thesis that the Medina del Campo approbation was for the religious volume of a 1552 two-volume collection, both of which were ready for print but may have not gone to press.[20] The poet's 1554 *Obras*, published

---

19. Darbord also observes the chronological contradiction in the manuscript (*La poésie religieuse espagnole*, 347.) Isabel Cid, curator of the manuscripts at the Biblioteca Pública in Évora, laments that no records about the manuscript itself are known to exist. What appear to be the original sections of the text are in a humanistic script; the alterations were done in a Gothic hand; both date from the mid-sixteenth century. I thank Pedro Cátedra for his paleographic evaluation of the manuscript.

20. Alonso Cortés, "Sobre Montemayor," 130; Jean Dupont, "Un *pliego suelto* de

in Antwerp, is a bipartite volume dominated by his *Obras de devoción* (*Devotional Works*), which follow the secular part of the collection.[21] His affinity for the secular pastoral is evident in several short pastoral poems and two long eclogues in this collection. Among the religious poems are included three *autos*, a second gloss of Manrique's "*Coplas*," a verse narration and commentary on the Passion, two poetic adaptations of Savonarola's expositions, one on Psalm 50 and the other of his Pater Noster, and three religious sonnets.[22]

The only religious work cast in any form of pastoral by Montemayor was his third "*Auto*," a short religious drama dated 1545–1557 by Florence Whyte, which was included only in the 1554 *Works* collection.[23] A simple and light piece, it follows in the popular dramatic tradition of Juan del Encina, Torres Naharro and Gil Vicente. Although on the surface it seems remarkable that Montemayor never developed the metaphor of Christ the shepherd in any of his works, the lack is perfectly consonant with his unwillingness to lower the divine to the human, a trait that will be shown to characterize his religiousness. Sonnets such as Lope de Vega y Carpio's later "Pastor que con tus silbos amorosos" ("Shepherd, You Who Beckon Me with Love"), or Fray Luis de León's chapter on the shepherd in his *De los nombres de Cristo* (*On the Names of Christ*, 1583), depend absolutely on such humanization, a fundamental theme of Christian humanism.

Like much of Montemayor's religious verse, that in his *Works* is doctrinal, narrative, and relatively impersonal; except for his adaptations of

---

1552 intitulé: 'Cancionero de las obras de devoción de Jorge de Montemayor.'"

21. The *Obras de devoción* begin on folio 75r [bis] of the *Obras* with a new colophon, a new dedication, and their own table of contents. The folio numeration, however, is consecutive with the *Obras*. All known copies of the *Obras* are bound with the *Obras de devoción*, except one standing volume of the first, at the Hispanic Society of America, and one of the second, at Yale University.

22. Montemayor was not the creator of the religious sonnet in Spain, but he did develop the form with some success. Juan Hurtado de Mendoza, with whom he exchanged verse epistles (GP, 351–62), published a collection of religious sonnets in his *Alvorada trovada* in 1549, and Montemayor was probably inspired by them. On this alderman of Madrid, the Latin translator of Manrique's "Coplas," known as "the philosopher" for his interest in the classics, see Dámaso Alonso, "Un poeta madrileñista, latinista y francesista en la mitad del siglo 16: Don Juan Hurtado de Mendoza" and Guillermo Antolín, "El traductor latino de las Coplas de Jorge Manrique."

23. "Three *Autos* of Jorge de Montemayor," edited by Florence Whyte, who discusses the work's date on p. 958; the text is on pp. 975–89.

Savonarola's works, there is little effective use of first person singular and no description of personalized religious or meditative experience, although his able use of dialogue and his imaginative interpretation of the Bible are well-established techniques therein. Using the categories suggested by Bruce Wardropper for classifying Golden Age religious poetry, one immediately observes a predominance of catechizing works as well as narrative (versus lyrical) verse about the Virgin and Christ, and a lack of the other, more intimate types. Dogmatic emphasis in this collection falls on the mystery of the Trinity and on the Christian's need for awareness of humanity's debt to the divine incurred by Christ's Passion.[24]

In 1558, Montemayor published a set of twin volumes in Antwerp, the *Segundo cancionero* (*Second Songbook*) and the *Segundo cancionero spiritual* (*Second Spiritual Songbook*). Of particular significance in the secular collection are his third and fourth eclogues, published with the first two, which had appeared in 1554, an entertaining pastoral narrative poem "La historia de Alcida y Silvano" ("The Story of Alcida and Silvano"), and other new pastoral verse. There is proportionately less cancionero-style poetry in this 1558 volume, more use of Italianate form, and more personalized introspection represented in all of the poems, both in traditional cancionero and Italianate form.

The *Second Spiritual Songbook* contains much more lyric religious poetry than its 1554 precursor. Only in this collection does Montemayor refer poetically to the *fuego de amor* (fire of love) so characteristic of sixteenth-century Spanish mystical literature, although he had described the fire of divine love in the "Spiritual Dialogue" in an officious manner, ultimately derived from Book 13 of Augustine's *Confessions* (DS, 51r). His major narrative/catechizing piece, "La pasión de Cristo" ("The Passion of Christ"), still dominates the collection, and he included several poems from his 1554 *Works* again, notably the gloss of Manrique's "Coplas." In spite of these repetitions (and again using Wardropper's typology), in the 1558 religious verse one observes an increase in penitential, devotional, and meditative verse compared with the *Works*. This *Second Spiritual Songbook* contains moving and personal poems, the most expressive of which are those revealing the poet's attempts to evaluate himself and the world he had come to know in light of his ideals, without overtly preaching at the

---

24. Wardropper proposes a typology for religious verse in his article "La poesía religiosa del Siglo de Oro," 18–19.

reader or his characters. Such are some of his new religious sonnets and his paraphrase of the psalm "*Super flumina Babylonis.*" Importantly, these poems share the introspective, sentimental, and melancholy nature that characterizes Montemayor's best pastoral works, the *Diana* in particular.[25]

In the prologue to the *Second Spiritual Songbook*, Montemayor repudiates an earlier publication of his religious verse, perhaps in reference to his *Works*, perhaps to the aborted 1552 volume described by Dupont. Therein he also declares that he had submitted the *Second Spiritual Songbook* to theologians in Flanders and at the Dominican College of San Gregorio in Valladolid before publishing it. Both were unfortunate claims. At that time, the Inquisition was busily ferreting out "heretical" elements in the Catholic reformists, several of whom had ties with San Gregorio (Bartolomé Carranza de Miranda and Luis de Granada, for example). The Holy Office was also immediately suspicious of religious books published outside Spain during this period, and Princess Juana herself signed on September 7, 1558, what Henry Kamen calls a "ferocious decree" of censorship restricting importation of books published abroad.[26]

The Spanish Inquisitorial *Index* of 1559 prohibited Montemayor's works touching on matters of devotion ("obras en lo que toca a devoción y cosas cristianas"); whether this affected only the religious poems in the *Works* volume or all of his religious works is not known. Most discussion of this prohibition has merely repeated and developed Menéndez Pelayo's dictum that their censoring was due to "the heresies that their author spilled forth out of his ignorance."[27] This may be an oversimplification of the problem, for even though there is no doubt that the Portuguese author's religious works contain theological errors, according to the Inquisitor General Valdés, so did those of many learned theologians. The extent to which any of them were actually heretical or erroneous was determined by political concerns of the moment; this is made clear by the *Index*'s sudden suppression of authors who had enjoyed official ecclesiastical support under reformist authorities such as Cisneros before Valdés came into power. Re-

---

25. The "*Super flumina*" gloss is not in the 1932 edition of Montemayor's poems, since González Palencia did not know of the existence of the *Segundo cancionero spiritual.* It is, however, included in Creel's *Religious Poetry,* 132–39.

26. Kamen, *Inquisition,* 80.

27. Marcelino Menéndez Pelayo, "La novela pastoril," 256. See Jesús Martínez de Bujanda's commentated edition of the Spanish *Index* of 1559, in the *Index des livres interdits,* 5:303–592; the reference to Montemayor is on 513–14.

gardless, when the works of men as erudite as Carranza and Granada were included on the *Index*, it is no surprise that Montemayor's were as well.

Although no historical evidence, such as a report by an Inquisitorial *calificador* or reader, has come to light explaining the prohibition of the Portuguese author's religious poems, their appearance on the *Index* is understandable for more concrete reasons as well. For unlike the many religious poets who were his contemporaries and his friends, such as Gregorio Silvestre, Montemayor turned his back on purely lyrical religious expression and persistently dealt with issues of theology and dogma in his works themselves, presuming to instruct. Such an intent was absolutely unacceptable to the Holy Office, which was surely sensitive to the dangers of allowing a man uneducated in advanced letters and totally lacking theological training to continue interpreting delicate issues of faith, especially in the vernacular. Further, it bears mentioning that the books prohibited in 1559 were not necessarily those containing doctrinal error. Inquisitor General Valdés's order of February 12, 1559, to the Inquisitors in Seville reveals his long-standing intentions to use the *Index* as a way to get at Bartolomé Carranza. In part to mask that intention, to which he admitted, Valdés included therein a mandate to withdraw from circulation all books in the vulgar tongues, "that touch upon Christian *doctrine*" (que toquen a *doctrina* cristiana; emphasis added) that had been printed outside Spain after 1550.[28] These books were also included in the 1559 *Index*, Montemayor's among them. Whatever the reason for their prohibition, no religious writings of his are known to exist after the 1558 *Second Spiritual Songbook*, and the *Diana* was published in the same year as the *Index*.

In 1560, Montemayor's final book was published, a translation of some of the *Cants d'amor* (*Songs of Love*) written by the medieval Catalan poet Ausias March (1397–1459).[29] His final turning to March is significant since it reaffirms Montemayor's long-standing commitment to medieval love literature; March's notions about human sentimental experience can be found throughout those of Montemayor's writings that were published

---

28. See Huerga, *Predicadores*, 31. Virgilio Pinto observes that the 1559 *Index* was prepared in great haste; it probably included some blanket prohibitions that more time might have spared ("La censura: sistemas de control e instrumentos de acción," 280).

29. Montemayor's translation of March was republished in 1990 by Martín de Riquer. A reprint of his 1946 rendition of the same, this edition likewise lacks essential poems by Montemayor himself, which Calatayud's edition, although less accessible, contains.

before his translation of the Catalan poet. This attention to March is complemented by the equal and constant devotion he demonstrated to the fifteenth-century Castilian poet, Jorge Manrique, in whose *"Coplas"* Montemayor seems to have found fertile ground for sowing the seeds of his own ideas.

Montemayor's secular poetry was a spectacular success. After appearing as the 1554 *Works* and the 1558 *Second Spiritual Songbook*, it was published posthumously, eight times before 1600 as simply *Songbook*, and once in 1579 under the title *Second Songbook* (this one differing from the 1558 volume of the same name).[30] These eleven editions of his secular poems (twelve counting the 1558 *Second Spiritual Songbook*) make Montemayor second only to Garcilaso de la Vega in number of editions printed of verse by any single poet published between 1543 and 1600. Further, the great majority of Spanish manuscript collections of verse dating from 1560 to 1600 contain at least one poem by Montemayor.

The course of Montemayor's writing career is notable for its direction; contrary to traditional passage from the worldly vanities of youth into religious themes of maturity, his works proceed from the divine to the secular, culminating in the *Diana* and his translation of March. One would expect, then, that his attitudes about religiousness, about love for God, and about the relationship between God and humanity influenced his interpretation of love between human beings, rather than vice versa. This seems to be the case, particularly in his vision of the devotional process as one directed toward a theoretically attainable but elusive goal, the realization of which is subject to the will of a force greater than that of the lover or worshipper. This conservative attitude about the relative powers of humanity and divinity is characteristic of the Catholic reformists with whom Montemayor's religious writings will be allied shortly. He seems to have readily identified with this vision, for it is the one represented not only in his religious works but in his secular writings, most conspicuously in the *Diana*.[31]

Although he published religious and secular poetry in the same collec-

---

30. Santiago González y Fernando-Corugedo studies the editions of Montemayor's secular verse in his "Ediciones de las poesía profana de Jorge de Montemayor."

31. Care must be taken to treat Montemayor's many translations and adaptations as exactly that. His own, original religious writings offer no expression of the positive attitude about God and humanity's relationship to the divinity that appears in, for example, his adaptations of Savonarola's expositions. While Montemayor may have been attracted to such a view, his works indicate that it was not naturally his own.

tions, Montemayor never mixed human and divine affairs in the same poem, except in his palinode religious piece recanting, in traditional fashion, his foolish devotion to women ("Pluma que en vanidades te ocupaste" [Pen, who spent yourself on vanities], GP, 280–84). That is, unlike his compatriot, fellow musician, and fellow poet Gregorio Silvestre, and unlike his much admired precursor Juan Boscán, Montemayor does not overtly intertwine what he has to say about God's existence and people's. Instead, a rigorous separation of reference is maintained between the two. The beloved is not evidence of heavenly beauty or goodness, as the Neoplatonists had it, nor is earthly life described as a microcosm of the heavens, as the humanists found it to be.[32] The force of fortune, which rules the world as it is represented in the *Diana* and shares marked qualities with God as represented by Montemayor in his religious works, is never overtly identified with the divinity. There is a distance between human and heavenly affairs that Montemayor respectfully represented throughout his career as a writer, as did the religious authors with whom his works share salient features.

The trajectory Montemayor's works follow is also interesting for the implications that it has on the nature of his secular writings, which may be expected to display the concerns he found increasingly problematic to write about in religious form. Why he never took religious vows or studied theology is open to speculation; his secular writings consistently express a vocation as a courtly representative of religious spirituality in the secular world, and his religious writings repeatedly prescribe monastic values only slightly adapted for the lay population, of the same nature as Luis de Granada's writings for Christians in general. It is possible that the "statutes of pure blood" (Spain's famous *estatutos de limpieza de sangre*) kept him from pursuing a religious career. These statutes limited entry into religious orders and lay fraternities to those who could prove their genealogies were untainted by Jewish or Arabic blood and whose families were untried by the Inquisition.[33]

Both Montemayor's writings and what others wrote about him reveal

---

32. Francisco Rico studies the theme of humanity as a microcosm of the divine during this period in his *El pequeño mundo del hombre: varia fortuna de una idea en la cultura española*.

33. About anti-Semitism in Spain during this period and about these statutes, particularly that of 1547, ratified by the Pope in 1555, see Kamen, *Inquisition*, 18–43, 114–24, 219–37; Kamen, *Spain: 1469–1714. A Society of Conflict*, 38–44; Albert A. Sicraff, *Los estatutos de limpieza de sangre: Controversias entre los siglos 15 and 17*.

that he apparently felt anxiety about his social status. Anecdotes indicate that he went to considerable lengths to prove himself an *hidalgo* (gentleman of noble upbringing) on one hand, and yet, on the other, he repeatedly insisted on writing about the importance of inner virtues—humility in particular—over social status and nobility by birth. To Fray Bartolomé Ponce's observation that his time would have been better spent writing about devout matters, Montemayor reportedly retorted, "Father Ponce, may the friars do penance for all of us, for the business of *hidalgos* is arms and love" (quoted in LD, CIV). He thereby included himself in a social class to which all historical evidence and his own writings reveal that he did not belong.[34] Ponce's anecdote as well as others indicate that humility does not seem to have been one of Montemayor's own virtues, and perhaps his insistence on its significance in his writings reveals awareness of that lack. Lourenço Craesbeeck, editing the *Diana* in Portugal in 1624, told of a garden party on the estate of Montemayor's patron, the Duke of Sessa; the noble company asked the Portuguese author questions about his pastoral narration, "to which he responded with many courteous words and no little arrogance over such good fortune" (quoted in LD, C).

Nonetheless, Montemayor's writings contain passages that undermine the value of the very social status he seemed to seek and lend a human quality to his works by the paradox they imply. His 1554 gloss of Jorge Manrique's "Coplas" admonishes

> From today on, let no one be named
> by the exalted bloodline from which he hails
> if he keeps himself in poverty,
> for the worth of the man
> is in only what he bears within.
>
> (De hoy más, ninguno se nombre
> de la alta sangre do viene
> si en pobreza se mantiene,
> pues no está el valor del hombre
> sino en sólo lo que tiene.)
>   (SCS, 138v; GP, 224)

Aside from the persistent devaluation of nobility by blood and emphasis

---

34. On the historical context of the word *hidalgo*, see Américo Castro, *La realidad histórica de España*, 219–23.

on humility in his religious works, there is a passage in the *Diana* in which the shepherd Sylvano defends the superiority of inner nobility, criticizing those who seek to prove their worth by their names (see *infra* 169–71). Interestingly, in the religious rapture described by Montemayor's hermit Dileto, social standing is one of the first things of which the Christian loses awareness:

> And the devout souls touched by divine love are so inflamed and enraptured and carried away that they forget themselves and the dignities and status and nature of their lineage, finally of all things of this world . . .
>
> (Y son así encendidas y enajenadas y transportadas [las ánimas devotas tocadas por el amor divino] que se olvidan de sí mismas y de las dignidades y estados y condición de linaje, finalmente de todas las cosas de este mundo . . .) (DS, 51v–52r)

This insecurity about social standing and authority, often described as typical of the converso, is important for its expression in most of Montemayor's narrative voices. As a vital posture, it can best be described as a poignant blend of self-righteous indignation and pained disillusion over the fact that the world does not function in accordance with the ideals of the speaking or implied "I." It also produces the haughty, vindictive, Old Testament tones that characterize most of his religious verse. For example, the narrator of his verse epistle to Juan Hurtado de Mendoza criticizes the classical authors whose opinions on the origin of the soul he reviews:

> Each one in his opinion, speaks and disposes
> of what the one whom they do not understand has done,
> nor do they know how to understand what he devises.
> If those who pretend with truth to know
> the origin of the soul, have known
> that it is God only, why do they offend him?
>
> (Cada uno en su opinión dize y dispone
> de lo que ha hecho aquel a quien no entienden,
> ni saben entender lo que él compone.
> Si los que con verdad saber pretenden
> el principio del ánima, han sabido
> que solamente es Dios, ¿por qué le ofenden?)
> (O, 248v; GP, 353)

He lashes out repeatedly at the Jews in his verse rendition of the Passion:

> Fall not, wicked people,
> since you have lances and sticks;
> but from such a low herd
> you are, that not even to be evil
> do I find you worthy.
> Charge, charge, heart,
> men made the wrong way.
>
> (No cayáis, gente malvada,
> pues tenéis lanzas y palos;
> mas de tan baja manada
> sois, que ni aun para ser malos,
> pienso que no valéis nada.
> Cobra, cobra, corazón,
> hombres hechos al revés.)
> (SCS, 76v; GP, 155)

This exaggerated vindictiveness against the Jews is unusual in sixteenth-century Passion literature, which tends to focus more on Christ's sufferings than on the errors of those who crucified him. A striking comparison emerges, for example, with the Passion poetry in Fray Ambrosio de Montesino's 1548 *Cancionero* (*Songbook*), or with Luis de Granada's passages describing the same event in the *Libro de la oración* (*Book of Prayer*, LdO, 20–97).

The same self-righteous posture is apparent in much of Montemayor's love poetry as well, in the lover's tendency to cast blame rather than accept or forgive it. For example, in a 1558 *"Canción"* ("Song") the narrator haughtily accuses Marfida of the same infidelity of which Sireno accuses Diana in the *Diana*:

> Marfida, that you should change your heart does not surprise me,
> but when I should change, oh my lady!
> may you see me live without life or hope.
>
> (Marfida, que te mudes no me espanto
> mas cuando yo me mude, ¡oh mi señora!
> vivir me veas sin vida ni esperanza.)
> (SC, 88r; GP, 420)

The writer's perception of himself as a worthy voice of authority, nonetheless represented more often than not as a humble figure, is correlational to the strongly didactic tone and material that can be found in almost all of Montemayor's secular and religious works. They display a reverence toward the rules of an ideology, rules which are themselves often set forth in his texts, contrasted with the irreverence and inconstancy toward that ideology of the world beyond the speaking self (or selves, as in the *Diana*). Because of this, many of his works appear designed not only to instruct, but also to make manifest the worth and implicit superiority of his narrative voices, be they characters or the narrator of a poem. Thus, in the "Spiritual Dialogue," an ex-courtier turned anchorite, never educated in theology, expounds at length on the most minute details of the Catholic faith. In a verse palinode, Montemayor abandons the limits of first-person examination to lash out at every reader individually, exclaiming,

> Here shall you see, man, who you are,
> and you shall see who God is and what he can do,
> and that without him you would not be as you are.
>
> (Aquí verás, hombre, quién tú eres,
> y verás quién es Dios y lo que puede,
> y que sin él no fueras como has sido.)
> (SC, 201v; GP, 283)

In his exposition on the *"Missus est angelus"* (Luke 1:26), the narrator preaches dogmatically at his readers:

> Humans, take note:
> that whatever word may be said
> by the divine majesty
> does not differ from that majesty's intention.
>
> (Humanos, esto notad:
> la palabra que dijere
> la divina majestad
> de la intención no difiere.)
> (SCS, 26v; not in GP)

Earlier in the same poem, he had presumed to instruct the Virgin about the rhetoric of Gabriel's message:

> The consummate messenger
> speaks very well, pure Virgin;
> he has proven himself to be a rhetorician,
> for we see that he takes
> the figure for the figured.
>
> (El mensajero extremado
> dice muy bien, Virgen pura;
> retórico se ha mostrado,
> pues vemos que la figura
> toma por lo figurado.)
>   (SCS, 19v; not in GP)

In the prescriptive poem "Regimiento de príncipes" ("Guidance of Princes"), that narrator teaches the prince which virtues become royalty (SCS, 30r–44r; not in GP). Finally, in the *Diana*, shepherds and shepherdesses are the mouthpieces of love doctrine and their relationships are held up as exemplary cases of amorous behavior.

The voice of the wronged one, heard constantly in Montemayor's writings, reveals a conflict between the strong self-esteem and confidence in his own authority projected in his writings, and the perception found therein of life's failure to recognize the ideals he sincerely defended. Although they are replete with self-examination, there is no penitence or self-criticism in the works of Montemayor, and his writings never reveal the self-doubt and self-deprecation one finds in the verse of his admired Ausias March. More typical is the point of view in which the narrator joins God or another authority to display the inferiority of the rest of the world. For example, at the beginning of this religious sonnet, published in both the 1554 and 1558 collections of his religious verse, the reader expects the subject to humble himself before God:

> If a fallen heart arises,
> and a dead spirit revives,
> and a soul, though it may lose, wins back what was lost,
> and disenchants the weary body,
> if your clemency, Christ, is not astounded
> by my grave evil and visits me,
> if in its grace it awaits me or brings me from danger
> and establishes my three faculties within itself,

(Si un corazón caido se levanta,
y un espíritu muerto resucita,
y un ánima, aunque pierda, se desquita,
y al cuerpo fatigado desencanta,
si tu clemencia, Cristo, no se espanta
de mi grave maldad y me visita,
si en su gracia me guarda o deposita
y mis potencias tres en sí las planta,)

Having established Christ's mercy, however, the narrator does not proceed to question whether he himself merits such generosity. Instead, in a technique repeated throughout his poetry, Montemayor abruptly changes the poem's point of view from first to third person, charging others with the errors that alienate God from the world, thereby implying his narrator's separation from them and his consequent superiority:

For what cause or reason are they dead in you
and alive to the world and its insistence,
they whom you bought with your blood?
For even today your arms are as open
to take in man as on the day
that on the cross you gave your blood for his.

(¿Por qué causa o razón en ti están muertos
y están vivos al mundo y su porfía
los que compraste tú con sangre tuya?
Que aún hoy están tus brazos tan abiertos
para acoger al hombre como el día
que en cruz tu sangre diste por la suya.)
                    (SCS, 205r-v; GP, 304)

In this poem, one may observe how Montemayor takes advantage of the sonnet's binary structure, using the quartets to set up a hypothetical situation—the ideal—and the tercets as a contrast to that ideal—the real. This technique is typical of most of his religious sonnets, which are not Petrarchan in an introspective sense, but rather comparative in that they establish a conflict between ideology and experience that is exposed as untrue to the ideal. It may be, as Bruce Wardropper proposes, that the adaptation of Italianate meters in Spanish religious poetry coincided chronologically with a shift in that same religious verse toward increased introspection, and that both this form and content therefore reveal a Petrarchan influence. It should be added, however, that the impressive flowering of devotional treatises teaching self-examination in Spain *also* coincided with this period; as Andrés Martín indicates, the problems of how to express intimate and personal experience through language were vivid in the minds of religious writers during the very early sixteenth century.[35] The increased intimacy and the emphasis on the theme of self-contemplation observable in some of Montemayor's 1558 religious sonnets were surely as much influenced by the Spanish religious environment in which he was immersed as by Petrarchism.

Although Montemayor's self-righteous posture, whether assured or disillusioned, is unattractive from the modern perspective, its didactic tone was quite typical of the preferred literature of his day, and continues in the tradition within which he settled himself with conviction: that is, the understanding of piety and human love that preceded Renaissance humanism and overlapped with it in prosperity. Furthermore, as presumptuous as Montemayor's attitude may appear, it is precisely what made possible the beautiful melancholy for which his works are so well known.[36] It is a melancholy that looks wistfully toward the past, seeing nothing but reason for sadness in the world. True to the pastoral mode, it is founded on a deep sense of loss. For example, from the prologue section to his moving paraphrase of the *"Super flumina Babylonis"*:

> I wish to sing, Lord, but who could do it?
> For since David moves me to write what I do,
> my song shall be weeping, although I would not wish it so.
> . . . .
> And thus the Israelites go, lamenting
> their sad captivity, and yet turning
> their eyes back from time to time.
> . . . .
> Now their grief brings them pleasure
> and makes more glorious their victory
> that came not from them, but from heaven.
> . . . .

---

35. Wardropper, "La poesía religiosa," 201–2. On the theme of intimacy in religious literature, see Andrés Martín, "Alumbrados, erasmistas, 'luteranos' y místicos, y su común dominador: el riesgo de una espiritualidad más 'intimista.'"

36. The classic study on Montemayor's melancholy is that of Bataillon, "¿Melancolía renacentista o melancolía judía?"

If one of them tells his or her passion to another,
what the other responds pains the listener;
thus one pain is exchanged for another.
Each one holds his or her own pain more dear than the other,
and upon seeing that the foreigners go happily along,
their sadness is refined and exalted.

(Cantar quiero, señor, mas ¿quién pudiera?
que pues David me mueve a lo que escribo,
será mi canto lloro, aunque no quiera.
. . . .
Y así los israelitas van llorando
su cautiverio triste, y aún volviendo
sus ojos hacia atrás de cuando en cuando.
. . . .
Ahora les da placer su desconsuelo
y su victoria hace más gloriosa,
lo cual no vino de ellos, mas del cielo.
. . . .
Si alguno su pasión al otro cuenta,
lo que responde el otro le lastima;
así que un mal por otro se descuenta.
Cada uno más su mal que el otro estima,
y en ver que van alegres los extraños,
se afina su tristeza y se sublima.)
                        (SCS, 180r–191r; not in GP)

From the same impulse was born the heartbroken complaint, uniquely forged by Montemayor through the eyes of the one who has suffered unjustly:

Sonnet
    I cannot believe of you, fortune,
judging by what we two have been through,
that you give or promise a good situation
to have therein any stability at all.
    You put my happiness higher than the moon,
oh greatest happiness, so high and extreme!,
and in an instant, it dropped by the same degree.
If I ask you why, you give me no reason.
    Do you wish, after you take my glory from me,
that my remembering it and that it is gone

bring me some consolation in this way?
Memory is such a charming consolation to one who is sad;
leave me to suffer, don't worry about it,
for the pain is not as painful as its cure.

(*Soneto*
No puedo yo creer de vos, fortuna,
según lo que los dos hemos pasado,
que dais ni prometéis un buen estado
para tener con él firmeza alguna.
 Pusistes vos mi bien sobre la luna,
¡oh sumo bien, tan alto y extremado!,
y en un punto bajó en el mismo grado.
Si os pido aquí razón, no dais ninguna.
 ¿Queréis, después que me quitáis mi gloria,
que el acordarme de ella y ser pasada
me cause algún consuelo en este medio?
 Gentil consuelo a un triste es la memoria;
dejadme padecer, no se os dé nada,
que no es tan malo el mal como el remedio.)
(SC, 138v; GP, 459)[37]

This disillusioned stance, typical in Montemayor's works, was readily accepted by his readers, who perhaps identified with the very human conflicts it captures: an exaltation of sincerity and humility superimposed upon a desire for status and authority, the inability to relinquish the ideal despite repeated proofs that it does not function in the world, and the feeling of isolation that ensues after severe emotional hardship. This is the pained but beautiful voice that sings in the works of Jorge de Montemayor, a literary voice of one trained in the service of God, who subsequently approached human devotion with the same reverence and idealistic expectations with which he approached religious devotion. His later works portray the failure of those ideals to function in experience: they are typified by a tone of melancholy discouragement and are dominated by the retreat motif, and the *Diana* is among them.

37. This sonnet appeared first in 1558 and is similar in many ways to messages presented in the *Diana:* the instability of fortune that rules over love, the insecurity of life, and the preference to suffer the memory of love lost blamelessly over forgetting that memory.

Montemayor and the Catholic Reformists

Montemayor's ideas about human love in the world do not differ greatly from those he expressed about righteous religious devotion in the same world. As has been indicated, the chronology of his works seems to indicate that his ideas about love of God influenced those about love between human beings, making his religious writings an important source for understanding the ideology of human love expounded in the *Diana*. However, the sources of Montemayor's religious ideas are difficult to trace for several reasons.

Identifying those sources is a biographical dilemma: it is not known which of the author's formative years were spent in Spain and which in Portugal. This problem is alleviated somewhat by the fact that sixteenth-century Portuguese religious life was dominated and to a large extent actually controlled by Spaniards sent to Portugal specifically for the purpose of reforming the Catholic religious institutions there. In 1536, King João III requested from his sister, the Empress Isabel, a report on the structure and workings of the Spanish Catholic reform movement, the one Francisco Jiménez de Cisneros had been largely responsible for setting in motion. The several earlier attempts at reforming Portuguese religious institutions (in a lamentable state of decadence at the turn of the century, according to José Sebastião da Silva Dias) had been carried out by Spanish reformists with less success than the monarch felt was necessary.[38] Spanish domination over Portuguese religious affairs is reported (by Spaniards) to have continued throughout the sixteenth century. In a letter to Felipe II dated September 11, 1580, the Duke of Alba, referring to the search for a Dominican Provincial, said that according to the Portuguese one had to be brought from Castile, "because there has never been any reform seen here at all, in any of the Orders, except with Castilian friars."[39]

Portuguese dependence on Spanish direction in reform efforts was par-

---

38. José Sebastião da Silva Dias, *Correntes de sentimento religioso em Portugal (séculos 16 a 17)*, 137; Vicente Beltrán de Heredia, *Historia de la reforma de la provincia de España (1450–1550)*, 221. Further similarities between the religious histories of Spain and Portugal are suggested by Charles Amiel's study of the Portuguese Inquisition, particularly as regards the persecution of marginalized castes and the history of Catholic indoctrination ("The Archives of the Portuguese Inquisition: A Brief Survey").

39. Quoted in Desiderio Díez de Triana, "Introducción," xlvi.

ticularly intense during the first half of the century: the famous Dominican reformist Juan Hurtado de Mendoza was working in Portugal from 1513–1517. He was followed by his own disciples, and eventually by Fray Luis de Granada, who was called upon to visit the Lisbon Dominicans during his service in Andalusia after 1535, and was finally brought to Portugal as the chaplain of Cardinal Prince Enrique in 1551. Granada lived in that country until his death at the convent of Santo Domingos (Lisbon, 1588). The Portuguese Archbishop of Lisbon, Fray Bartolomeu dos Mártires, was himself trained by Dominican reformists from Spain.[40] This substantial Dominican influence may explain the predominance of Dominican ideology in Montemayor's works; based on their content, one could reasonably postulate an innate attraction to the Order's way of thinking, which could have been reinforced by his exposure to it during his youthful years. Historical events make that a possibility: the Portuguese court fled the plague in Lisbon and took refuge in Coimbra during the early 1530s.[41] Montemayor was only twenty-three kilometers away in Montemôr-o-velho, and he might well have had contact with the court in Coimbra. It is unlikely that he attained the prestigious position of singer in the royal Spanish chapel in 1548 coming straight from his small hometown along the Mondego.

Portuguese and Spanish royalty had intimate political and familial relationships during the years Montemayor was serving the latter, years during which his works indicate a personal as well as professional alliance with both houses. It seems safe to assume that, whether in Portugal or Spain, Montemayor had contact with a group of Catholic reformists, mostly Dominicans, who influenced the religious beliefs expressed in his writings.[42] Given Luis de Granada's extensive work in Portugal and visits to the Por-

---

40. Dias, *Correntes de sentimento religioso*, 82–161.
41. Vasconcelos, editor of Sâ de Miranda's *Poesias*, xviii.
42. Most religious historians describe the early sixteenth-century reform movement by categories of religious Orders, which indeed serve to make important distinctions. However, it is important to note that those reformists with whose works Montemayor's share significant themes were not limited to the ideals of their own Orders. For example, the Dominican Luis de Granada was personally and ideologically close to Franciscans and Jesuits, Juan de Ávila in particular. Indeed, the Jesuits defended him against accusations of Illuminism brought against him by a fellow Dominican in 1577. On these interrelationships see Resina Rodrigues's chapters (*Granada y la literatura*, 519–44) and Andrés Martín, LR.

tuguese court in Évora before his 1551 appointment, it is not surprising to find that Montemayor's religious writings can be most strongly allied to those of this eloquent and personable Dominican.

It may never be determined when, or even if, Montemayor ever had direct contact with Luis de Granada; there is no specific mention of the friar in his works, but neither is there mention of any other contemporary theologian or religious figure. Regardless, the thematic and ideological similarities between Montemayor's post-1548 religious works and those of the Dominican are undeniable. The first half of Montemayor's "Spiritual Dialogue" is fundamentally based on Peter Lombard's scholastic masterpiece the *Sententiae*, and the second half is an adaptation of St. John Climacus's *Scala paradisi* (*The Heavenly Ladder*; St. John, one of the Desert Fathers, was canonized in 649). This balance between medieval scholasticism and ascetic meditative piety is characteristic of the Dominican spirituality then prevalent at the College of San Gregorio de Valladolid, where Luis de Granada was educated and where Montemayor boasted that his 1558 religious works were examined. According to Vicente Beltrán de Heredia, "Perfectly harmonized medieval scholasticism, Savonarolian idealism, and a bit of Erasmist humanism are, then, the factors which figured in Dominican life in these Castilian centers [San Esteban, San Gregorio] during the second quarter of the century."[43] Climacus's text was among those which Cisneros personally had translated from Greek into Latin and printed (Toledo 1505), and the *Scala*, a prescriptive exposition about virtues and vices, was one of the most popular works of the Catholic reformists. Luis de Granada himself translated the *Scala* and, although that translation was not published until 1562, works from his earliest on contain material taken directly from it.

A persistent and peculiar attention to certain events of the Passion also links Montemayor with Granada. The former's devotion to the sufferings of Christ is manifest in his long verse narrative and commentary on the same, published in both his 1554 and 1558 volumes of poetry, and also in the persistent way in which he returns to the values of the redemption in his other works. Luis de Granada's *Book of Prayer* begins with a detailed and lengthy exegesis of the same topic that shares remarkable details with Montemayor's poetic version. For example, the Dominican friar develops

---

43. *Las corrientes de espiritualidad entre los dominicos de Castilla durante la primera mitad del siglo 16*, 50.

the encounter between Jesus on the cross and Mary, emphasizing the mother's compassionate suffering when he says of her to Christ, "The woman who 'you knew so well' was crucified with you on the cross" (La cual tan de cierto sabías contigo estar crucificada en la cruz, LdO, 70). Montemayor likewise observes that Mary was transformed into her son during his sufferings on the cross: "because she was transformed / into the one who was suffering," (porque estaba transformada / en aquel que padecía, SCS, 110v; GP, 192).

The parallels continue: as Granada observes, "The pain of the son grew with the presence of the mother" (Crecieron los dolores del Hijo con la presencia de la madre, LdO, 70). Montemayor says, "There was the pain doubled / when the two saw each another" (allí fue el dolor doblado / cuando se vieron los dos, SCS, 110v; GP, 193).[44] After relating Christ's death, Granada also describes Mary's soul as more dead than alive, "her soul, without death [still alive], already more than dead," and later exclaims of her life after the crucifixion, "Oh dead life!" (su ánimo sin muerte ya más que muerto; ¡Oh vida muerta!, LdO, 70, 80). Montemayor uses an identical paradox to describe her: "The Virgin lives without life" (La virgen vive sin vida, SCE, 123r; GP, 206). The piercing of Christ's side by Longinus releases the blood to cleanse the sins of the world in Granada's prose version: "Water and blood were released with which the sins of the world are cleansed" (Salió agua y sangre con que se lavan los pecados del mundo, LdO, 78). Montemayor's verse adaptation likewise says

> water and blood by the hand
> of Longinus ran down
> . . . .
> buying back the human race
>
> (Agua y sangre por la mano
> de Longinos fue corriendo
> . . . .
> comprando al linaje humano.)
> (SCE, 123v; GP, 207)

44. In the scene of Mary's compassion at the foot of the cross, Granada is adapting from the Pseudo-Tauler's *Exercitia super vita et passione Salvatoris* (Latin transl. 1548), as Fidel de Ros has indicated ("Los místicos del norte y Fray Luis de Granada," 149–51). It may be that Montemayor is as well, although other parallels between his works and Granada's make it more likely that he was using the Dominican's ideas directly.

These are but a sampling from a multitude of specific turns of phrase that Montemayor seems to have borrowed from Granada. They are complemented by fundamental similarities of vision, which will be discussed in the next section.

A number of possibilities arise to explain this relationship. It may be that the two have a source in common which has yet to come to light. Montemayor may have met Granada or may have heard him preach while in Seville; upon returning to the court from Seville some time before 1552, Montemayor exchanged poems with his friend Gutierre de Cetina, which later appeared in his *Works* (GP, 63–64). For his part, before being sent to Portugal in 1551, Granada was the most sought-after religious speaker of the Andalusian aristocracy. As mentioned above, it is likely that the two had contact during Montemayor's years of service as Princess Juana's chamberlain, while Granada was serving the Archbishop, Juana's brother-in-law. The Dominican's *Book of Prayer* was finished by 1546, and although it remained unpublished until 1554, it likely served Granada for sermon material during those intervening years and may also have circulated in manuscript.[45] Luis de Granada's own spirituality, however eclectic, had its roots in the heart of traditional Spanish Catholic reformism.

Perhaps because of its conservative nature, perhaps because of its unquestioning alliance to the Catholic Church as an institution (a generally unpopular stance in the modern era), or perhaps because it constituted the simple but solid trunk from which more dramatic and modern spirituality flowered in Spain, this type of piety has been relatively little attended until very recently. Its extremely complex history intertwines with the heresies that flourished with it across the first quarter of the sixteenth century, that is, religious currents that were declared unacceptable by the Catholic Church in the middle of the same century. Spanish Catholic reformism shared many ideals with types of piety from which it was subsequently forced to divorce due to events in European and Peninsular history. Careful attention to its salient features is important as a foundation for study of sixteenth-century Spanish literature such as Montemayor's, religious and secular alike, for it was the Catholic reformists who were

---

45. On Granada in Andalusia, see Huerga, "Fray Luis de Granada en Escalaceli. Nuevos datos para el conocimiento histórico y espiritual de su vida," 479. On the dates of the *Book of Prayer*, José María Balcells, editor of Granada's *Guía de pecadores*, 107.

largely responsible for the spiritual formation of the Spanish empire during the first half of that century. It was they who taught Montemayor to interpret the world and humanity's role in it as he did in the *Diana*.

The intricate relationship between Catholic reformism and other types of sixteenth-century piety has produced inaccuracies in the interpretation of Spanish Golden Age literature in general, and of Montemayor's religious works in particular. As a consequence, his religiousness has been mistakenly categorized as pertaining to spiritual currents outside the confines of the one to which they rightly belong. Reconsideration of his religious works and their relationship to those of writers like Luis de Granada makes possible not only a clear understanding of his ideology, but also an interpretation of the *Diana* different from the one offered by literary scholarship until now, one more faithful to his works as a whole as well as to the age in which he lived.

Spanish Catholic Reformation and the Recogidos: Texts and Contexts

Sixteenth-century Catholic reformism in Spain was the product of a long movement of Christian reform, the origins of which are debated by historians. José Sebastião da Silva Dias traces it back to the end of the twelfth century. Andrés Martín maintains that foundation of the Hieronymite order in 1373 makes manifest its beginnings, and he opens his history of recogido piety, which he named after the meditative method practiced by many of the Catholic reformists, with the last quarter of the fifteenth century. Luis Sala Balust holds that the reform itself began with the founding of the observant convent Escalaceli in Córdoba by Fray Alvaro de Zamora (d. 1430). From there, he says, other reforms were generated that took place before the Catholic Kings became the patrons of Cisneros: the foundations of San Esteban in Salamanca and San Gregorio in Valladolid.[46]

---

46. On the early reform almost all of the studies of sixteenth-century spirituality published since 1937 have supported or challenged Bataillon's strong statement about the pervasive influence of Erasmus in Spain, which begins with a chapter on Cisneros (E&E, 1–71). Since the book's publication, judicious studies have attempted to reestablish the balance between native Spanish piety, founded on the ascetic tradition that is quite alien to Erasmism and Christian humanism, and foreign influences, a balance that was offset by critical enthusiasm for Bataillon's monumental study. The French

All agree that the Spanish Catholic reform movement reached a climax at the turn of the century under the decisive leadership of Cisneros, who was responsible for stabilizing a deep and far-reaching reform in the religious organization and the spiritual life of the emerging nation.[47] Among his most significant activities were the reestablishment of the Franciscan observancy, the founding of the University of Alcalá de Henares, and patronage of the translation and printing of many books about ascetic and meditative experience. Cisneros's projects represented the balance between faith and works, between retirement from the world and activity in it, that characterized most of the Spanish Catholic reformists.

Bataillon and Dias both use the term "pre-reform" to distinguish Cisneros's activities from Luther's "reform." However, the term "Catholic reform" suffices to mark the difference between the two and does not imply the temporal rupture or change in focus implied by the historically nonexistent distinction between "pre-reform" and the Catholic reform itself. Most who study the sources of sixteenth-century Spanish piety agree that there was a direct relationship between the spirit of discovery fundamental to religious reform and the same spirit evident in European maritime expeditions, scientific discoveries, and culture in general. There is agreement that the reform movement in the Low Countries, the *devotio moderna* and the Brothers of the Common Life, conjoined at the end of the fifteenth century and overlapped in Spain with influences from Italy, Italian Dominicans in particular and Savonarola most notably, although the relative importance of the Flemish and Italian movements is debated.[48]

---

scholar's monograph continues to be the strongest statement about the reform initiated by Cisneros as one fundamentally related to European spirituality. See Dias, *Correntes de sentimento religioso*, Andrés Martín, *Reforma española* and LR, Sala Balust, "La espiritualidad española en la primera mitad del siglo 16."

47. Sala Balust's article on sixteenth-century Spanish spirituality ("La espiritualidad española"), Angela Selke's article about illuminism ("El iluminismo de los conversos y la Inquisición. Cristianismo interior de los alumbrados: resentimiento y sublimación"), and Eugenio Asensio's response to Bataillon's ideas about Erasmism ("El erasmismo y las corrientes espirituales afines") all stress the importance of this continuity. Pedro Sainz Rodríguez's book describes the spirituality fostered by Cisneros (*La siembra mística del Cardenal Cisneros y las reformas en la Iglesia*). Bataillon reserves the term "Catholic reform" for the generation including Constantino de la Fuente and Francisco de Borja (E&E, 714).

48. A representative listing of some sources on each side of the argument will suffice here: for Erasmism, Pierre Groult's *Los místicos de los países bajos y la literatura*

It is now generally affirmed that, although it assimilated some influences from abroad, Spanish reformism had acquired characteristics unique to itself by the time Cisneros began to mold the Franciscan reform at the turn of the century. Spain's reformist practices and piety demonstrate a marked continuity with a long Christian tradition of asceticism and meditative, affective piety, from which the movement never separated, a heritage that marks it as distinct from religious expression of other countries during the same period. Held up to comparable English religious literature, for example, its "passionately exuberant religious sensibility" and "extravagant hyperbole" are notable. Considering the influence of Ignatian meditative techniques on sixteenth- and seventeenth-century English religious verse, Edward Wilson observes, "The religious poetry of Spain became capable of expressing itself in completely human terms. Religion and life thus remained to an extraordinary degree in contact with one another."[49] These qualities may reflect the concern with popular piety consistently displayed by the Catholic reformists.

This sentimental Spanish religiousness had developed within early Christian monasticism and prospered in the hands of sixteenth-century Catholic reformers of all orders. It was the only type of Catholic reformism to emerge, battered but triumphant, through the crucial years of Tridentine reform and Inquisitorial repression of the mid-sixteenth century, and is the brand of piety that made possible the works of a woman like Santa Teresa, whose mysticism is so characteristically Spanish. The saint's relationship to foreign currents of devotion and religious scholarship is clearly insignificant when compared to the influence exercised on her religious practice by native sources of recogimiento, such as Francisco de Osuna's *Tercer abecedario espiritual* (*Third Spiritual Alphabet*, 1527).

Osuna's treatise and Luis de Granada's famous *Book of Prayer* constitute the two best-known manuals of Catholic reformist meditation called

---

espiritual española del siglo 16, Marcel Bataillon's "Une source de Gil Vicente et de Montemôr: la Méditation de Savonarole sur le *Miserere,*" and his "Sur la diffusion des oeuvres de Savonarole en Espagne et au Portugal (1500–1560)." Among those supporting other sources are Alonso's "Sobre Erasmo y Fray Luis de Granada," Asensio's "El erasmismo," Castro's "Lo hispánico y el erasmismo," and Whinnom's "The Supposed Sources of Inspiration of Spanish Fifteenth-century Narrative Religious Verse."

49. R. V. Young, *Richard Crashaw and the Spanish Golden Age,* 1; Edward Wilson, "Spanish and English Religious Poetry of the Seventeenth Century," 43.

recogimiento.[50] The relationship between the recogidos and the Catholic reformists was not absolute; although many of the Catholic reformists practiced recogimiento meditation, not all did. Nonetheless, the recogidos' contemplative ideals were directly related to the mission of the Catholic reform. Specifically, there was a strong correlation between the private recogido practice of asceticism as a part of meditation and the public concerns of the Catholic reformists, such as the observant monasticism and the general social reform they endorsed.

As the vogue of recogido piety within Spain gathered momentum, other types of private spirituality and communal reformism developed, trends with which the Catholic reformation shared some important features and for which it is often confused with them. These are currents that either arrived from abroad or surged forth from the country's own spiritual energy, trends that were determined to be heretical by the Inquisition and so were removed from Spain, often violently. The most important ones for the matter at hand include Illuminism (1512–1525), Erasmism (1516–1559), and Lutheranism (1517–1563). The illuminists themselves claimed to have been practicing what was eventually branded as Illuminism as early as 1512; although there were four more important outbreaks of Illuminism in Spain after the initial illuminist flare-up in Toledo that ended with the 1525 edict against them, the second outburst was not until 1579. Erasmism officially began in Spain when Cisneros invited Erasmus to work on the polyglot Bible in 1516 and officially ended when the Valdés *Index* of 1559 prohibited the Dutch scholar's works or any trace thereof. The dates for Luther are that of his posting of his theses in Wittenberg, and the last

---

50. Although San Ignacio de Loyola's *Ejercicios espirituales* (1548) might appear related, they are radically different in tone, form, and content from books like Osuna's and Granada's. Because they lack both imaginative imagery and rhetorical devices related to preaching, the *Ejercicios* may be considered tangential to recogido treatises for literary reasons, just as Loyola's activities in his later life separate him from the Catholic reformists (on the latter, see Andrés Martín, *La teología española en el siglo 16*, 1:194–96). The Dominicans in general, Carranza, Bartolomé de los Mártires, and Granada in particular, did participate in recogido spirituality, although the official Dominican position with respect to mysticism was generally critical by the 1550s, when that order led the Counter-Reformation. Logically, in that context both Granada and Carranza's works were prohibited in 1559. See Andrés Martín, "Trayectoria del recogimiento entre los dominicos," LR, 392–449.

year of the Council of Trent, by which time the Lutheran religious and political separation from the Holy Roman Empire was absolute.[51]

Elements of all three of these movements have allegedly been found in Montemayor's religious writings, Lutheranism typically being mentioned in relationship to Illuminism. About Montemayor's "Spiritual Dialogue" alone, for example, these opinions emerge: Creel, echoing part of Mario Martins's interpretation, finds it Erasmist; López Estrada finds it contains elements of mysticism (LD, XV); Estevá, likewise developing an idea proposed by Martins, unnecessarily goes all the way back to Sabunde and various other medieval philosophers for Montemayor's sources. Martins himself interprets it in light of humanist theology.[52] Although the correctness of all of these interpretations may be chronologically imaginable, it is ideologically impossible. The fact that Bataillon, whose signature figures on the list of people who saw the manuscript of the "Dialogue" in Évora, passed over this and Montemayor's other works in silence, would seem to put the question of Erasmism and humanist theology in the works of Montemayor to rest. His suggestion that the works of Carranza and Granada are the appropriate sources of inspiration for the Portuguese author (E&E, 608), on the other hand, has gone unheeded. However, these seemingly disparate elements of religiousness do indeed all pertain to the ideals of Spanish Catholic reformism without contradiction. The time has come to lay aside modern prejudice against Montemayor's most important precursors, for not only did they influence him, they held Golden Age Spain in rapt attention for years.

Catholic Reformism in History

The age of Cardinal Cisneros at the turn of the century was the culmination of attempts at sweeping monastic reform, beginning with the mendicant orders, which sought to reinstate those orders' original rules. Although others participated, the central protagonists in this reform were the Franciscans and the Dominicans, both committed to contact with the

---

51. Andrés Martín provides dates for all of the illuminist movements in *Nueva visión*, 33. Bataillon describes Cisneros's unsuccessful attempt to lure Erasmus to Spain in E&E, 72–73.

52. Creel, *Religious Poetry*, 60; Mario Martins, "Uma obra inédita de Jorge de Montemayor"; María Dolores Estevá, "El 'Diálogo spiritual' de Jorge de Montemayor."

lay population, with which they worked zealously to spread their ideals. Concurrent to practical monastic reform, Spanish Catholic reformists developed ideological and contemplative piety designed to re-form the meditative process as well, specifically recogimiento, mentioned above, whose essential "withdrawal" or "recollection," follows the process of purification in mystical experience.[53] The origins and early developments of recogimiento are amply studied by Melquíades Andrés Martín (LR, 21–107).

In very broad terms, Spain's recogimiento is distinguishable from other sixteenth-century types of piety by the three qualities mentioned above: its foundation in asceticism, its representatives' concern with teaching Catholic doctrine as well as techniques of meditation, and the balance between contemplation and action upon which its practitioners insisted. The word *reform* is important, for emphasis in this context was consistently placed on renewed contact with the Christian past, on reestablishing religious purity in form and in spirit. It was a return to something perceived as lost.[54] Spanish Catholic reformism was a self-consciously conservative movement; its participants made an effort to rediscover and conserve traditional ideals and practices which they felt had been abandoned, and in the process they did not pretend to be original (LR, 782). The Counter-Reformation, which was well under way by the mid-sixteenth century, actively undercut this type of conservatism in favor of another.

The early ideals of the Catholic reformists, many of which were common to European currents of piety, inspired variations on themselves in Spain that eventually proved to be the downfall of the early reform. The illuminists or *alumbrados*, Bataillon's *dejados*, practiced an exaggerated form of lay piety based on ideas that were actually imparted to them in the early sixteenth century by the practitioners of recogimiento.[55] Since no illuminist manifesto or treatise is known to exist, all beliefs attributed to its practitioners have been deduced from letters and Inquisitorial records,

---

53. Evelyn Underhill's 1911 book on mysticism remains the most eloquent description of the mystical process; she discusses recollection in chapter 6, part 1: "Introversion: Recollection and Quiet" (*Mysticism: A Study in the Nature and Development of Man's Spiritual Consciousness*, 298–327).

54. See José Ignacio Tellechea Idigoras's study for interesting descriptions of Melchor Cano's violent reactions to writers who exalted the primitive church (*El catecismo del Arzobispo Carranza*, 17–26).

55. For example, Francisco de Osuna took part in illuminist meetings before 1524 (see Andrés Martín, *Nueva visión*, 14–22).

leaving us with an irrevocably slanted perspective. It seems, however, that the alumbrados displayed alarming tendencies toward exhibitionism, an anxiety for supernatural experiences, disdain for Church hierarchy and even for civil law, and general lack of decorum and control in favor of total abandon to God's love. None of these practices were shared or encouraged by other reformist movements of the age.

The aberrant and extreme nature of Illuminism's theocentricity, along with its practitioners' other imprudences, led to two definitive ruptures between the illuminists and those whom they apparently believed they were imitating: one in 1524, the date of the Franciscan Provincial Capital's decree against Illuminism; the other in 1525, the date of an Inquisitorial edict condemning the movement and anything like it.[56] By the time Montemayor began to write, it was extremely dangerous to display any form of Illuminism in religious writings; there is no reason to assume that he was not aware of exactly the extent of the danger.

Importantly, Illuminism was not born heretical, rather it became so in the changing political environment of western Europe during the first quarter of the sixteenth century. A movement such as Illuminism was could have only come about under the universality of religious experience that the Catholic reformists exalted by taking their spirituality out of the monasteries and into the world at large. The ideals of the reform were effectively communicated via the pulpit and to the reading population through the multitude of self-help books and pamphlets written to instruct the reader on how to attain holiness and grace. Kamen describes preaching during the years referred to here, saying, "Sermons were to the public of those days what television is to the twentieth century: the most direct form of control over opinion." The preaching and publication system appears to have backfired eventually, since by the end of the sixteenth century, congregational awareness of doctrinal matters had risen to such

---

56. The 1525 edict appears in Antonio Márquez, *Los alumbrados, orígines y filosofía (1525–1559)*, 229–38. Studies of Illuminism have proliferated over the last twenty years; several are mentioned here as their authors are cited. Its characteristics cited above are from Asensio, "El erasmismo," 72–77, and Andrés Martín, *Nueva visión*. José C. Nieto's article provides extensive bibliography on the subject: "El carácter no místico de los alumbrados de Toledo, 1509?–1524." The intricacies of Toledan illuminism are made evident in Milagros Ortega Costa's edition of María de Cazalla's Inquisitorial trial, *Proceso de la Inquisición contra María de Cazalla*.

heights that the preachers felt threatened, and obliged to entertain their audiences as well as instruct them.[57]

The spiritual inquietude of the age is captured in the veritable plethora of instructional treatises on doctrinal material published in the vulgar tongue, some of which were intended for the professional religious, while others were written for lay readers. These treatises differ from those on which Bataillon concentrates in *Erasmus and Spain*, in that they attend to popular piety and professional devotion, and are thus only tangentially related to the more elite Christian humanists to whom the French scholar devotes most of his thorough attention.[58] The overwhelming popularity of this literature among the reading population cannot be denied, and it surely exercised a significant influence on sixteenth-century culture as a whole; it bears repeating that Luis de Granada's *Book of Prayer* was published more, by far, than any other book in sixteenth-century Spain and would have been printed even more had Granada not been forced to take time to rewrite it after its inclusion on Valdés's *Index* in 1559. This type of treatise was a fundamental part of the apostolic mission being carried out by the Catholic reformers, who, like reformers of any age, were using all resources at their disposal to communicate their message.

A significant body of Spain's ostracized population, the conversos, found in recogido spirituality a type of piety with which they could identify, one which exalted inner, individual qualities that defied measure and control, and recognized inner worth over social standing and name. Such an attraction is understandable, given their circumstances. Among Spanish Jews converted to Catholicism, there were many who converted sincerely. Others were less sincere, but either way the conversos found themselves in a homeland that denied them inclusion in mainstream society, a situation aggravated as the statutes of pure blood accumulated across the sixteenth century. The marginality to which they were subjected made the ideals of reformist Catholicism, which exalted inner piety over ritualistic

---

57. Kamen, *Inquisition*, 205. Otis Green, "Se acicalaron los auditorios: An Aspect of the Spanish Literary Baroque." A work comparable to Hilary Smith's *Preaching in the Spanish Golden Age: A Study of Some Preachers of the Reign of Philip III* remains to be done for the sixteenth century.

58. For a sampling of the more popular treatises, see Pedro Sainz Rodríguez's *Antología de la literatura espiritual española (Edad Media, Siglo 16)*; Andrés Martín studies a great number as well in *Los recogidos*.

observance, particularly meaningful to them. Some of the members of the religious orders who practiced recogido meditation are believed to have been conversos, notably the Franciscan Osuna and the Jesuit Ávila, and the great majority of illuminists are believed to have been conversos as well.[59] This does not mean that the conversos were seeking an indirect way to return to Judaism via reformism or Illuminism; none of the convicted illuminists were engaged in crypto-judaizing, although they were of converso heritage. On the contrary, the illuminists, like many of the conversos, were doubtless sincere in their practice of their Catholicism.

The intimate relationship between the Catholic reformists and the illuminists, many of whom were women and most of whom were uneducated, stands as testimony of the popular nature of native Spanish reformism in the form in which it spread to the lay people. Importantly, although the most well-known authors of recogido treatises were as well educated as the humanists, theirs was a piety that strove to touch the Christian's soul, emotions, and conscience, not the individual's intellect. It is a notably sentimental piety, quite purposefully directed at an all-inclusive audience. Thus, this reformist trend was separate from, although given impulse by, Christian humanism in Spain such as the scholarly activities at the newly founded University at Alcalá de Henares. In cases of conflict, however, Spanish Catholic reformism was true to faith at the expense of the intellect: the story of Cisneros's refusal to alter the text of the Vulgate for publication in the polyglot Bible, where humanist scholar Antonio de Nebrija insisted there was an error, is telling (E&E, 35–39).

There was, then, a reformist environment prospering on the Peninsula, under the leadership of men such as the Franciscan Cisneros and the Dominican Hurtado de Mendoza, by the time Erasmism became a known entity there. The illuminist movement, however distinct from Erasmism

---

59. On Osuna, see Andrés Martin, *Nueva visión*, 22; on Avila, Sala Balust "La espiritualidad española," 178. Selke ("El iluminismo") repeats Sala Balust's insistence that the converso illuminists were not attempting to return to their old faith; Selke points to the uniquely Spanish quality of illuminism because of the converso population's significant participation in it and that group's relatively new relationship with Catholicism. Her thesis, which is also Nieto's ("El carácter no místico"), that the *alumbrados* constituted a strictly Hispanic phenomenon (618) might be reexamined in light of Carolyn Walker Bynum's discussion of the fourteenth-century Free Spirit movement, fundamentally identical to that of the *alumbrados* (*Holy Feast and Holy Fast: The Religious Significance of Food to Medieval Women*, 16–18).

on many points, shares the idealistic fervor and some of the theoretical ideals of the Dutchman's intellectual piety; those similarities and the illuminists' dramatic history produced an entanglement between the two that led to their mutual destruction and continues to this day. As mentioned above, Isabel de la Cruz and Pedro Ruiz de Alcaraz were among those already practicing Illuminism by 1512, and Erasmus's unique popularity on the Peninsula was surely made possible by the reformist environment that included the recogidos and the illuminists alike, one in which the need for return to original Christian ideals and monastic reform had already been recognized and a campaign to realize those ideals begun. The same chronology is applicable to Lutheranism, which touched Spain shortly after the illuminists had begun their practices and after Erasmism had begun its meteoric climb there. Luther's works were introduced in Spain by Froben in 1519, and, judging from Inquisitorial records of the 1525 trials of the illuminists, none of the German friar's works were in any of their libraries; the illuminists were sparked by the Catholic reformists, not the Lutherans.[60] This order is important to establish, for it makes clear the fact that the Catholic reform movement itself predated all three of these spiritual currents in Spain, and although based on a common idealism, it did not emerge from them nor was it dependent upon them for existence.

Illuminism, Erasmism, and Lutheranism, and ultimately the Catholic reformation itself, all threatened the establishment in Spain by challenging the Church hierarchy as it then existed. Once Spanish Catholic reformism gathered a certain momentum beyond its monastic origins, it was swept into the greater tide of European religious issues and was irrevocably associated with extraneous circumstances. The Church did not hesitate long before labelling the threatening elements as heretical and beginning to extract them from Spain. Consequently, all elements of Illuminism, Erasmism, and Lutheranism were forcibly exorcised from Catholic reformism, and along with them went some of the dearest ideals of the most devoutly Catholic men in Spain. The Catholic reformists, all deeply committed to the Church, did not hesitate to conform, however sadly and bitterly.[61] Of particular importance in this context was the reformist ideal of

60. See Andrés Martín, *Nueva visión*, 33–35, and *Reforma española (1517–1536)*.
61. For example, Loyola supposedly burnt all his manuscripts upon hearing of Valdés's 1559 decree ordering that all unpublished writings dealing with matters of the

superseding the intermediary between the worshipper and God, a common feature of all these types of reform, one clearly unacceptable (to the ecclesiastical order then in power) as a universal practice, since that order's power depended on such mediation for existence. As Andrés Martín observes, "The Inquisitors calibrated the political transcendence of radical negation of all mediation."[62]

The ideal of unmediated contact between the worshipper and God serves as a paradigm for other Catholic reformist ideals, such as the practice of retirement from the world and the translation of the Bible into the vulgar tongues, which suffered a similar fate. Acceptable in their original context, that of monastic communities, these ideals were originally meant to be interpreted in very specific, controlled ways, interpretations that were lost once they were passed on to the Spanish community at large. In their Christian zeal, the Catholic reformers did not distinguish between the professional religious population and the lay people, an omission that offended what Dias calls the *"falange conservadora,"* or conservative troops that fortified the Counter-Reformation. Melchor Cano, a bulwark of that fortification, censored Luis de Granada for three reasons: "for having pretended to turn everyone into a perfect contemplative, and teaching the whole population, in Castilian, what is appropriate for only a few, . . . for having promised to all a common and general path to perfection, without vows of chastity, poverty, or obedience."[63] That is, Melchor Cano was offended that Granada would offer the benefits of Christ to the general population without exacting the forms of piety required of the professionally religious to attain the same benefits.

In spite of their differences, the Catholic reformists tended not to break with the Church across the years, even when it became clear that, as Bataillon says, "people were being burnt in 1558 who, a few years earlier, would have expiated their sins with penances of short duration" (E&E, 709). One would search in vain for a work written by a Spanish Catholic reformist denying the rightness of Church hierarchy and ceremonies for the average Christian, or questioning the importance of regular contact

---

faith so disappear. Immediately thereafter, so the story goes, he took to his bed, sick at heart (Kamen, *Inquisition*, 83).

62. *Nueva visión*, 24.

63. Dias, *Correntes de sentimento religioso*, 31. Huerga, *Fray Luis de Granada*, 147. Huerga quotes from F. Caballero's 1871 biography of Melchor Cano.

with and control of the individual by a superior.[64] Originally intended to *encourage* individual spiritual experience without interfering in the proper functioning of Church order, recogimiento was increasingly associated with *discouraging* individual subjection to established Church authority as the sixteenth century progressed. At the point where this contamination became unavoidable, the Inquisition intervened, and the nature of Catholic reformism itself was forced to change. Thereafter, issues such as blanket belief in the workings of the Holy Mother Catholic Church, which had been implied in their ideology all along, had to be spelled out, and carefully.

A case to illustrate this point is whether an error on the point of justification led to Inquisitorial intervention or not. It was largely a matter of chance before 1547, because the interpretative breadth of the issue was then wide and its enforcement somewhat arbitrary. Even though the decree clarifying the matter, published after the sixth session of the Council of Trent, did away with that interpretative plurality, it did not dictate how its exposition would be enforced. Sala Balust maintains that Juan de Ávila, who had himself participated in the early sessions at Trent, waited for the final decree on justification to settle in Spain before publishing an authorized version of his *Audi, filia*. Although he died before its 1574 publication, the book had been finished by 1548 and, according to Sala Balust, was published without Ávila's approval in 1556. This first edition was on the 1559 *Index*.[65] It was extremely difficult to remain a Catholic reformist and an orthodox Catholic at the same time. To write about one's reformist convictions was to ask for trouble.

In the process of this conservative "reformation" of the Spanish Catholic reform movement itself, indeed a counterreformation, many of the participants in earlier reformist activity were tried by the Inquisition, some were convicted as heretics, and several saw their works censored by Val-

---

64. Isolated sentences challenging the contemporary Church and its practices may indeed be found. However, Andrés Martín (LR, 28) and others point to the need to examine spiritual treatises as entire works; focus on single sentences produces the analytical anarchy that typified Inquisitorial censure of religious literature around 1558. With this in mind, quotations from religious texts are limited here to those which respect the ideological integrity of each work.

65. See Sala Balust's introduction to his edition of Ávila's text and, on Ávila's participation in the Council of Trent, Ricardo García-Villoslada, "Pedro Guerrero, representante de la reforma española," 124–45.

dés. The very disturbing case of the Dominican Archbishop Bartolomé Carranza de Miranda, whose seventeen-year-long trial ended eighteen days before his death (whether of illness, disillusion, or old age is unknown), is poignantly representative of the spiritual environment in which Montemayor's religious writings were prohibited, along with Carranza's. The Archbishop's *Comentarios sobre el Catechismo christiano* (*Commentaries on the Christian Catechism*) were on the 1559 Spanish *Index;* they were subsequently approved by the third session of the Council of Trent (1561–1563). Modern interpretation of these cases seems almost as fraught with tension as the original events; the personal and political conflicts that figured into Carranza's conviction by Melchor Cano are as completely described by Kamen as they are ignored by Andrés Martín.[66]

It was in this environment that the Jesuit Francisco de Borja left Spain, fearing for his life. As church and state organized their defense against "heresy," orthodoxy was redefined in procedures, investigations, and decrees that proliferated until well after the Council of Trent ended in 1563. Nonetheless, the definition of heresy was extremely malleable throughout the mid-sixteenth century. Indeed, one of the sentences from Carranza's *Catechism* most harshly censored by Melchor Cano as irrefutable evidence of Illuminism was actually a rigorous translation of a passage from Saint Thomas's *Summa theologica*. During this period of redefinition, the Spanish Catholic reformists struggled to maintain their loyalty to the Church without compromising their spiritual integrity. The struggle cost some of them their lives.[67]

Although the theoretical ideals of Catholic reformism remained unmodified by the Council of Trent, the ways in which they could be expressed without a breach in orthodoxy changed dramatically, and the ways in which they could be expressed in Spain were extremely problematic. Luis de

---

66. Kamen, *Inquisition*, 155–60; Andrés Martín, LR, 301–2. On the history of Carranza's *Catechismo*, see Tellechea Idigoras's introduction to his edition of it, 3–96. Kamen's peculiar article, "Toleration and Dissent in Sixteenth-century Spain: The Alternative Tradition," does little to alter established historical opinion about this period (opinion largely established by Kamen's own previous publications).

67. On the passage from the *Summa*, see Tellechea Idigoras, *El catecismo*, 22. The reform did not die with the reformists who died for it, as Saint Teresa proves so well. It did, however, take on different qualities in the second half of the century, changes that do not figure in a study about Montemayor. Bataillon (in the final chapters of E&E) and Andrés Martín (LR) deal with the Counter-Reformation.

Granada did not discard his prohibited works, rather he altered them by lengthening them and reordering passages, attending carefully in the reworkings to points of doctrine centered around form that he had not felt the need to mention in the original versions, and eliminating direct references to prohibited authors such as Serafín de Fermo, Bautista de Crema, and Girolamo Savonarola. That is to say, much of what Cisneros had not only accepted but supported himself as orthodox reform in 1516 was heresy by 1559. Such, for example, was the ideal of biblical translation into Spanish, made impossible by Valdés's prohibition of the Bible in the vulgar tongues.

What truly calls attention to the 1559 *Index* is its display of a concentrated effort to efface the very school of meditative piety that Cisneros had encouraged by his publication of instructional and mystical treatises: Tauler, Fermo, Herp, Rickel, Castello, Osuna, Palma, Granada, Ávila, de Borja. The Inquisitors Valdés and Cano were clearly as committed to shutting the general population off from the secrets and mysteries of Catholic spirituality as their predecessors had been to opening it up to those same people. Cano maintained, "There is no mystery where there is no secret" (No hay misterio donde no hay secreto).[68] Luis de Granada's reaction to Inquisitor General Valdés's censorship of his own books is worth repeating, for, after speaking to Valdés himself about the *Index* which had just gone to print, he wrote to his friend Carranza that the Inquisitor was "so set against things, as he calls them, about contemplation for carpenters' wives" (tan contrario a cosas, como él llama, de contemplación para mujeres de carpinteros). The quote is extremely revealing, not only because Valdés therein disdains the Virgin Mary, but because it indicates how significant women's participation in reformist piety was.[69]

---

68. Andrés Martín comments on the prohibited authors in *La teología española*, 2:621. Cano's statement is in Tellechea, *El catecismo*, 16. This mentality is by no means limited to Spanish Inquisitor Generals; I recall, with Edgar Wind, its support by Saint Augustine, Pico della Mirandola, and, along the same lines, "the pernicious axiom of [Edmund] Burke that 'a clear idea is another name for a little idea'" (*Pagan Mysteries in the Renaissance*, 22–23).

69. Granada's letter is reproduced in Huerga, *Luis de Granada*, 143–44. On women's participation in the reform movements, see Bataillon, E&E, 69–70, 177–78, 452–53; Ronald E. Surtz, *The Guitar of God: Gender, Power, and Authority in the Visionary World of Mother Juana de la Cruz (1481–1534)*; and Jodi Bilinkoff, *The Avila of Saint Teresa: Religious Reform in a Sixteenth-century City*.

It is also remarkable that some of the very works Cisneros had taken care to publish personally, such as Savonarola's commentary on Psalm 50 *Miserere Mei Deus* (Alcalá, 1511), were found to be heretical in the altered religious context that followed the age of the Cardinal. Montemayor wrote a verse adaptation of Savonarola's commentary on the *Miserere* and published the poem in his 1554 *Works*, with another adaptation of Savonarola's exposition on the Lord's Prayer.[70] Caught between the changing tides of Catholic orthodoxy, Montemayor wrote religious literature that, although acceptable at the moment he wrote it (all his collections of religious works were approved by officers of the Inquisition), read like heresy in 1559 and after. The modern perspective similarly tends to brand as illuminist, Erasmist, and Protestant all spirituality that does not conform to conservative Catholic standards of orthodoxy, even when the literature in question was written before those standards existed. Interestingly, Andrew Weiner finds that a similar problem exists in traditional interpretation of reformed Puritanism's influence on the works of Sir Philip Sidney, the essence of which is identical to that indicated here with regard to the role of Catholic reformist piety on those of Montemayor. He suggests, "The difficulty, I think, is one of terminology and chronology. One cannot apply a term which later in its history comes to acquire certain meanings to a period before those meanings were clearly developed without doing a certain amount of damage to the clarity of his argument."[71]

The difficulties of interpretation can be overcome, however, with the aid of hindsight. Bataillon, reflecting on this decisive point in the history of Spanish Catholicism and the problems implicit in interpreting literature related to it, makes important distinctions:

> The Catholic reformers forcefully affirmed their fidelity to Roman discipline, to the formal religious cult, to the theological tradition. But since they did not dwell constantly on those issues, they came to be suspected and fought against by the appointed defendants of orthodoxy as participating more or less in the errors of the Protestant reform. They have been treated, if not as Lutherans, at least as illuminists.

He goes on to emphasize that absolute definitions of Spanish recogi-

---

70. Bataillon ("A Source") and Darbord (*La poésie religieuse espagnole*, 405–19) study Montemayor's adaptation.

71. *Sir Philip Sidney and the Poetics of Protestantism: A Study of Contexts*, 6.

miento and other currents of piety are difficult to make because of the common themes they initially shared, themes which originally served to unite them, not divorce them: "The Spanish school of prayer . . . daughter of the spiritual restlessness of the waning Middle Ages, was the sister of the Protestant reform, a sister long a rival more than an enemy."[72] The changing nature of orthodoxy across the century and the Catholic reformists' constant battle to remain within the confines of that orthodoxy do not, however, undercut the several outstanding qualities of this piety and its literature that serve to separate it unto itself, the qualities that allowed it to survive the spiritual and physical violence of the mid-sixteenth century.

Ideological Distinctions

Like most of the reform movements of its age, the ideals of Spanish Catholic reform centered around the incorporation of religious beliefs into the entire experience of life. It was an affective, personal piety directed toward loving imitation of Christ, in support of which its representatives attempted to educate and thereby guide the mystical body back to its original Christian principles. Like Illuminism, Erasmism, and Protestantism, in its pre-*Index* era, the Catholic reform worked toward making God's word available to all of the faithful and held forth Christian ideals as attainable goals for everyone; its proponents recommended intimate, personal acquaintance with the Bible, and biblical texts form the mainstay of treatises written by them. Although its defenders criticized the abuses of the Church and lamented superficiality in religious practice, as did the Erasmists, they tended to support ecclesiastical order, papal authority, and the virtue of obedience, with its constituent conformity, for Christians in general and themselves in particular.[73]

While concurring with the Erasmists' motto *monachatus non est pietas* (meaning the monastic life is not the equivalent of piety), in that they found all Christians capable of attaining holiness, Spanish reformist Catholics

---

72. Bataillon, "Jeanne d'Autriche," 260.
73. Some of the important studies that point out distinctions between the Catholic reformists, the illuminists, the Erasmists, and the Lutherans are Andrés Martín's *Nueva visión*, his "Introducción general" to Francisco de Osuna's *Tercer abecedario espiritual*, and his *Reforma española;* Sala Balust's "La espiritualidad española"; Bataillon, E&E, 62–71, 172–90; and Asensio's "El erasmismo."

supported the ideal of professional religiousness and most of them were active members of religious communities, not university professors or intellectuals as were many of the Christian humanists. Their support of monastic culture is evident in the values they held forth to the lay population, values derived from ascetic practices centered around renunciation. Erasmism and Illuminism, on the other hand, took a more critical stance before monasticism as it was then practiced, emphasizing the need for individuals in every walk of life to undertake the imitation of Christ and expect to reap the same benefits as the professional religious. In this context, the lay population was discouraged from indulging in the renunciations called for in monastic life. This was not the case with Spanish Catholic reformists who, while not exacting monastic vows from all Christians, did exalt the monastic virtues those vows represented as appropriate for everyone. This ascetic vein was pronounced in sixteenth-century Dominican spirituality, and is likewise apparent in Montemayor's religious works.[74]

Universally, Christians were encouraged by the Catholic reformists to practice good works as a complement and natural result of their faith, to renounce worldliness, to practice moral sex only and chastity when possible, and to obey the mandates of the Church. All of these recommendations are present in Montemayor's religious writings; it is in this spirit that his hermit Dileto begins to instruct Severo, saying that mortification of the flesh and of one's own will is the road to God, "for which you must first believe what the Holy Mother Church believes, which is God's truth, and you must believe it sincerely and clearly, not needing any reason or cause, but believing as our Lord commands that we believe" (para lo cual primeramente has de creer lo que la santa madre Iglesia cree, que es la verdad del Señor, y háslo de creer clara y sinceramente, sin pedir otra razón ni causa sino como manda Nuestro Señor que los creamos, DS, 84v–85r). Since it was originally a monastic religiousness, Catholic rites and ceremonies, particularly the sacraments, do enter into recogido spirituality but are not emphasized; emphasis on ceremonies

---

74. Observation of what few things the Erasmists and illuminists have in common is not an attempt to ally the two, rather to point out how they both differ from Catholic reformism. Likewise, the term "Catholic reformism" is used for purposes of distinction, not to challenge the Catholicism of other reformist groups, such as the Erasmists. Although the characteristics discussed in this chapter are common denominators of the Catholic reformists, their selection and presentation purposefully highlight Dominican piety because Montemayor's works predominantly display that piety.

and sacraments figures more prominently in post-1559 treatises for obvious reasons.

Belief in the need to participate in holy rites is constant in the texts chosen by sixteenth-century reformers for perpetuation and commentary (Augustine, Jerome, Gregory, Climacus, Cassian). Climacus, for example, entreated his monks, "ecclesias et collectas frequentate" (1540, cxlv, v), and Granada translated, "frecuentad las iglesias y los sermones" (frequent churches and sermons).[75] Montemayor shows, rather than tells, about this facet of Christian life: book two of his "Spiritual Dialogue" begins, "As soon as Dileto and Severo got up the next day, they went to mass in the morning at a hermitage very close by" (Como Dileto y Severo se levantaron otro día, en la mañana fueron a oír misa a una hermita muy cerca de allí, DS, 83r). Vocal prayer and the use of physical objects to inspire piety were considered perfectly acceptable for those who found inspiration in them, and were prescribed as necessary for the initiate. The practiced worshipper, however, did not need such assistance, but did not deny its worth either.

Catholic reformism and Erasmism shared this temperate attitude about the role of material objects in piety; quite contrary to this, the illuminists rejected all physical elements of the cult as well as any relationship between faith and activity in the world to manifest it. Not surprisingly, then, Montemayor's characters and poetic narrators practice conservative if essentialist Catholicism, not devoting special attention to any sacraments except baptism, communion, and the mass. All of these are among Catholicism's most sacred mysteries.

Catholic reformism of the first half of the sixteenth century was a spirituality that balanced education in the field of doctrine and practice of ritualistic faith with private experience and always emphasized the latter after instruction in the former. As was secular love in the secular context, the worship of God was interpreted by these reformists as an art that had to be practiced and could be validated by experience alone.[76] Touch by the divine hand was believed to overcome all worldly shortcomings, and it was toward that moment of grace that the Catholic reformists led their

---

75. Luis de Granada, translator of Johannes Climacus's *Scala paradisi* (the Spanish *Escala epiritual*), 290b.
76. Cf. Fray Alonso de Madrid's *Arte para servir a Dios* (1521); on the concept of religious practice as an art, see Andrés Martín, *La teología española*, 2:19, 146.

flock. The only preparation necessary to receive the descending divine touch was a humbled heart and a disposition to delve into oneself, collecting the self into the spirit (*recogerse*), abandoning the world. Andrés Martín characterizes the movement, saying, "the most characteristic thing about recogimiento will be love without previous or concomitant knowledge" (LR, 783).

Although quite learned themselves, the writers of recogido treatises were extremely sensitive to the superior value of spiritual experience over intellectual pursuits; they regularly extolled the former and denigrated the latter. Luis de Granada wrote to Bartolomé Carranza saying: "with regard to what you tell me of your desire to see yourself free from those studies and occupied in divine study [meditation], that desire is very just. . . . Ministers of the Gospel need not be like Cicero, but like Christ" (En lo que me dice del deseo que tiene de verse libre de esos estudios y ocuparse en los divinos, muy justo es el deseo . . . Los ministros del Evangelio no han de ser semejantes a Tulio sino a Jesucristo). The letter's closing invoked the psalm that inspired one of Montemayor's most important religious works, his poetic interpretation of the *Super flumina Babylonis* (Ps. 137). Revealing a key attitude in his piety, Granada took advantage of the original psalm's lament of loss to communicate his personal disillusion with a world in which theology was divorced from faith and was dangerously engrossing. Blending phrases from both Psalms 62 and 137, he says:

> There is reason to be careful of this, since your soul is planted in an isolated and dry desert land, among willows and among beech trees, where those exiled from Jerusalem silenced their organs and halted their celestial music. It is a great wretchedness that letters today are so vitiated, for we have abandoned the fount of living water.
>
> (Hay razón para tener de esto cuidado, por estar plantada [su ánima] *in terra deserta, invia et inaquosa*, entre sauces y entre hayas, adonde los desterrados de Jerusalén pusieron silencio en sus órganos y suspendieron la música celestial. Gran miseria es estar tan estragadas las letras de hoy, pues que hemos dejado la fuente de agua viva.)[77]

The *agua viva* to which Granada refers is the "pure river of water of life,

---

77. Huerga, *Luis de Granada*, 63.

clear as crystal, proceeding out of the throne of God and of the Lamb," referred to in Revelations 22:1; it is grace, the effect of the descending Holy Spirit on the human soul. Montemayor laments the same loss in his gloss of Psalm 137 mentioned above, likewise referring to a situation that has led to the loss of divine presence, and subsequently produced the lament:

> The grace we lost, we understand
> is represented by these instruments we hang,
> which we can recover by means of God.
>
> (La gracia que perdimos, entendemos
> por estos instrumentos que colgamos,
> la cual por medio de él [Dios] cobrar podemos.)
> (SCS, 187v; not in GP)

One of the primary consequences of the reformist belief in the superiority of infused over acquired wisdom was the disdain of intellectual pursuits, common to all of the major figures of the movement. Study, particularly of classical authors, was not recommended for those learning to pray and know God. Indeed, pre-Christian authors are often repudiated in the recogido treatises: after insisting on the wealth of meditative material available in the Christian tradition and setting forth a few examples, Luis de Granada sharply concludes, "May all the deceitful miracles told by the Greeks and Latins in histories be silent in the face of this truth" (Callen ante esta verdad todos los mentirosos milagros que escriben en sus historias los Griegos y los Latinos, LdO, 3). Or, from Montemayor's 1554 gloss of Jorge Manrique's "Coplas":

> The poets that dealt
> with gods of falseness
> were so blind
> that they invoked lies,
> fleeing from the truth.
>
> (Los poetas que trataron
> con dioses de falsedad
> fue tanta su ceguedad
> que a la mentira invocaron
> huyendo de la verdad.)
> (SCS, 128v; GP, 214)

He displays the same suspicion of classical philosophers in his "Epístola a Juan Hurtado de Mendoza" ("Epistle to Juan Hurtado de Mendoza," GP, 351-54). This characteristic distinguished these men from the Erasmists, who found in letters an important complement to faith: for example, from the 1526 Spanish translation of Erasmus's *Enchiridion*, "I tell you also that for this soldiery and Christian combat, I do not wholly reprove, nor does it seem detrimental to me, that as a novice knight a person like yourself practice and take exercise in the decent and pure gentile poets and philosophers, as long as it be with temperance. . . ."[78]

The notion that by virtue of divine grace, the humble (and unlettered) Christian was illuminated by divine wisdom, and thus in no need of formal education, is a standard theme of spiritual renovation of all ages, and it circulated widely in the late fifteenth and early sixteenth centuries. Such an idea complemented the reform movement's concurrent exaltation of humility and, like most Christian reformist ideals, it can be traced back to the Bible ("for the letter killeth, but the spirit giveth life," 2 Cor. 3:6). Taken to an extreme, the rejection of study meant profession of belief in the Holy Spirit's power to overcome the worshipper completely, making moral and doctrinal error impossible in the illuminated individual even if that person were illiterate; this was one of the fundamental heresies of the Toledan illuminists.[79]

In a more decorous fashion, the affective experience of God was interpreted to entail rejection of intellectual curiosity for its own sake, an attitude exemplified in Luis de Granada's writings for both the lay and monastic populations. In his *Book of Prayer*, study is considered to be a temptation for any Christian if it leads to "knowing too much," at which point it is held to be impertinent. Imitating Climacus, Granada dedicates an entire

---

78. Desiderius Erasmus, *El Enquiridión o manual del caballero cristiano*, translated by Alonso Fernández de Madrid, 132. This translation differs substantially from the Latin text; it is, however, perhaps truer to Spanish Erasmism than Erasmus's own version, and it is quoted for that reason. See Bataillon's introduction to the Alonso edition (9-90).

79. The illuminists were not the only ones to run into difficulties putting this ideal into practice: because of intellectualism's detrimental effects on piety, the Franciscans refused so absolutely to participate in formal studies that the Order's survival was endangered, for that lack disqualified them from ecclesiastical posts. They subsequently modified their position (Andrés Martín, *La teología española*, 1:82-118).

chapter to "too much appetite for study and knowing," in which intellectual pursuits are determined to be dangerous for the negative effect they have on one's devotion: "Study dries up one's affection for devotion" (LdO, 387-93). The Dominican mixes his criticism of studying worldly subjects ("estudio de letras humanas") with study of divine letters ("la palabra de Cristo"). Both, he insists, are secondary to affective worship. Ironically, Granada, like Montemayor in his "Spiritual Dialogue," makes ample use of erudite sources to prove the worthlessness of study, including quotations from patristic and classical authorities. (Unlike Montemayor, Granada had a superb education at the service of his powerful mind and his sources are seamlessly integrated into his works, whereas Montemayor's retain a patchwork of quality.)

Love of God, insists Granada, will be the fount of all wisdom: "Everything you can know in the world is nothing. And should you exercise yourself in the love of God, quickly you will reach him and in him you shall see all things" (Todo lo que puedes aquí [en el mundo] saber es nada. Y si te ejercitares en el amor de Dios, presto lo irás á ver y en él verás todas las cosas, LdO, 394). The contemplative life is represented as the way to communicate with that love and so gain that knowledge or vision: "And since it is clear to us that exercise of and acts in the contemplative life help more for this than any other, it follows that such acts will be the best and most successful of all" (Y pues nos consta que los ejercicios y actos de la vida contemplativa ayudan más para esto que otros ningunos, síguese que éstos serán los mejores y más acertados de todos, LdO, 394).

The only complete knowledge, then, is that achieved by "the devout man who day and night engages in nothing but crying and feeling the things of God" (el varón devoto que día y noche no entiende sino en llorar y sentir las cosas de Dios, LdO, 397). Divine wisdom, imparting itself to the lowly soul, will teach humanity all it needs to know, not only about faith but about doctrine as well.[80] Such is the doctrine that one learns at the foot of the cross, sharing Christ's suffering as intimately as possible. Dileto holds up this ideal for Severo, exclaiming, "How many things one learns at the foot of the cross, contemplating the Lord's death, crucifying ourselves with him on his cross!" (¡Cuántas cosas se aprende al pie del crucifijo, contemplando en la muerte del Señor, crucificándonos con él en

---

80. Carranza states and elaborates on this dangerous notion in his *Catechismo*, 2:356-66; his ideas are cited in detail, *infra* 96-97.

su cruz!, DS, 6v). Thus Luis de Granada included a chapter dealing with the same infused wisdom in his *Book of Prayer*, "On the doctrine that is learned at the foot of the cross, by Fray Baptista de Crema" (De la doctrina que se aprende al pie de la cruz, de F. Baptista de Crema, LdO, 71). Although Crema's name was removed from the subtitle of the section it heads in the post-*Index* edition of the *Book of Prayer*, the text itself remained basically unaltered. This infused wisdom, clearly of fundamental importance to the Catholic reformists, is upheld as the only source of things worth knowing.

Preparation for the experience of enlightening love involved long practice of virtues and uprooting of vices which are studied in detail in Spanish Catholic reformist treatises. Before engaging in actual meditation, the proper attitude of humility had to be acquired, one which involved adopting a world view unique to this current of piety in the sixteenth century.

The humanists found in earthly life a microcosm of heaven, and in the human soul potential for divine goodness and eternity. The Neoplatonists captured the direct relationship between the good and beautiful of the earthly world and the spiritual realm beyond it in a particularly inspiring fashion: "Corporeal beauty is the shadow and image of the spiritual" (la belleza corporea è ombra e immagine de la spirituale, DA, 101v).[81] Goodness for the human soul, therefore, was to use earthly beauty as a tool for transcendence to the divine: "to ascend from corporeal beauty to the spiritual, and to know by means of inferior things perceived by the senses the beautiful and intellectual superior things" (ascendere de la belleza corporale ne la spirituale & conoscere per l'inferiore sensibile le superiore belle e intellettuale, DA, 113v). This is the ascending ideal that can be found in precursors of the Christian humanists such as Raymundus de Sabunde, whose *Theologia naturalis* (*Natural Theology*), also known as the *Liber creaturarum* (*Book of the Creatures*), is based on the notion that God is knowable through the material world.[82]

Dominican recogidos such as Carranza, on the contrary, insisted that

---

81. Hebreo's *Dialoghi* are treated more extensively in the section about Chapter Four of the *Diana* (*infra* 174–89). As their relationship to Montemayor's religious works is antithetical, so their essential meaning is at odds with the overriding message of the *Diana*.

82. Sabunde's text was adapted by Peter Dorland and published as the popular *Viola animae* in 1499; see Martínez de Bujanda's "Introducción" to Juan de Cazalla's adaptation of Dorland's text, entitled *Lumbre del alma*.

this type of ascension was knowing things backwards ("conocer las cosas por las espaldas"), and constituted an imperfect road to God. This conservative attitude insisted that God could only be known directly through the spirit and via a descending touch to the mortified soul (versus the ascending Neoplatonist). The idea was twisted into an even more conservative posture by Melchor Cano. In his censure of Carranza's *Catechismo*, he maintained that since human experience is inherently imperfect for its ties to the flesh, human knowledge of the divine, necessarily tied to the human condition, was inevitably *experimentum fallax* and was thus impossible. The window through which divine light descended in recogido ideology, across which Carranza had intended to place something of a diaphanous curtain, was quickly shuttered, leaving darkness.[83] In this context, the inner mystic space of Santa Teresa's *Moradas de castillo interior* (*Dwellings of the Interior Castle*) and San Juan de la Cruz's dark night of the soul acquire triumphal poignancy.

Throughout the tumultuous sixteenth century, Catholic reformist piety such as Carranza's was based on systematic attempts to compensate for the imperfect human condition, learned from authors like Climacus, whom the Christian humanists did not use. Climacus's *Scala paradisi* is not the Neoplatonic treatise its title would indicate; rather, it describes the rungs on Jacob's ladder as vices to be overcome and virtues to be won by progressive elimination of worldly life, not display of its beauty. One's attachment to the world and people in it likewise must be overcome to attain holiness, for union with God means rejecting, from the very outset of the spiritual experience, all earthly existence, which is considered merely another temptation to be conquered.

The way to know God, according to the recogidos, was to escape from the world into the refuge of contemplation, delve into the self, purging worldliness from the soul, and await God's descent. Thus, Osuna refers to the act of recogimiento as a refuge in his *Alphabet*, and Granada does the same throughout the *Book of Prayer*.[84] For the recogido, readiness for grace was accomplished through bodily and spiritual mortification and unabating abnegation. In a humble state, meditation on divine mysteries

---

83. The quotation from Carranza is in the *Catechismo*, 1: 359. There are lengthy excepts from Cano's censure of Carranza's text in LR, 427–33; the reference to human *experimentum fallax* is on p. 431.

84. Osuna, *Abecedario*, 214.

could begin and, when and if God chose, the Holy Spirit invaded the soul and raised it to consciousness of the divine. Perfect knowledge of the divinity and the world was only attainable after the Holy Spirit had illuminated the humbled individual. Although all mystical experience is passive at the moment of union, in recogido piety, emphasis on human passivity before divine power was absolute: the worshipper could only prepare for God's touch, perceived as an action of lowering oneself to then be raised, and wait. It is to this passivity that Luis de Granada refers, writing to the young Dominican Fray Luis de la Cruz, when he compares the falling of divine grace upon the human soul to dew that descends imperceptibly from heaven. As Santa Teresa was to observe later, Granada instructs that the Holy Spirit descends lightly upon the worthy one like rain and cannot be fetched like water from a well ("recibirse tiene como agua llovida y no cabarse como agua de pozo").[85]

This vision of life, which Montemayor's works impart as well, places an abyss between heaven and earth that can be crossed only by divine will. Such ontological limitation was inherited by Catholic reformists from the Middle Ages, and pertains to the moral realm, secular and divine. In a passage that could refer to the recogidos of sixteenth-century Spain, Alberto Várvaro describes the ideological foundation of the medieval lyric, referring to the concept of refuge mentioned above in the process: "An insurmountable distance exists between humanity, tied to the suffering of life and sin, crushed by faults, and the divinity; the poet does not hope to overcome this distance, or even dare to aspire to do so. It may happen, nonetheless, that the divine may come down from its heights to the earth and take it to a 'safe haven' [saque a puerto] an act not representing a reconciliation, rather a 'freeing from discomfort and sadness' [librar de malestar complido e de tristura]."[86] It is in this spirit that Granada says, "Since the distance between the divine being and all the other creatures is

---

85. This letter is in Huerga, "Fray Luis en Escalaceli" (333). These water metaphors are fundamental in Treatise Nine of Osuna's *Abecedario*, 308-33; Saint Teresa repeats it in her *Moradas del castillo interior* ("Cuartas moradas," ch. 2, 3) and throughout chapters 15-18 of her *Libro de la vida*. A thorough study of Teresa's relationship to the recogidos is needed to complement Catherine Swietlicki's study of Christian cabala in her works and Alison Weber's *Teresa of Avila and the Rhetoric of Femininity*.

86. Alberto Várvaro, *Literatura románica de la Edad Media: Estructuras y formas*, 113. He quotes from poems by Juan Ruiz, Arcipreste de Hita.

infinite, thus is also infinite the distance between divine works and human ones" (Como sea infinita la distancia que hay del ser divino al de todas las criaturas, así lo es también la que hay de las unas obras á las otras, LdO, 376). God is not one with the world, as the Neoplatonists had it: "God being one in the most simple unity, it follows that what comes from God be also one in complete unity, because one comes from the other, and from pure unity, perfect union" (essendio Iddio uno in simplicissima unità, bisogna che quel che procede da lui sia ancor' uno in intera unità, perche da uno uno proviene & de la pura unità, perfetta unione, DA, 72r).

The polarized universe of the *recogidos* encourages a passive, observant, and sensitive mentality on the part of the worshipper, whose imagination and memory become finely tuned instruments in the service of devotion. When the only thing the devout Christian can do to attain union with God is prepare relentlessly for the undeterminable moment of embrace by the Holy Spirit, that same Christian is destined to perpetual self-examination in hopes of living in readiness. In his later poetry, Montemayor returns again and again to this need for the inward glance and the awareness of one's nothingness brought about by that self-examination: "Recollect yourself, my distracted mind / . . . / take care, for you are leading me to perdition" (Recógete, mi seso distraído / . . . / cata que me lleváis a ser perdido, SC, 202r; not in GP). In the next poem, he addresses Christ saying

> My soul raises itself to imagine you,
> . . . .
> through you will I be taken up to heaven;
> on myself, I never cared to count.
>
> (Levántase mi alma a imaginarte
> . . . .
> Por ti he de subir allá en tu cielo,
> por mí jamás me quise hacer cuenta.)
>   (SCS, 202r; not in GP)

Or, from a sonnet that follows:

> At the point at which divine love ignites the tinders
> of my soul, with its fire
> it inflames and purifies it . . .
> . . . .

it understands that without God, no good is accomplished.
Oh man, oh world, oh wasted time,
turn back upon yourself, for you have lost your way!

(Al punto que el amor divino enciende
la yesca de mi alma, con su fuego,
la inflama y purifica . . .
. . . .
entiende que sin él [Dios] no hay bien cumplido.
¡Oh hombre, oh mundo, oh tiempo mal gastado
revuelve sobre ti, que vas perdido!)
(SCS, 203r–v; not in GP)

The recogidos' vision, contrary to that of the Italian Neoplatonists, was aligned with the medieval interpretation of the world as God's creation, but not God's habitat. Life on earth inspired them to contemplation of the divine only by encouraging rejection of its instability and unworthiness, which, they insisted, could be deduced from anyone's contemplation of his or her own human experience. Granada exhorts his reader to consider, "how much change there is in the life of all of man, who is subject to all the vicissitudes of fortune, which never remains the same, rather is ever rolling from one state to another" (cuánta [mudanza] la de todo el hombre que está subjeto á todos los vaivenes de la fortuna, la cual nunca permanesce un mismo ser, sino siempre rueda de un lugar en otro, LdO, 115). Montemayor makes the same observation in his gloss of Manrique's "Coplas":

for nothing endures
more than time wants;
. . . .
if fortune gives contentment,
it will quickly take it from us.

(pues cosa ninguna dura
más de lo que el tiempo quiere;
. . . .
si da fortuna un contento
presto nos lo tomará.)
(SCS, 139v–140r; GP, 225)

Over life itself, the realm of God's eternity has control: "For time will triumph over life / as it has triumphed over everything" (que el tiempo triunfará de ella [la vida] / como de todo ha triunfado, "Coplas," SCS, 141r; GP, 227).

Human life, then, is worth only disdain: "If this life is as you have heard, that is, brief, uncertain, fragile, inconstant, deceitful and miserable, how long can the building constructed on such a foundation endure?" (si esta vida es tal cual aquí has oído, conviene á saber, breve, incierta, frágil, inconstante, engañosa y miserable, ¿qué tanto podrá durar el edificio que se armare sobre este cimiento? LdO, 136). In order to find the divine, one must reject and release the world: "One should take the direct road to two main goals, among others: one, the knowledge and disdain of worldly glory, and the other, knowledge and disdain of oneself" (debe el hombre enderezar á dos fines principales, entre otros: el uno, el conoscimiento y desprecio de la gloria del mundo, y el otro, el conocimiento y desprecio de sí mismo, LdO, 135–36). The narrator of Montemayor's "Coplas" gloss exclaims: "Oh how much the Christian wins / by being dead to the world!" (¡Oh cuánto el cristiano gana / de estar al mundo difunto! SCS, 126r; GP, 211). Recogimiento, then, is directed toward retreat from an unworthy world and realization of one's insignificance in the face of a greater power. This is basically what the characters of the *Diana* are led to realize as well.

The setting aside of time devoted only to self-examination was a personal contemplative exercise consistently recommended by the recogidos and Erasmists alike. The orthodoxy of the practice was confirmed when the Council of Trent prescribed it as an essential prelude to confession.[87] The Erasmists' inward glance, however, reinforced virtuous humanity's positive relationship with God, for it was inspired by an interpretation of the Socratic maxim that stressed the worth of the spiritual human soul, even while denigrating the "hombre exterior," or outer person. As Bataillon observes, Erasmus's invocation of this classical precept is allied to the Dutch scholar's belief in the worth of ancient philosophy and the emphasis on the spiritual soul taught therein.[88]

The same exercise carried out by the Catholic reformists, although perhaps ultimately derived from Socrates as well, was more immediately inspired by the patristic tradition in which self-examination and self-knowledge inspired self-abasement and subsequent realization of human nothingness compared to divine glory. This type of inward glance, a different

---

87. Charles Henry Lea, *A History of Auricular Confession and Indulgences in the Latin Church*, 2:413.
88. E&E, 195. See also chapter 3 of the Spanish translation of Erasmus's *Enchiridion* (1526), "Que lo principal de la sabiduría es conocerse el ombre a sí mesmo," and chapter 4, "Del ombre interior y exterior," 149–57; 157–64.

exhortation to self-knowledge than that of the Christian humanists, came to the sixteenth century from the rich tradition of medieval theology.[89] Self-awareness, in that context, was to produce unquestioning subservience to and awe of divine will. Attempting to inspire the humility necessary to attain grace, Granada chastises his reader, "What makes you so haughty, dust and ashes? Why do you glorify and magnify yourself, little creature made of dirt?" (¿De qué te ensorberbeces, polvo y ceniza? ¿Por qué te magnificas y engrandesces, hombrecillo de tierra? LdO, 137). In his palinode, Montemayor repeats, using the same lexicon:

> Know yourself and you shall see how you are dirt;
> know yourself and you shall see how you perish:
> so you can say without shame:
> Oh mire!, you, why are you so haughty?
>
> (Conócete y verás como eres tierra;
> conócete, y verás cómo pereces:
> porque puedas dezir sin afrentarte:
> ¡oh lodo!, tú, ¿por qué te ensoberbeces?)
> (SCS, 201r; GP, 283)

The difference between this disparagement and the positive humanistic vision of humanity as the microcosm of the entire universe could not be more stark: "man is the image of the entire universe" (l'huomo è immagine di tutto l'universo), Hebreo joyously affirms (DA, 17r). For the recogidos, self-examination leads to a pained awareness of the human condition: "and so, he who wishes truly to humble himself, let him work to know himself, and thus he will be humbled" (por tanto, el que desea de verdad humillarse, trabaje por conocerse, y así se humillará, *Guía*, 343).[90] Montemayor says the same:

> Take account of yourself
> and you shall find yourself so overcome by yourself
> that you are humbled.

---

89. Carolyn Walker Bynum describes the broad characteristics of that tradition in "The Body of Christ in the Later Middle Ages: A Reply to Leo Steinberg."

90. Granada's *Guía de pecadores* was intended to be the third book of his *Libro de la oración* and was included on the 1559 *Index* with it; the *Guía* was probably written by 1549 and was first published in Lisbon, 1556. A post-*Index* version was printed in 1567, modifying the original in the expansive method described above. The edition cited herein is that of 1567, which is much more accessible than the earlier version.

(Entra en cuenta contigo
y hallarte has de ti tan alcanzado
que quedes humillado.)
(SCS, 201r; GP, 283)

In his *Guide for Sinners*, Granada concludes, "Then who will not wish to flee from such a world?" (Pues, ¿quién no deseará huir de tal mundo? *Guía*, 312). After describing the ways of that same world, Montemayor concluded in his gloss of Manrique's "Coplas": "Then who is there who would not flee / from such manifest vice?" (Pues, ¿quién habrá que no huya / de vicio tan manifiesto?, SCE, 127v; GP, 212). This sentiment is the essence of the flight from the corrupt world that takes place in pastoral literature.

Such an interpretation of the world and humanity's place in it cannot but produce total dependence upon God for grace and salvation. Free will is never questioned by the Catholic reformists (or Montemayor), but neither is its inferiority to divine will. Granada writes of John 6:44: "Leading to understand that neither human free will nor the entire package of human nature suffices in itself to raise a person from sin to grace should the arm of divine power not intervene" (Dando a entender que ni el libre albedrío del hombre, ni todo el caudal de la naturaleza humana basta por sí solo para levantar un hombre del pecado a la gracia si no entreviniere aquí el brazo de la potencia divina, *Guía*, 46–47). Montemayor concurs, again echoing the Dominican's idea almost word for word:

> True that my salvation is in my hands,
> and free will is not a fallacy
> but a very noble gift that humanity has.
> However, should God withhold his grace,
> any grace of ours would be worthless,
> for his grace moves and sustains me.
>
> (Bien que mi salvación está en mi mano,
> y que el libre albedrío no es falacia
> sino un muy alto don que el hombre tiene.
> Pero si retuviese Dios su gracia,
> cualquier gracia nuestra sería en vano,
> que su gracia nos mueve y nos sustenta.)
> (SCS, 200r–v; GP, 282)[91]

---

91. Montemayor never challenged humanity's free will, rather he seems to have taken care to mention it; see, for example, GP, 219. Or, from the "Spiritual Dialogue": "God gave

Granada encourages the total dependence on God that such an attitude toward free will inspires, suggesting that the worshipper think: "Lord, I have nothing, I am worth nothing and can do nothing without you but sin" (Señor, nada tengo, nada valgo, y nada soy, y nada puedo hacer sin Ti, sino pecados, LdO, 101). Montemayor, never much given to self-abasement, lashes out at his reader in second person: "Oh you! Without God with you / could you ever do anything? No, surely not" (¡Oh tú!, sin Dios contigo, / ¿podrás acabar algo? No, por cierto, SCS, 200r–v; GP, 282).

When God is perceived as exercising such absolute control over the events of human life, divine omnipotence pervades the world in a controlling, almost threatening, fashion. A piety similar to that which had been characteristic of the Middle Ages flourishes whenever such a perception prevails, resounding with passages from Job and Ecclesiastes, founded on fear, "for fear of God is the beginning of love of God" (porque el temor de Dios es principio de su amor, LdO, 164). Montemayor advises the worshipper, "Fear hell and purgatory / and look at yourself, mortal" (Teme infierno y purgatorio, / y mírate, hombre mortal, SCS, 142r; GP, 228). By the recogidos, God was perceived as forgiving and merciful, under the proper circumstances, but was also a distant and absolute authority, one who was ever-watchful, whose glorious accomplishments only served to enhance divine might. In his translation of the *Contemptus mundi* (1536), Luis de Granada says: "For one's road is not always in one's own hand, rather it is for God to give and console when he pleases and how much he pleases and whom he pleases, as it pleases him and no one else" (Porque no está siempre en la mano del hombre su camino: mas a Dios pertenece el dar y consolar cuando quiere y cuanto quiere y a quien quiere, como a él le place y no más).[92] Granada himself observes, "For truly God is present everywhere, not only by potential and by presence, but also by

---

man free will, which was one of the most precious things he bestowed upon him" (Dios dio al hombre libre albedrío, que fue una de las cosas más preciosas que le dotó, DS, 18v).

92. Fray Luis de Granada, *Contemptus mundi. Cōpuesto por el famoso maestro en sancta theologia Juā gerson*, 49v. Bataillon believes that this translation was done by Juan de Ávila, not Granada (E&E, 594). Yet many phrases from this particular translation/adaptation reappear in other treatises by Granada. This, for example, is in the 1567 edition of the *Guía:* "Happiness and contentment of heart is a gift of God given when he wishes, to whom he wishes . . . and he takes it away when he wishes" (la felicidad y contentamiento del corazón humano es dádiva de Dios, y que él la da cuando quiere, y a quien quiere . . . y la quita cuando quiere, *Guía*, 198).

essence. . . . All that is in God is God, and therefore, wherever is anything of God's, there is God in his entirety" (de verdad Él [Dios] está presente en todo lugar, no sólo por potencia y por presencia, sino también por esencia. . . . porque todo lo que hay en Dios, es Dios, y por eso, doquiera que está algo dél, está todo Él, LdO, 295). In Granada's context, this is a reminder not of universal oneness in the divine, but of the need to be constantly on guard against sin; the rest of the chapter is instruction on how to maintain that vigilance. Montemayor agrees:

> In any place, God is the whole;
> neighbor to each one he is, and very close,
> since he sees, knows, and judges all.
>
> (En cualquier lugar, Dios es el todo,
> vecino es de cada uno y muy cercano,
> pues él lo ve, conoce, y juzga todo.)
> ("*Super flumina,*" SCS, 186v; not in GP)

Under these circumstances, the individual's lot is to conform to a superior power and will, and be aware of the omnipotent divine eye.

Acceptance of human dependence on a greater power and will emphasizes the chasm between God and God's own creation. As in medieval Spanish piety, that chasm is not bridged, but rather is opened and examined to produce the humility that leads to grace.[93] Granada describes this separating abyss effectively: "For when the soul considers, on one hand, the greatness of God, and on the other the abyss of its own vileness, the more it is overawed by the distance between these two extremes, the more it marvels over such incomprehensible goodness that thus inclines itself and condescends to care to take its pleasure with such a poor creature" (Porque cuando el ánima por una parte considera la inmensidad de la grandeza de Dios, y por otra el abismo de su vileza, cuanto más se espanta de la distancia destos extremos, tanto se maravilla más de tan incomprehensible bondad que así se inclina y condesciende á querer tener sus deleites con tan pobre criatura, LdO, 101). In this spirit, Montemayor's hermit Dileto reminds Severo, "Considering the very great love that God had for man since he made him, and considering the innumerable good things he did for him, as much as man can love God in comparison . . . is a

---

93. On the nature of this Spanish medieval piety, see Whinnom, "Supposed Sources."

puff of air" (Considerando el grandísimo amor que el Señor tuvo al hombre desde que lo formó y considerando los innumerables bienes que le hizo, cuanto el hombre le puede amar en comparación . . . es un poco de aire, DS, 179v).

Although the human soul is described as having been created in God's image, that image displays God's power, not humanity's dignity:

> Oh soul, which was made in the image
> of him who created and was not created!,
> nor was there beginning in him, nor end attains him . . .
>
> (¡Oh alma, que a la imagen hecha fuiste
> de aquel que crió y no fue criado!,
> ni hubo principio en él, ni fin le cabe . . .)
> (SCS, 199r; GP, 281)

The God of the Catholic reformists and Montemayor's as well is the active agent who lowers himself to earth without compromising his power and majesty, to raise the awaiting soul, the passive agent, to divine heights: "The divinity came down / without lowering its power" (Bajó la divinidad / sin bajarse su poder, "Coplas," SCS, 133r; GP, 218); "Then who raised me up? / Who lowered himself to raise me?" (Pues, ¿quién me hizo subir? / ¿quién se bajó por subirme? "Coplas," SCS, 156r; GP, 243). The concept of a descending divinity is one of the most frequently developed by Montemayor, particularly in his poetry describing the Incarnation, of which he wrote a substantial amount. For example: "He made use of the Virgin, for he came down / to raise us to heaven" (usó de ella [la Virgen], pues bajó / para nos subir al cielo, "Sobre *Missus est angelus*," SCS, 2v; not in GP). Christ incarnates the opposition between heaven and earth, and in Montemayor's verse on the Passion, the human, weaker Christ does battle with the divine and immutable, "because there was great difference / between the human and the divine" (porque hubo gran diferencia / de lo humano a lo divino, SCS, 70v; GP, 149). Evaluating the relative powers of God and humanity in this fashion leaves but one door open for human happiness: preparation for the moment of grace, when happiness is awarded, albeit temporarily, by the active divine agent. It is toward that moment that all meditative skills and even daily activities are directed in recogido piety.

In the same context, God descends only to the soul willing to imitate Christ in His moment of supreme selflessness: the Passion. The worshipper's humility having been established by keen awareness of human lowliness, contemplation of Christ's actual sufferings may begin. The more the individual identifies with that suffering, the closer to Christ she or he comes. With this goal in mind, moments of Christ's most excruciating pain are typically called up and elaborately developed in recogido treatises, as are the moments of spiritual and emotional torment of those who most loved him (LdO, 20–97; Montemayor's "Pasión de Cristo") (Passion of Christ, SCS, 64r–124v; GP, 141–208). After enumerating Christ's many agonies on the cross, Luis de Granada exclaims, "Finally, wherever you look at him, you will find that there is not one single part free from pain" (finalmente por do quiera que le mirares, hallarás que no hay en él una sola parte libre de dolor, LdO, 220–21). Under consideration here is the essence of love, *charitas*, in Catholic ideology, the willing and innocent endurance of pain and eventual death. Its echoes reverberate throughout Catholic culture, secular and religious alike, from courtly love to mystical asceticism. According to Granada and those who believe as he, this special type of suffering is the goal toward which all Christian behavior should aim, and their interpretation of it as a positive experience is fundamental to the character of their religious practice.

The distinction between suffering love in general and guiltless suffering is fundamental in distinguishing this concept from a multitude of others like it, from other periods and other cultures: whether focused on emotional or physical pain, recogido piety holds that in the undergoing of pain, innocence is the key to the imitation of Christ. Therefore, the more innocently one suffers, so much the closer that experience draws one to the Savior, and hence to heaven: "If you suffer for your sins, you suffer on the cross of the good thief; but if you suffer without sin and without blame, you should be so much the more consoled, for that is suffering on the cross of the Savior" (Si padesces por tus pecados, padesces en la cruz del buen ladrón: mas si padesces sin pecados y sin culpa, por eso te debrías más de consolar, porque eso es padescer en la cruz del Salvador, LdO, 87).

So love begins with the glad endurance of trials for the sake of the beloved. It is pain: "Where there is love, there is pain" (Donde hay amor, hay dolor, LdO, 59).[94] Love, a positive experience, transforms pain and

---

94. The idea was widespread and enduring: cf. Cervantes's shepherd Lenio, who criticizes love saying, "And thus one concludes that where there is love, there is pain" (Y así se concluye que, donde hay amor, hay dolor, LG, (1585) 2:46).

suffering into equally valuable experiences for the confirmation they provide of the individual's alliance with Christ. The suffering of trials becomes an honor, granted only to those who merit it by virtue of their assumption of Christ's spirit and his cross, and, importantly, virtue is allied with the enduring of trials: "In God's house, there is no greater honor than suffering for God's love. . . . And beside this, there is no work in the world that more declares true virtue than undergoing trials for love of God" (En la casa de Dios no hay otra mayor honra que padecer por su amor. . . . Y demás desto no hay obra en el mundo que más declare la verdadera virtud que el padescer trabajos por amor de Dios, LdO, 85). Importantly, the amount one suffers is directly proportional to one's worth, as was Christ's: "Such that in this case, the greater closeness to God does not mean greater pampering, rather greater trials" (De manera que no se tiene aquí respecto á la mayor privanza para mayor regalo, sino para mayor trabajo, LdO, 86). This is the spirit expressed in Montemayor's interpretation of Savonarola's meditation on the *Miserere*, in which he says of Jesus:

> He was in glory being in jail,
> he embraced tribulations.
> Neither the chain frightened him
> nor the cruel lashes that they gave him
> . . . .
> but instead he showed to the entire world
> that the more afflicted he was, the happier.
>
> (Gloriábase en las cárceles estando,
> con las tribulaciones se abrazaba.
> No le espantaba entonces la cadena
> ni los crueles azotes que le dieron
> . . . .
> mas antes se mostraba a todo el mundo
> cuanto más afligido, más contento.)
> (SCS, 234v; GP, 334–35)

As Christ demonstrated his humility and his selflessness by his willing submission to a real and agonizing death, so the lovers of the *Diana* sing of a metaphorical death caused by human love that displays exactly the same dynamics of proportion as the one the recogidos derived from the Passion: those who suffer the most are the best ("pues los que sufren más, son los mejores," LD, 167; see *infra* 166–68). This belief that innocent suffering constituted the foundation of the love experience, which in itself was perceived as the most meaningful facet of existence, was to have great consequences for the human lovers who followed in Montemayor's writings.

Unlike Granada, Montemayor does not conjure up Christ's physical torments for his reader. Instead, he evokes the Savior's inner sufferings and disappointments, in the same fashion that he focuses consistently on his own and those he invents for his characters, centering the poetic experience on sentimental, not physical, reality. He imagines on Christ's behalf ("yet you silence your pain" [mas tú callas tu dolor]), speaks for Gabriel ("'Do not fear death, Lord'" ["No temas muerte, Señor"]) and to the Virgin as well, as one participating directly in the scenes he describes, indignant at what he sees: "Look Virgin, how / this people loses itself" (Mira, Virgen, la manera / con que este pueblo se pierde, SCS, 97r, 72r, 74r; GP, 178, 150, 153).

The consideration of emotional and physical pain as a positive experience in the confirmation of religious faith is an outstanding feature of sixteenth-century Spanish recogido piety, whose practitioners found therein not only the foundation of a meditative method, but the very key to salvation through the imitation of Christ. It distinguishes them from the illuminists, Erasmists, and Protestants alike, whose supporters preferred to focus on more positive moments of Christ's life, the Beatitudes in particular. For example, in the 1525 Spanish translation of the *Enchiridion*, Rule 17 is entitled: "That the most effective remedy for all temptations is the cross and the Passion of Jesus Christ our Savior." Although this title would seem to indicate Passion literature like Granada's, the benefits of Christ's death and the positive inspiration to be derived from its consideration are evoked instead, and the rule contains no detailed reference to Christ's suffering. Indeed, Erasmus chides those who use meditation on the physical circumstances of this biblical event to achieve an empathic experience of pain or to provoke the devout weeping that was a hallmark of recogimiento (as of Christian mystical experience). Erasmus, no mystic, logically then concludes, "This is not the true fruit of that tree of life."[95] However, the Passion was at the ideological core of recogimiento, so much so that Andrés Martín's study of its practitioners includes a chart comparing the various stations of the cross as they were presented in a series of recogido treatises (LR, 95).

95. *Enquiridión*, 368–74; 369.

This intense concentration on Christ's moments of pain and effort to share them is another feature strongly allying this current of spirituality with medieval religiousness in general, and late medieval female piety in particular. Carolyn Walker Bynum observes, "Medieval piety (at least in the fourteenth and fifteenth centuries) speaks far more urgently of life coming from death, of significance located in the body, of pain and suffering as the opportunity—even the cause—of salvation.... Late medieval theology stressed crucifixion more than resurrection." Medieval women's piety characteristically explored the depths of physical pain and emotional denial as ways to identify with Christ's humanity.[96] It is this spirituality that Montemayor represents by portraying the psychological torments and the betrayals of Christ's death story in his Passion poem, ending it with the placement of the dead body in the tomb, and devoting but two shallow stanzas to Christ's life after death and its meaning for Christians (GP, 208).

The recogido interpretation of the *imitatio Christi* philosophy meant that those who suffered as Christ did would receive illumination, the fleeting, ineffable truth of God, the only bliss on earth. All of their prescribed practices are preparation for receipt of that grace during life, within the confines of human experience. Like all mysticism, it is directed toward manifestation of the divine in history, in earthly experience, even as the soul attempts to flee from that history (time and space) and human life (the body). For except in death, return to earth is inevitable. Therefore, the divine touch, which is treated in varying degrees of depth by the many recogido authors, is depicted as the transitory yet self-defining experience that typifies all mystical ecstasy. It is within this tradition, which represents the positive moments of mutual love as necessarily limited by humanity's own nature, that Montemayor's human lovers can be best understood, for they also perceive love between women and men as subject to the same flux imposed by human limitations.

Luis de Granada unites all the benefits of grace, which the recogidos attributed to union with the divine, including "perfect prayer, contemplation, the consolation of the Holy Ghost, God's love, and the wisdom of heaven, and that most blessed union of our spirit with God, which is the goal of all spiritual life" (la perfecta oración, y la contemplación, y las

---

96. "The Body of Christ in the Later Middle Ages," 439. Bynum delineates the features of late medieval women's piety throughout *Fragmentation and Redemption: Essays on Gender and the Human Body in Medieval Religion.*

consolaciones del Espíritu Sancto, y el amor de Dios, y la sabiduría del cielo, y aquella beatísima unión de nuestro espíritu con Dios, que es el fin de toda la vida espiritual, LdO, 278). Just as the recogido authors practiced works and faith, so their literature depicts preparation for union with God as well as that union itself. The more austere authors concentrate on the former; Luis de Granada describes his mystical experiences only in his letters, clearly keeping that experience within the confines of private religiousness, to which he prudently declared it belonged. For his general readers, mystical ecstasy is represented as a remote but attainable goal and is itself fleetingly described, particularly in the *Book of Prayer*. If Granada scarcely treats the moment of union and the benefits of suffering piety, Montemayor does not treat them at all, and prefers to dwell instead on the suffering that precedes union. From Montemayor's writings, it cannot be affirmed that he ever had a mystical experience of the intensity for which he apparently longed.

For the Catholic reformists, in the context of life at large as well as in specifically religious experience, salvation and ecstatic meditation can only follow the patient endurance of endless trials, which are exalted. Again in imitation of Christ, love is perceived as the unquestioning submission to torments. Juan de Ávila insists that the Christian "accept fully in his or her heart that if he or she wants to go to heaven, he or she must endure many trials and must be ridiculed and persecuted by many." Luis de Granada claims further, "But perfect love does not content itself with overcoming the trials that arise, but also desires those trials for the sake of that love" (Mas no se contenta el perfecto amor con vencer los trabajos que se le ofrecen, sino desea también que se le ofrezcan por lo que ama, *Guía*, 293). Montemayor's courtier Severo responds with joyful anticipation to the hardships his friend the ascetic has promised await him in the name of Christ, exclaiming, "How happy is my soul to see how discreetly you teach it the way to salvation! Do go on with your doctrine, for you are giving me new strength to suffer all the difficulties and persecutions that may come to me for love of Christ" (¡Cuán alegre está mi ánima en ver cuán discretamente le enseñas el camino de su salvación! No dejes de proceder en tu doctrina, porque me vas dando nuevas fuerzas para sufrir todas las fatigas y persecuciones que por amor de Cristo me puedan venir, DS, 89r). In such an ideology, suffering out of love becomes not only an accepted part of life, but its very objective. This is one of the primary traits of human love as it is represented in the *Diana*.

One of the natural complements to the focus on the Passion and the ideal of suffering love that typifies recogido piety is concomitant attention to the pained figure of the Virgin Mary. The Erasmists and Lutherans, on the contrary, concentrated on Christ, alive or resurrected, and God, and the illuminists on God alone. Unlike Luis de Granada, who does not pay her any extensive homage, Montemayor devotes many poems to the Virgin, although she does not appear at all in his "Spiritual Dialogue." The Portuguese author's attention to the Holy Mother would seem to indicate either a trait of his personal devotion or the influence of Franciscan piety, in which she figured prominently. As the vehicle of the Incarnation and the metaphorical tabernacle of Christ's humanity, she is the protagonist of numerous works of Montemayor's, most notably his 1548 exposition on Psalm 86, which is based on the metaphor of Mary as God's holy mountain. The strength of Marian themes in his works is interesting for the sensitive attention to a suffering female figure it entails, which is also one of the salient characteristics of his secular works.

Finally, and interestingly, the devil figures prominently in recogido treatises as the one who pursues devotees of Christ with emphatic zeal, one who has specific powers that are regularly invoked to torment the faithful; Satan appears little modified from the figure of "The Enemy" he is in writers such as Lombard, Climacus, and Cassian. The Erasmists and other Christian humanists tended to interpret human frailties more as precisely that, rather than attributing them to external forces. Particularly interesting are Granada's chapter "About some precautions one should take in these exercises against the deceits of the enemy" (LdO, 405–32); Ávila's "Not conversing with the devil" (*Audi,* 116–17); Osuna's "On the devil's tempting wiles." As a contrast, Rule 19 of Erasmus's *Enchiridion* serves well. Entitled, "Who is God and who the devil," it presents an antagonism between these two figures rather than between God and humanity, and the attention allotted to diabolical intervention in human affairs is minimal. Satan, not personified at all, represents the absence of goodness and thus is a different type of threat from the vividly portrayed tempter of the recogidos.[97]

This seemingly minor point acquires great significance in the context of

---

97. Osuna's chapter heading in Spanish reads, "De las astucias que el demonio tiene en tentar," *Abecedario,* 566–69. In Fernández de Madrid's translation of Erasmus's *Enchiridion,* see "Quién es Dios y quién es el diablo," 374–75.

Montemayor's vision of love. A poem published in his 1554 *Works* and again in the 1558 *Second Spiritual Songbook* begins, "From hell there emerged a Moor / whose name was Satan" (Del infierno salió un moro / que Satanás se decía, SCS, 62r; GP, 138–39). The fact that it features a personified devil as its main protagonist, the same crafty character who appeared in the "Spiritual Dialogue," is symptomatic of another, broader disposition that Montemayor shared with the recogidos: the tendency to attribute power over human life to extra-human forces, whether they be God, fortune, personified Christian virtues and vices, or the devil, calls attention to this type of piety. For all its emphasis on meditation and self-contemplation, for all its astute analysis of human nature, this is nonetheless a spirituality in which the individual is represented struggling not as much with the self as with powers described as separate from that self, powers that modern psychology attributes more to the realm of individual psyche. Although affective experiences and memories are described as coming from within, the circumstances that produced them are inevitably represented as being imposed from without.

While this is a natural consequence of other Catholic reformist ideals, such as humanity's dependence on the divine for grace and salvation, it accentuates the feeling of victimization that the same ideology imposed by externalizing inner problems, thereby allowing the individual to feel helpless and passive. This same helplessness and passivity, a function of Montemayor's particular religiousness, marks his most expressive literary voices, his shepherds and shepherdesses. The nature of those characters is illuminated by special attention to the features of his own religious writings, which, although based on the tenets of recogimiento, have their own individual qualities.

Montemayor's Vision

One of Montemayor's earliest and most curious texts is his "Spiritual Dialogue," a prose exposition of Catholic doctrine. The work merits special consideration, for it is faithful to the spirituality about which he wrote all of his life, as well as the way in which he wrote about it. Furthermore, the "Dialogue" contains the first expression of numerous specific ideas that resurface in varying contexts throughout his later works. It subtly repeats authoritative doctrine in piecemeal fashion and stresses the worth of emotional suffering and retreat from the world resulting from disillusion over failure to see the ideal made real, a flight from reality to contemplative experience, represented didactically. Stylistically, it captures his interest in ideological exposition and his tendency toward self-righteous lament, two traits that reappear forcefully in the *Diana*.

In fairness to Montemayor, the "Dialogue" must be taken into account as the primary source of any description of his religious ideology, for all of his other religious writings are poetry or poetry with prose as a complement to the verse, and thus respond more to an affective impulse of expression than to exposition: as Michel Darbord says, "It is evident that religious poetry is never truly put in the service of doctrine."[98] Since the dialogue has been somewhat misrepresented by those who have written about it to date, and since it expresses Montemayor's spirituality well, this early work is worth considering with some care. Without dwelling on the intricate theological problems of the treatise, it is possible to discover in it the type of spirituality that Montemayor used to express his vision of the life experience, a vision he never abandoned. In the course of this overview, his alliance with the trends of Spanish Catholic reformism described above stands out clearly. The characteristics of that alliance, in turn, form the ideological foundation of the *Diana*.

The "Dialogue," like many of Montemayor's works, is imitative and may well be his Spanish translation of another, probably Portuguese, treatise that has yet to be identified. His other works, in poetry and prose alike, indicate an avid enthusiasm for copying, translation, and commentary. As mentioned above, the dialogue's second part is a free adaptation of Climacus's *Scala paradisi*, the prescriptive treatise about ascetic practices required to attain paradise. The *Scala* constitutes the ideological and thematic basis of many fifteenth- and sixteenth-century monastic treatises, and its fundamental monasticism is little altered in Montemayor's adapta-

---

98. *La poésie religieuse espagnole*, 18. In his analysis of Montemayor's religious verse, Creel runs into difficulties distinguishing between "poems whose piety is of a traditional variety and poems which, in spirit or doctrine or both, are of an essentially reformist character" (*Religious Poetry*, 57). This difficulty stems at least in part from the fundamental difference in mode between the poetry Creel studies and the theological texts according to which he evaluates the poetry. Other studies devoting particular attention to Montemayor dialogue include Estevá's "El 'Diálogo spiritual'" and Martins's "Uma obra inédita."

tion of it.[99] Climacus's work describes the virtues that lead to salvation and the vices in which the devil invites the faithful to indulge along the way. From among the original author's carefully ordered thirty-one topics, Montemayor rather haphazardly included several that he probably felt suited for his courtly audience, losing in the process the symbolism of Climacus's thirty-one stairs plus the final one into heaven. The "Dialogue" presents the following topics in this helter-skelter order: renunciation of the world, dreams and fantasies, patience, endurance of trials, prayer, chastity, confession, penitence, the memory of death, humility, vainglory, gluttony, lying, hope, and charity.

It bears repeating that Climacus's *Scala* is an ascetic, not Neoplatonic, treatise, in spite of its title's implication of human ascent to the divine. In it, the ladder is used to emphasize the difficulties encountered by the Christian who progressively abandons material life to focus on spiritual existence. In his adaptation, Montemayor eliminated the concept of the spiritual ladder joining heaven and earth and used instead the metaphor of the twelve gates of Jerusalem (Rev. 21:12). He thereby altered the dynamics of the entire piece from an ascension to a lateral movement, holding humanity on one level of existence and more forcefully locking it into the same, human, condition.

The first half of Montemayor's manuscript surely follows another source as closely as the second follows Climacus: it is replete with quotes from Peter Lombard and treads heavily on delicate matters of faith such as the definition of God and the Trinity, explanations of the creation and the Christian cosmos, including angels, heaven, earth, purgatory, hell, the devil, and finally the mystery of Christ's resurrection. Montemayor's recourse to Lombard supports the argument that his piety was largely inspired by the Dominicans, whose spirituality and theology alike were characterized by a strong current of scholasticism. At the beginning of the sixteenth century,

---

99. Cisneros had Climacus's book translated into Spanish by 1504, and sponsored a new Latin translation from the Greek which was published in 1505. It was previously available in Italian (Venice 1491; 1492). Aside from being a favorite of the Archbishop, Climacus was also the author most quoted by the illuminist Alcaraz during the initial stages of his Inquisitorial trial. (This was clearly for purposes of appearing orthodox, however, for the illuminists' trial documents repeatedly reveal that they wanted nothing to do with the corporeal suffering that Climacus found healthy, Antonio Márquez, *Los alumbrados*, 115).

the *Sententiae* had long been the undisputed theological text of authority at Spanish universities. Cisneros, however, initiated a triangular base for theological study at the University of Alcalá de Henares (Thomism, Scotism, nominalism) that reduced the book's hegemony, even though it continued to be a basic reference text for all theological commentary. Montemayor's recourse to such a vast and complex source reveals his interest in issues of doctrine, not only faith, and displays well his obsessive commitment to expounding on "the rules" of behavior without ever attending to the reasons for following them or the benefits that result from their practice.[100]

The "Dialogue" is a dogmatic exposition divided into two parts. It has the traditional medieval form of a conversation between a wise hermit and a wandering Christian that takes place over an afternoon, evening, and the following morning. Contrary to what its form might imply, it is not a Renaissance dialogue, based on intellectual interchange of opinions; it is an exposition in which one individual imparts information to another, with its few rhetorical strategies harshly subjected to the content being taught. Dileto, who lives in solitary retirement, is visited in his refuge by Severo, a courtier travelling on his way to "a certain land" ("una cierta tierra"). Severo lives in a "desierto" or wilderness, the term used for dwelling places of ascetics who had retired from the world, sometimes close to a village, more often in isolation. Covarrubias's 1611 dictionary defines "desierto" as "the solitary place that no one inhabits or cultivates. The holy fathers who are hermits retire there, and monks, and in the primitive Church it was populated by saints."[101] The word was used for Carmelite houses of retreat later in the century.

Severo refers to Dileto's life as "removed from comfort" (fuera de descanso, DS, 2r); he happens upon Dileto in the nondescript meadow next

---

100. On Lombard's *Sententiae* in Spain, see Andrés Martín, *La teología española*, 2:32, 77, 442–43. I have been unable to find any Spanish translation of the *Sententiae* from the fourteenth to the sixteenth centuries. Montemayor may have used the Latin text, although it seems more likely, considering his tendency to copy from other texts in Romance languages, that he copied his quotations from Lombard from another work in Portuguese or Spanish. A comparison between the "Dialogue" and a sixteenth-century Latin edition of the *Sententiae* reveals numerous errors in translation, whether Montemayor's or another source's is unknown.

101. Sebastián de Covarrubias y Orozco, *Tesoro de la lengua castellana o española*, 310.

to the hermitage, the same place where their second conversation takes place. There is no indication in the manuscript of what Martins refers to as "the bucolic peace of that afternoon," or what Creel calls its "lovely bucolic setting."[102] That is, the correspondences between Dileto's environment and that of the *Diana* are limited to removal from the urban world, the practice of suffering, and the emphasis on conversation in that removal. The approach Montemayor takes to that traditional conversation is significant, for Dileto, like the pastoral characters later to appear in the Portuguese author's works, has lived another life before the one he is living when Severo happens upon him, a life that acquires a certain relief across the dialogue: he had been a courtier, as Severo is, dedicated to frivolous worldliness, and he knows the court well. Disillusioned over the secular world's failure to recognize his spiritual ideals, he retired to his "desert" lodging, turning his back on physical reality to focus on his inner life.

Dileto's relationship to Montemayor's personal ideal is clear: he has abandoned the court and lives in virtuous retirement from worldly distraction. From this contemplative solitude, he is nonetheless disposed to emerge to display his firsthand understanding of the intricacies of Catholic faith. He sets his doctrine forth with the same casual familiarity that Montemayor's human lovers will expound on love doctrine in the *Diana*, from a vantage point as unlikely as theirs. Dileto seems to be a projection of the desire Montemayor's works betray to be wise in matters of faith without study of theology. In the prologue to the "Dialogue," the author had affirmed both his own lack of theological training and his vivid interest in Bible reading, claiming as his own the Catholic reformist ideals of intimate familiarity with the Holy Writ and disdain of letters in favor of infused wisdom. One is led to believe that the lengthy exposition that follows, as well as Dileto's wisdom itself, arises from the latter. Montemayor addresses his reader:

> Prudent reader: If it seems reprehensible to you that a man with neither years nor experience should pretend to deal with such difficult matters, so distinct from my profession and custom, understand that although I reside in a palace among gentlemen and ladies and not in a monastery among theologian monks, this has never kept me from the practice and reading of the Holy Scriptures, for which I have had an affection since childhood.

102. Martins, "Uma obra inédita," 403; Creel, *Religious Poetry*, 59.

> (Discreto lector: Si te parece cosa digna de reprensión que un hombre sin edad ni experiencia pretenda tratar materias tan dificultosas y tan diferentes de mi profesión y hábito, ten entendido que puesto caso que resido en palacio entre caballeros y damas y no en monasterio entre religiosos teólogos, nunca esto ha sido parte para estorbarme el ejercicio y lección de la Sagrada Escritura, a quien desde mi niñez he sido aficionado.) (DS, IIIv)

Dileto proffers a similar explanation for his wisdom: he first says he knows what he does (everything worth knowing, he feels) from contemplation of Christ crucified, the Catholic reformist theme of meditation par excellence and a metaphor of the life of hardship he is happily enduring for his ideal. This immediately prompts him to provide another source for his knowledge, however, one that would seem to contradict what he has just said about his wisdom acquired through grace:

> And do you know how people can attain those humanly attainable things of God, without wasting time on study or money on books? Well I shall tell you, and I do not tell you this because I am so confident in my justification that I count myself among them, because if I tell you anything, it is what I have learned from reading or from having heard it said by some learned men of sound doctrine with whom I used to converse when I lived at court.
>
> (¿Y sabes de qué manera los hombres alcanzan las cosas que humanamente se pueden alcanzar del Señor, sin haber gastado el tiempo en el estudio ni la hacienda en libros? Pues yo te lo daré a entender, y no te digo esto porque esté yo tan confiado en mi justificación que piense ser de los tales, porque si yo alguna cosa te digo es por haberlo leído e oído decir algunos hombres doctos y de buena doctrina con quien conversaba el tiempo que en la corte residía.) (DS, 6v–7r)

Like Montemayor's shepherds and shepherdesses, Dileto's life detached from court depends absolutely on that court for authority and values, while at the same time he, like the pastoral characters, appears to have rejected both. His conflicting stories about how he learned such an amazing amount of doctrine are clearly an autobiographical contradiction, for Montemayor doubtless gleaned his own "wisdom" from preachers at court and books, and idealized that knowledge into the enlightening touch from the Holy Spirit that Dileto claims to have experienced. Regardless, Dileto's lack of formal theological studies hinders neither his personal understanding of his faith nor his understanding of what he has heard "certain theologians" say about it. He proceeds to expound upon the doctrine of infused wisdom, in terms that ring true to the same ideas set forth by Carranza, Ávila, and Granada, concluding that he knows God even better than those who have studied theology. The presumption this implies is typical of Montemayor's early works; the ideal it supports is quite true to pre-*Index* Spanish Catholic reformism.

Dileto's first approach to the theme is literal and reveals clearly the theme of enlightening love, central to the "Spiritual Dialogue":

> And those in whom God infuses understanding without learning of those things are the ones who taste God because God tastes good to them, and such people attain those things that can be known of God better than those who study, to whom God does not taste good because they preach and do not act, they speak and do not do, and these are the ones who know God by science, but they do not know or taste God well by experience.
>
> (Y aquellos en quien Dios infunde el entendimiento sin aprenderlas [cosas de Dios] son los que gustan a Dios porque les sabe bien, y estos tales alcanzan mejor las cosas que de Dios se pueden saber que en los que estudian, y Dios no les sabe bien porque predican y no obran, dicen y no hacen, y éstos son los que saben a Dios por ciencia, mas no les sabe a ellos bien Dios por experiencia.) (DS, 7r)

His next attack is metaphorical but carries the same message:

> Now you see a child at its mother's breasts, with what vehement desire and what extreme pleasure it is tasting that milk, such that it seems to that child that there is no created thing that tastes better. Oh, how much better that child would speak, then, should nature make it possible, about milk and its effects and qualities than the philosopher or physician who by means of natural philosophy or anatomy understands what sort of thing milk is! And this is because the physician knows milk, but the child tastes it. Thus the one who tastes God knows God better than the one who knows God by virtue of studies completed and years of education.
>
> (Ya ves a un niño a los pechos de su madre, con qué agonía [deseo vehemente] y con que extremado gusto está gustando aquella leche, que le parece que no hay cosa criada de mayor sabor. ¡Oh cuánto mejor hablaría, pues, aquel niño, si naturaleza le diese lugar, de la leche y de los efectos y particularidades de ella que el filósofo o médico que por filosofía natural o por anatomía entiende qué cosa es leche o qué particularidades tiene! Y esto es porque el médico sabe la leche, mas al niño sábele la leche. Así que muy mejor sabe a Dios quien le sabe porque lo gusta que quien lo sabe por virtud de las letras que tiene y de los años que ha estudiado.) (DS, 7v)

Belief in the superiority of experience over book learning was obviously an attractive type of piety for a man like Montemayor, who himself declared the limited nature of his education and revealed his own anxiety about acquiring authority in the world. Although it may have complemented his personal situation well, however, the idea was not his own. One finds this passage in the Dominican Bartolomé Carranza's 1558 *Catechism:*

> And the milk acquired without work or labor whatsoever at the breasts of a woman is understood to mean the infused wisdom reached by good Christians at the breasts of God with prayer and holy readings, from which spiritual people emerge learned.
>
> (Y por la leche que se alcanza sin labor ni industria alguna a los pechos de la mujer se entiende la sabiduría infusa que la alcanzan los buenos cristianos a los pechos de Dios con oración y con leción santa, donde salen enseñados los hombres espirituales.) (CC, 1:362)[103]

The differences between the two passages are substantial enough to imply a common third source, but Carranza's attention to the theme indicates how significant the notion was in the piety of the Catholic reformists.

All of the major recogido authors emphasize the same difference between *ciencia*, or knowledge, "acquired by study of books and exercise of letters," and wisdom infused by the Holy Spirit, "acquired by infusion of the Holy Spirit" (CC, 1:361). According to Carranza, union with the divine provides familiarity with both and is thus what makes study as unnecessary as Dileto claims it is: "The gift of knowing is another light that comes to the understanding from union with the Holy Spirit with the soul in which it resides. . . . By means of this light we know what we need to about things of religion; we know how to distinguish the things of faith from those that are not" (CC, 1:364). Elaborating on the same theme, Luis de Granada makes the acquisition of this wisdom a function of one's virtue, or practice of the proper behavior: "The third privilege conceded to virtue is a special light and wisdom that our Lord communicates to the just, which proceeds from the same grace to which we referred earlier" (El tercero privilegio que se concede a la virtud, es una especial lumbre y sabiduría que nuestro Señor comunica a los justos, la cual procede de la

---

103. Bynum treats feminine attributes of the divine such as this one in *Jesus as Mother: Studies in the Spirituality of the High Middle Ages;* she returns to the theme of a nursing God and Jesus in *Holy Feast, Holy Fast,* esp. 172–80; 270–75.

misma gracia que dijimos). He continues to say that faith and prudence themselves have enlightening powers: "they illuminate our understanding so that it knows what to believe and how to act" (alumbran nuestro entendimiento para saber lo que ha de creer and lo que ha de obrar, *Guía*, 133).

The notion of individual betterment via the process of love, compounded with the acquisition of specific knowledge to formalize that betterment, creates a substantial union between Dileto and the pastoral characters of the *Diana*. All are courtly figures disguised as seemingly humble individuals who claim to have rejected the very society in which their wisdom has value; shepherds have no more use for love theory than anchorites have for theology. Both are literary incarnations of important Spanish Catholic reformist ideals, rejection of worldliness and exaltation of the wisdom that love brings to the humble. The concept of infused knowledge allowed for Montemayor's peculiar brand of literary shepherds and shepherdesses, wise not only in the ways of love as a consequence of their experience in it, but equally wise in love theory. By carrying their wisdom out of the context of the civilization they claim to have rejected, these characters all validate that civilization by imposing its forms and knowledge on people who claim to be escaping it for a better life. Simultaneously, the constant attention Montemayor devotes to dogmatic exposition reveals how pervasive was the attention to lay indoctrination in sixteenth-century Spain.

After having established this bilateral source of his wisdom (God on one hand, books and theologians on the other), Dileto begins to teach Severo about the articles of the Catholic faith. Across their conversation, which consists of long sermonic sections punctuated by Severo's leading and uninteresting questions, it becomes clear that Dileto's courtly friend has been practicing a faith he did not understand. The hermit thus takes it upon himself to draw Severo toward his own way of life, and thus save his soul. He proudly urges his friend to follow his own example in the path of righteousness, a way of life as extreme as the doctrine he preaches: absolute renunciation of the world, including family and friends, and complete dedication to the ascetic life in the hopes of attaining the worth necessary to be touched by divine grace. These qualities, retirement from the world and self-righteous lament of its failures, a humble way of life in the absence of material comfort, enlightenment via a love experience, and a tendency toward extremism, remain constant in Montemayor's writings and are notable features of the *Diana*.

In this as in all of his writings, Montemayor outlines no meditative process through which the Christian can seek the experience of grace. Rather than dwelling on contemplative exercises, Dileto chooses the ascetic practices that lead to possible worthiness for the reception of that grace. His chapter on prayer (book two, chapter 7) follows Climacus closely, returning insistently to ways to discipline a mind that wanders during devotional exercises. Only the hardships of that preparation interest Dileto, psychological suffering such as the loneliness brought about by solitude and the thoughts with which the devil tempts the Christian. The moment of the divine touch is treated cursorily and in what at first glance seems a remarkably anti-climactic fashion: once the individual has attained a state of worthiness, after enduring immeasurable torments and grief, he or she will not experience the divine kiss of Saint Bernard or anything similar, but instead can expect to hear an angelical voice reply to the query of where is God: "Oh fervent lover! You may not know my beauty until such time as you be released from the prison of human nature" (¡Oh amador herviente!, no podrás conocer mi hermosura hasta que seas suelto de la cárcel de la naturaleza humana, DS, 181r). This disappointing moment is important, and reflects a process that Montemayor will repeat in his pastoral narration: human access to the superhuman can reach the very portals of the beyond, but it can progress no further. At the instant when contact with the ideal seems on the verge of occurring, the individual is turned around, directed back into the course of human events, to wait out divine will, to overcome the human condition itself through death. This is perfectly in keeping with the reform spirituality that directed more attention to humanity's limitations than to its potential; for example, there is an important chapter in Osuna's *Third Spiritual Alphabet* entitled, "About how while we live we cannot know God in God's self."[104]

The worshipper's ultimate distance from the divine is understandable in light of how Dileto describes both the worshipper and that divinity. The Christian is depicted as one who must attend to the need to be good out of obligation, in repayment of the debt accrued by Christ's crucifixion. Dileto's religious vision is the sum of numerous equations, calculated by a watchful God who never loses count. Thus it is that getting out of purgatory becomes a mathematical affair, a business of "doing time," in which

104. "De cómo mientras vivimos no podemos conocer a Dios en sí mismo," 181–83.

one earns release by enduring infernal tortures proportionate with one's mortal errors:

> Those who are there little and receive harsh pain are those who commit serious sins and remain a little time in sin and return to God. And those who are there a long time and have little pain are those whose sins were not as grievous as was the time they remained in sin. And those who are there little and have little pain are those who committed small sins, and so also was little the time they remained in sin. And those who are there a long time and receive very harsh pain are those who committed grave sins and were in a state of sin many days without returning to their creator.
>
> (Los que están poco y reciben grave pena son aquellos que hacen graves pecados y están poco tiempo en ellos y se vuelven a Dios. Y los que están mucho y tienen poca pena son aquellos que no hicieron tan grandes pecados como fue el tiempo que en ellos estuvieron. Y los que están poco y tienen poca pena son los que hicieron pequeños pecados, y así mismo el tiempo que en ellos estuvieron. Y los que están mucho y reciben pena gravísima son los que hicieron graves pecados y estuvieron muchos días en ellos sin volverse a su criador.) (DS, 67r)

God is the indecipherable authority who keeps track of these accounts, the same figure who dominates recogido piety; obviously not malevolent, but not the loving, approachable divinity adored by the Christian humanists. Dileto defines God in superlatives, adapting from Peter Lombard: "God is a spiritual substance with such very great power, with such incomparable wisdom, with such most excellent love, that his power cannot be judged, his wisdom cannot be grasped, nor his love calculated" (Dios es una espiritual sustancia con tan grandísimo poder, con tan incomparable sabiduría, con tan excelentísimo amor, que ni el poder suyo se puede arbitrar ni su sabiduría se puede pensar, ni el su amor se puede numerar, DS, 3r). Of the Trinity, he says much the same: "Three persons and only one true God, who cannot be understood by any means, by anyone" (Tres personas y un solo Dios verdadero, el cual por ninguna vía puede ser comprendido por ninguno, DS, 6r). The external divine cannot be captured in the human state, imperfect as it is.

True to the recogidos and antithetically to Neoplatonists such as Plotinus, Marsilio Ficino, and Leone Hebreo, Dileto invokes the distance between God and God's creation, not the unified harmony of the universe. The easy and natural interchange between heaven and earth that characterizes Neoplatonism and its most eloquent representations, such as Botticelli's "Primavera," is alien to Montemayor and his sources.[105] Not even Raymundus de Sabunde, whose *Theologia naturalis* Montemayor quotes twice in his dialogue, can be considered a true influence on the work. The references to Sabunde are deceiving, as a reading of his Latin text or any of its many adaptations reveals. The Catalan theologian joyfully exalts universal harmony and humanity's kinship to the Almighty, an optimistic attitude quite opposed to that of the Portuguese author's melancholy delight in the world's imperfections. The use Montemayor actually made of the *Theologia naturalis* could not be more superficial: from Sabunde's profound book, he quotes only the definition of baptism, and the fact that hell is very far from heaven (DS, 59r; 12r).[106] Thus Montemayor takes advantage of Sabunde's deliverance of doctrinal material, and virtually ignores the nature of his treatise; this taste for dogma was characteristic of the recogidos, who sought to fulfill their apostolic mission by teaching not only the spirit, but the Catholic Church's letter as well, meaning precisely its doctrine.

Unlike the recogidos, however, Montemayor never turned his pen to optimistic exaltation of divine majesty, in spite of his repeated expression of that majesty itself; indeed, there is little if any joyous anticipation of the future to be found in his works at all. This is precisely what facilitated his access to the pastoral mode, which emphasizes the past at the future's expense. In his religious works, the attention devoted to the painful path to glory without consideration of the glory itself is a constant and serves to distinguish his own personal piety from that of the Catholic reformists, the Erasmists, and the illuminists as well. Unlike them all, Montemayor does not contemplate the benefits of Christ, of God, or evidence pointing to God's goodness on earth.

Any of Granada's lengthy and numerous passages on the benefits of

---

105. On Plotinus's Neoplatonism in this context, see Wind, *Pagan Mysteries*, esp. 57–61. Wind later says of Ficino, "his Neoplatonism is marked by a curiously antiascetic strain" (69), which signals one of the many differences between the mystical tendencies of Italian Neoplatonism and the recogidos. Wind's book contains a Neoplatonic reading of Botticelli's painting (100–111).

106. Montemayor's passing mention of Sabunde in the "Dialogue," highlighted in the margins of the manuscript, seems to have been what led Martins to posit Sabunde as a significant source of the "Dialogue" (Uma obra inédita). His thesis was apparently what provoked Estevá to elaborate on that supposed relationship ("El 'Diálogo spiritual' ").

God would serve as a contrast to Montemayor's vision. For example, the Dominican elaborates on the eighth Psalm, saying, "What walks on the earth and what swims in the seas, what flies in the air . . . is yours. For all those things are benefits of God, works of God's providence, proof of God's beauty. . . ." (Lo que anda sobre la tierra, y lo que nada en las aguas, y lo que vuela por le aire . . . tuyo es. Ca todas esas cosas son beneficios de Dios, obras de su providencia, muestras de su hermosura . . . . , *Guía*, 31). This optimism of Granada's does *not* express transcendence of the human experience; rather it is pure exaltation of divine power and majesty. Whereas Montemayor extolled the same divine majesty, he did not delight in its earthly manifestations with the warm zeal of his Dominican mentor. Thus, the end of Montemayor's poetic version of the Passion lingers on Christ's placement in the tomb instead of on the resurrection, the "Spiritual Dialogue" stops at the final gate of heaven, the *Diana* concludes on the verge of the characters' happiness. Transcendence or passage to another stage from the one dedicated to suffering proof of worth does not seem to have interested Montemayor, and thus lovers of God and of women and men alike are represented with a desire they can neither attain or abandon. This temporal and psychological suspension is fundamental to pastoral art, which does not propose to go anywhere narratively, rather serves for dwelling on the moment, collapsing like a house of cards at the first indication of movement.

As he provides Severo with the formulae to pass through the holy gates, Dileto does not invoke humanity's kinship with God or Jesus and harps instead on the importance of works, a curious and exaggerating permutation of the ascetic virtues recommended by writers like Juan de Ávila and Luis de Granada. To Severo's question of what exactly are the things that can win heaven, the anchorite launches into the following exposition, typical of the "Dialogue" and quite extraordinary, considering Montemayor was supposedly writing this prescriptive treatise for courtiers like himself:

> Hunger, thirst, the suffering of injuries, the negation of one's own will, patience in the face of offense, the like suffering, without talking about it, of those who despise us, which means not becoming angered at those who speak badly of us, humiliating ourselves before those who pursue us. Ah, Severo mine, blessed are those who travel this road! See that it is appropriate, if you want to follow God, to renounce three things: principally . . . to renounce all riches and leave

your relatives and the company of your friends. Second, is to deny your own will. Third, to renounce the vainglory that can come to you from having renounced these two things. And after you have made these excellent renunciations, should your heart become inflamed with the love of your relatives and of the riches of the world, truly believe that it is nothing but the devil who is dying of envy upon seeing how you are going to take possession of the seat from which he was brought down. And then it behooves you to take up the weapon of prayer against him, and remember the fire of hell, and then you will see how passion for these temporal things that you have left behind is a puff of air in comparison to those which you will receive in hell should you depart from the path of the Lord.

(La hambre, la sed, el sufrimiento de las injurias, el negamiento de la propia voluntad, la paciencia en las ofensas, el igual sufrimiento, sin murmuración, de nuestro desprecio, que es no nos ensañando contra los que dicen mal de nosotros, humillándonos a los que nos persiguen. ¡Ay Severo mío, bienaventurados aquellos que van por esta carrera! Mira que te conviene, si quieres seguir a Dios, renunciar tres cosas: principalmente . . . renunciar todas las riquezas y dejar todos los parientes y la conversación de tus amigos. La segunda es negar tu propia voluntad. La tercera, renunciar la vanagloria que de haber renunciado estas dos cosas te puede venir. Y si después de haber hecho estas excelentes renunciaciones se encendiere tu corazón del amor de los parientes y de las riquezas del mundo, cree verdaderamente que no es otra cosa sino el demonio que se muere de envidia de ver como vas a tomar posesión de la silla de adonde él fue derribado. Y entonces te conviene tomar contra él las armas de la oración, y ten memoria del fuego del infierno, y entonces verás como es un poco de aire la pasión de estas cosas temporales que has dejado en comparación de las que recibirás en el infierno si te apartas de la carrera del Señor.) (DS, 88r–v)

Such exaggerated piety can only be practiced in isolation from the typical experience of daily living, not in the world. Granada preaches the same retirement and identical abandon of family and friends, at least during meditation and, if possible, in a general sense: "Flee from public places, flee likewise even from the members of your household, separate yourself from friends and from enemies, and even from the very people who serve you." (Huye de los lugares públicos, huye también aun de tus domesticos y familiares, apártate de amigos y de enemigos, y aun de los mismos que te sirven, LdO, 305). The monastic nature of these ideals is clear, and their pervasiveness in Montemayor's writings provides reliable evidence of recogido influence on his works. This disciplinary and rigid approach to salvation is similar to Erasmus's ideas only in its concept of prayer as a weapon (*enchiridion* means "dagger") and is also well removed from the illuminist approach to God, which is facile in comparison.

The "Spiritual Dialogue" confirms that Montemayor's literary universe is ideologically identical with that of the Spanish Catholic reformists in most of its fundamental qualities. In that universe, humanity depends absolutely on divine grace for ascension to the ideal, as Augustine, and Lombard commenting on him, insisted as well. In the *Diana*, this grace assumes a secular form, that of happiness in human love, represented as an unpredictable gift from a distant, omnipotent, and incomprehensible force called fortune. Like virtuous, and temporary, earthly happiness attained through the experience of divine love, fulfillment in human love is likewise represented as a possible event, but one dependent first on sufficient suffering of trials by the lover and second on the time being right for such an event to happen. Just when the time is right is not discernible by the human mind, rather it is determined by powers beyond humanity.

Montemayor's dedication to themes of renunciation and emotional pain, his explicit preference for an interventionist God over an encouraging one, as well as his fixed attention on the self at the expense of the other, kept him from expressing joy in life as a harmonious whole. These qualities, however, seem to have been as much a function of his personality as his religious beliefs, for those writers with whom his works have the most theological ideals in common do indeed communicate purely positive aspects of the ascetic life. But unlike Climacus, Ávila, and Granada, Montemayor never devoted any literature to the attainment of the rewards for all the sufferings his characters endure in his writings, nor does he ever express the tranquility of soul to which their piety or amorous devotion led them. The emphasis is always on the sad present, the lost and better past, with no hope for a bright future without the intervention of an uncontrollable and external force.

Although Montemayor's "Spiritual Dialogue" provides evidence of the theological foundation of his ideology, the melancholy quality of his spirituality does not figure significantly therein because it is primarily an expositional work. It is in his poems that expound on biblical passages, particularly the Psalms, that his spiritual lament is most powerfully expressed. Montemayor's primary role in the development of Spanish psalm poetry is thus easily understood. One of the psalmist's most characteristic postures was very much Montemayor's own, from his first religious writings to the end of his career: pain and indignation before an unjust world in which the singer calls out to God for attention without daring to challenge the divine authority that has apparently allowed the injustice to take place and go uncorrected. This self-righteous lament combined artfully with his focus on remembrance and, echoing the psalmist's cry, his best religious poetry sings of the individual's inability to do anything except recollect the past and invoke, by lamenting the present, a better life that would be forthcoming if it were possible to live out the ideal. He thereby implicitly affirms the rightness of a system he does not pretend to understand. Instead, his later works proffer a melancholy resolution to hand himself over to the ways of life, the ways of God, in humble acceptance.

In Montemayor's exposition on the psalm "*Super flumina Babylonis*," the songs of a lost and captive people are presented in expressive terms, identical to those used by the shepherds and shepherdesses in his pastoral works.[107] The poem takes place in a remote environment which the characters, because of their sadness, cannot appreciate:

> By the sad rivers of Babylon,
> we sat, and with our eyes
> we swelled the tempestuous current.
>   There a thousand woes, a thousand troubles
> led us to understand quite clearly
> that we were the spoils of war.
>   We did not see the current of the rivers,
> nor the greenness of the high grove,
> for we saw only sadness.
>
> (Sobre los ríos tristes nos sentamos
> de Babilonia, a quien con nuestros ojos
> la impetuosa corriente acrecentamos.
>   Allí mil desconsuelos, mil enojos
> nos dieron a entender muy claramente
> que de la guerra fuimos los despojos.
>   No vimos de los ríos la corriente,
> no de la alta arboleda la verdura,
> que a la tristeza vimos solamente.)
>   (SCS, 182v; not in GP)

In the *Diana* as well, the natural world is the fixed and idealized back-

---

107. Wardropper notes that there is a relationship between Montemayor's "*Super flumina*" and the secular pastoral voice in the *Diana* (*Historia de la poesía lírica a lo divino en la cristiandad occidental*, 36).

drop against which the unhappy states of the characters are described. This is a transformed version of the classical *locus amoenus* and the ascetic's desert dwelling, not the Neoplatonists' optimistic microcosm. The scene is static, significant only for its relationship to the characters' feelings.

There is a kinship between Montemayor's exiled Israelites and his pastoral characters, founded on their common dedication to lament and recollection, as well as on the spirit of community in which they share their pain:

> If one tells his passion to another
> what the other responds pains him,
> and so they go exchanging one pain for another.
> . . . .
> There endure the sad tears,
> there sad sighs are heard,
> and they cannot even weep as much as they would like.
> . . . .
> There again their cares are renewed
> seated by the rivers, as David
> had prophesied in his Psalm,
> who, with sad song told them
> what I shall now tell.
>
> (Si alguno su pasión al otro cuenta
> lo que responde el otro le lastima,
> así que un mal por otro se descuenta.
> . . . .
> Allí lágrimas tristes perseveran,
> allí sospiros tristes son oídos,
> y aun no pueden llorar cuanto quisieran.
> . . . .
> Allí de nuevo vuelve su cuidado
> sobre los ríos sentados, como había
> en su salmo David profetizado,
> el cual con triste canto les decía
> lo que ahora diré. . . .)
>
> (SCS, 181v–182r; not in GP)

The narrator's perspective in this poem is identical to that of the narrator in the *Diana*, who retells individuals' recollections of the past with its lost happiness and their reactions to those memories. The practice of self-contemplation through memory is the essence of religious meditation and of the pastoral mode alike, and Montemayor depended on that essence in his exposition on the psalms, his holy sonnets, and his secular pastoral poetry. In his pastoral narration, he continued the same technique with even greater success, creating a narrative present that exists as a consequence of the individual's own intimate recollections of quotidian experiences gone by. It is likely that Montemayor's sensitivity to the power of the past in the human mind was heightened by the Catholic reformists' insistence on the use of memory as one of the soul's three faculties. They dwell repeatedly on the need to remember, be it the fires of hell or the rewards of heaven. They also insist that part of each day be spent in quiet recollection, remembering daily activities and devotional readings, and imagining biblical scenes. Memory in this context is the affective evaluation of quotidian experience in one's mind and reviving the past in the present to compare it with the individual's expectations. As such, it was perfectly adaptable to a secular context.

The significance of the religious tradition in which Montemayor wrote is revealed in his holy sonnets, where he repeats the verb *recoger,* saying: "Collect yourself within, my distracted mind / hold back, unruly thoughts" (Recógete mi seso distraído / teneos, pensamientos desmandados) and in another, "Collect yourself within, my soul, and let your memory / turn back into itself" (Recógete alma mía y tu memoria / revuelva sobre sí, SCS, 202r; 203r; not in GP). The recogidos themselves were so called because of their central use of the verb *recoger,* which means, as mentioned above, "to collect the self within itself" or "to withdraw." Montemayor's use of this particular word may have been fortuitous, but it may well have been a tribute to the current of spirituality within which he had learned to contrast the real and the ideal, to appreciate the virtue of suffering and humility, to make full use of his feelings, his imagination, and his convictions. Significantly, Montemayor's poetic lexicon reveals an increased concentration of recogido vocabulary in his 1558 *Second Spiritual Songbook.* He was probably working on the *Diana* during the same years he was writing that poetry.

Montemayor's religious literature, the publication of which preceded and coincided with his secular works, supports an ideology that is opposed to the humanistic vision, particularly Neoplatonism, but faithful to the essential tenets of reformist Spanish Catholicism: the faultiness of the human condition and the perfection of the divine; respect for ceremony, authority, and hierarchy without aggressively insisting on any; the need to combine moments in the world with moments without it; disdain for the material, and emphasis on the spiritual, with particular development of contemplative skills and self-examination; and the imitation of Christ through innocent suffering of whatever divine will is pleased to offer.

This ideological foundation is colored by Montemayor's own ideas about both religious experience and human life. For their persistent focus on the earthly, the human, and the fallible, for their refusal to acknowledge the consequences of divine righteousness or the benefits of Christ's humanity, and for their unwillingness to release the exaltation of suffering for the reaping of its benefits, his devout writings disclose the themes that concerned him particularly. They are replete with ideas and voices that likewise fill his pastoral works: humility and submission to the ways of the world; rejoicing in innocent suffering and the willing participation in trials and torments; the rejection of formal letters in favor of infused wisdom; a contradictory interest in appearing superior without sacrificing humility.

The practice of waiting and of reflecting on one's past behavior, combined with Montemayor's propensity toward affirmation of the self as the behavioral exemplar, offered him rich preparation for the expression of the lament of loss in a secular context. Having begun to approach the representation of life in literature with the tender melancholy of one gazing sadly on the misfortunes of the innocent in reality, and determined to assume and represent those trials on earth, he drew his own particular retreat around him, his *locus amoenus*. Therein, his characters recollect the experiences he attributed to them, encounters with human love and its ways in the world.

2
FORMAL VEHICLES OF IDEOLOGY
Character Typology and Narrative Structure in Spanish Pastoral Narrations

"Some readers cannot enjoy the shepherds because they know (or they say they know) that real country people are not more happy or more virtuous than anyone else; but it would be tedious here to explain to them the many causes (reasons too) that have led humanity to symbolize by rural scenes and occupations a region in the mind which does exist and which should be visited often. If they know the region, let them try to people it with tram conductors or policemen, and I shall applaud any success they may have; if not, who can help them?"

(C. S. *Lewis*, The Allegory of Love)

he concluding remarks of the previous chapter touch on the fundamental similarity of pastoral and religious experience as represented by Montemayor and his sources. The cornerstone of that common ground is memory, the contemplation of the past, remote or recent, in light of the desired ideal and the present. This entire process is mental and by nature implies no movement of bodily limbs; indeed, physical motion tends to undo the fragile knots that join the recollective experience to the rest of reality. As a cerebral event by which information is processed through the mind of one individual, the act of memory is conditioned absolutely by the subject doing the remembering. It is among the primary subjective experiences. As such, it is vulnerable to the irregularities of individual personality and does not pertain to the realm of the empirical. The remembered is real only in the mind of the one who remembers.

In recent years, literary scholars have established the need to look away from empirical realism in evaluating the representative features of pastoral literature, realizing that artistic representations of the type exemplified by pastoral characters are not meant to be mirror images. They are, however, representative in their depiction of something more subtle than physical reality. It is this fidelity to the intangible that strongly allies pastoral to literary expressions of religious experience, also centered on the psychic, intangible world. One would expect the inherent alliance between the pastoral and the religious impulses to acquire a significant dimension in the works of an author like Montemayor, whose most successful vehicles of literary expression were precisely these two modes. Yet the relationship between the pastoral and the religious is by no means limited to him. Most of Spain's sixteenth-century literary shepherds and shepherdesses have characteristics that distinguish them from the same type of literary characters of other ages and other peoples; these are typically the very qualities that exclude them from studies of European pastoral tradition and also tie them to Spain's own history, a heritage strongly marked by conflicts of faith.

In this context, the most highly productive responses to the need to concentrate on pastoral's positive attributes are studies that create a modal system of evaluation (versus one of genre), adaptable to all versions of pastoral that emerge across the ages and in different forms.[1] In evaluating a book such as the *Diana*, critical strategies that identify the common traits of universal pastoral—its mode—yet also allow room for the distinctions found in the various genres that accommodate it, are of primary importance.

Montemayor's pastoral narration has long come under attack for not conforming to certain standards, typically dominated by criteria of empirical realism; critical approaches to it most often hold the book up for scrutiny next to a wide array of representative forms. Such comparisons typically draw in the Spanish sheepherder's union, the *mesta*, adduced as evidence of growth in real pastoral activity just before Montemayor wrote the *Diana*. Another commonly quoted source is one of Cervantes's short novels, "El coloquio de los perros" ("The Dogs' Colloquy"), in which his dog-character Berganza totally deflates the pastoral myth, observing that real shepherds spend their days shouting at each other and removing

---

1. The word "mode" is used here in reference to pastoral's capability to function in many formal environments (elegy, drama, prose fiction) and evoke a consistent meaning, in accordance with the definition of it proposed by Robert Scholes ("Towards a Poetics of Fiction: An Approach through Genre").

their fleas, not singing in dulcet tones and speaking of love. About the pastoral narrations, his canine dialogist concludes that "all those books are dreamed up and well-written stuff . . . and without any truth whatsoever." Third, critics typically invoke Fernando de Herrera's prescriptive formula for pastoral, included in his commentary on the works of Garcilaso; the famous passage is the one beginning, "The material of this poetry is the things and doings of shepherds, particularly their loves, but simple and harmless." Indeed, Herrera's passage has come to be held as "the canon to which the pastoral was to conform" (NPE, 206).[2]

Such comparisons are important for the light they shed on the historical and literary context in which the pastoral books were appreciated. They are, however, inherently incongruous because they compare figures from four different versions of pastoral without distinction of kind: the historical, the parodic, the theoretical, and the one exemplified by the variety of characters found in the *Diana* and its imitations. The fact that Herrera does not treat the pastoral narrations in his 1580 treatise indicates that he perceived a categorical difference between Garcilaso's poetry and sources, on one hand, and Montemayor's text and its imitations, on the other. Herrera also laments, but nonetheless describes elaborately, the mythical version of the mode's origins, thereby acknowledging its relationship to psychic, not physical, reality.[3] In the following analysis of the pastoral characters' representative nature, focus will remain on one version of pastoral: the protagonists of the pastoral narrations, narrations which include poetry as a complement to the prose. Pastoral characters may be defined as those who participate in activities in the *locus amoenus* as part of their normal lives within the fiction. This excludes, therefore, those such as Montemayor's Felicia, more allied to other literary modes. Felismena, also from the *Diana,* and characters like her, are pastoral to the extent that they evidence the qualities outlined on the following pages.

2. Francisco López Estrada elaborates on the relevance of professional livestock keeping to Spanish pastoral narrations (LdP, 281–85). Cervantes's Berganza delivers his opinion in "El coloquio de los perros," 309. For Herrera's text, see Antonio Gallego Morell, *Garcilaso de la Vega y sus comentaristas,* 437.

3. See Gallego Morell, *Garcilaso,* 472. Aurora Egido discusses the development of eclogue theory and practice in Golden Age Spanish literature as distinct from what happened with the pastoral narrations; see her article, "Teoría de la égloga en el Siglo de Oro."

Most characters who are not natives of the pastoral enclosure are hybrid beings whose nature combines pastoral elements with those of courtly or chivalresque literature, as does Felismena.

Since Montemayor's works are so clearly dominated by the inner experiences of his characters, an especially helpful system of analysis for the pastoral mode is the one offered by Paul Alpers. The lives of shepherdesses and shepherds constitute what Alpers calls the representative anecdote of pastoral, meaning that "pastoral works are representations of shepherds, who are felt to be representative of some other or of all other men."[4] He thus specifies the characters as the defining element of pastoral literature, not the scene or the action within it; although both scene and action are generally fixed, they are functions of the characters and not vice versa. Working from Kenneth Burke's theory of representative anecdote, Alpers reminds us that literature, as representation, is a selective phenomenon that signifies a reality separate from that which it represents. Hence the word "anecdote" to describe it, whose association with limitation is a reminder that literature by nature is a combination of represented characteristics that is less than the actual experience of reality, and therefore necessarily prejudiced toward a specific end.[5]

This selective nature of the anecdote frees the representation from unconditional historicity, providing it with a core that can be transformed to meet the needs of successive generations, and pastoral characters have long provided writers with a protean code through which human experience is meaningfully depicted: "Various writers at various times modify the conventional depiction of shepherds on the grounds that it either does not truly represent them or that it deprives them of their representative force."[6] The pastoral anecdote's adaptability across time is important in the description and analysis of Spain's sixteenth-century pastoral literature, which responded to needs of representation quite distinct from those

---

4. "What is Pastoral?" 456. Alpers refers to men, following established critical practice. As mentioned in the Introduction, in the context of sixteenth-century Spanish pastoral narrations such usage is productively altered to include women, whose participation is generally more significant than that of the men.

5. Burke's text says: "Men seek for vocabularies that will be faithful reflections of reality. To this end, they must develop vocabularies that are selections of reality. And any selection of reality must, in certain circumstances, function as a deflection of reality" (*A Grammar of Motives*, 59).

6. Alpers, "What is Pastoral?" 456.

that led to Virgil's *Eclogues* or Sannazaro's *Arcadia*, even while continuing in the tradition of the mode they established.

Like all literary types, the shepherds and shepherdesses are neither diachronically nor synchronically exact; their representative qualities do not encompass the entirety of human life, or the whole of human existence at any given moment. However, their primary function being the lament of loss, they do capture certain inner states with a high degree of fidelity, a quality lending itself to the representation of such events as exile, death, and love.[7] The pastoral characters' exalted talents in poetry and self-expression are delivered at the expense of their physical existence and physical prowess. Insofar as they are pastoral, what activities they do engage in center around recreation, such as conversation and poetic or sportive contests, although the latter two do not appear in the *Diana* or books directly imitating it. In Spain's pastoral books, any violence engaged in by the characters is typically of an allegorical nature and enhances their moral recreation; human aggression may be recalled but not witnessed in the *locus amoenus*. Thus, representation of non-allegorical violence in the narrative present, of the sort committed by Cervantes's Lisandro in the opening book of the *Galatea*, constitutes a temporary rupture in the pastoral mode.

Sixteenth-century literary shepherds and shepherdesses, like all characters cast in the pastoral mode, derive their representative qualities from inner experiences, not outer; the basic nature of their psychological and emotional trials—death of a loved one, rejection, separation, jealousy—is generally familiar, whereas the mask they wear of perfectly beautiful, highly literate sheepherders who rarely tend their flocks, is not. Alpers summarizes this particular configuration of characteristics when he observes that, relative to the world around them, pastoral characters universally display outer weakness but inner strength, to the extent that they are pastoral.[8] They are typically superior to the seemingly humble context in which they operate with respect to inner faculties such as intellect, mem-

---

7. Alpers considers the lament of loss to be the fundamental characteristic of the pastoral mode ("Mode and Genre: The Example of Pastoral"). To define mode, he employs Angus Fletcher's use of the word, which finds that a protagonist's strength relative to the world makes [her or] him "a modular for verbal architechtronics" (*The Singer of the Eclogues: A Study of Virgilian Pastoral*, 7). Scholes's definition of mode, mentioned in note 1, is much the same and perhaps more straightforward.

8. See his *Singer of the Eclogues*, 1–8.

ory, and feelings, but are equal or inferior as regards their relationship to that same humble world in terms of physical strength, wealth, political power, and social status.

Since the emphasis in their representative nature falls squarely within the realm of spiritual experience, shepherdesses and shepherds are especially appropriate figures to portray emotional suffering. Characters whose inner lives are deemed more significant than any other aspect of their existence, they offered an attractive vehicle for expression to Montemayor, whose interest in religious spirituality was well established by the time he wrote any pastoral literature. Indeed, as he molded the pastoral narration into the form it assumes in the *Diana*, he exaggerated this inherently spiritual quality of literary pastoral characters by substituting talk and song about love for what had previously been the commonplace pastoral activities of rustic games, sport, and dance or extensive description of the natural world. Montemayor's pastoral narration implicitly represents its characters' competition to suffer the most in love, not prove themselves superior in artistic performance, in intellectual activity, or in sportive contests, as do Sannazaro's shepherds in his *Arcadia*. Neither they nor their narrators perceive at any length the lush natural world around them, as did their Italian predecessors.[9]

In effecting such a change, Montemayor transferred into prose what Garcilaso had begun in poetry, the total sentimentalization of the pastoral anecdote. Both his religious literature and his pastoral narration insist on the relative insignificance of formal aspects of life and devotion, stressing instead its spiritual events and their examination. This shift in values from aggressive to contemplative heroism was typical of the age's movement away from active heroic ideals toward more thought-oriented values, both of which surfaced in the development of prose fiction: the wane in chivalresque narrations, which coincided with the vogue of pastoral ones. Sentimental fiction might be considered an important precursor of pastoral narrations but for the fact that such books exalt a courtly code of behavior,

---

9. Jacopo Sannazaro's *Arcadia* (1504, first authorized Italian edition) was read on the Peninsula well before its translation/adaptation into Spanish was published in Toledo in 1547. For different evaluations of Sannazaro's influence on Spanish pastoral books, see LdP and Michele Ricciardelli, "La novela pastoril española en relación con la *Arcadia* de Sannazaro" and his *Notas sobre* La Diana *de Montemayor y* La Arcadia *de Sannazaro.*

directed toward individual participation in society—the court—not in contrast to that society, as does the pastoral. In books like Diego de San Pedro's *Cárcel de amor* (*Prison of Love*), emphasis falls on formal manifestation of inner experiences, and hence their propensity toward elaborate allegory.[10] Pastoral narrations, on the contrary, tend to focus on individual experience for its own sake, in isolation from society, and depict moments of passive experience, not active.

The dynamics of the picaresque mode, which flowered at the same time as pastoral fiction, are much closer to those of pastoral than first glance might indicate: although picaresque fiction parodies where the pastoral over-idealizes, both assume a critical posture toward society. Significantly, picaresque narrations, like the pastoral, are devoted exclusively to memory via their pseudo-autobiographical form. Although purporting to be objective recollections, they are as deeply conditioned by their protagonists' inner worlds as are the pastoral narrations. The new emphasis on subjective, individual experience, evident in the *Diana*, closely followed the same trend in religious experience during Montemayor's most productive years.[11]

The "heroic" nature of the literary shepherdesses and shepherds, meaning the sum of those characteristics that make them imitable, differs greatly from that of the goal-seeking, physically motivated heroines and heroes that generally typify Western culture. In the context of pastoral, based on dialogue about thoughts and feelings (reactions, not actions), aggressive pursuit of goals is inappropriate. For this reason, bursts of energy or violence in this type of fiction still manage to make the reader uncomfortable, as every reader of Cervantes's *Galatea* knows. In strictly pastoral terms, characters who engage in aggressive behavior while in the *locus amoenus*, such as Montemayor's shepherdess Felismena, are less "heroic" than those who seek the contemplative ideals truer to the pastoral mode. Modern readers persist in making Felismena the "heroine" of the *Diana* because she is active and she appears to solve her own problems. Such a reading denigrates the very purpose of pastoral, while satisfy-

---

10. Alan D. Deyermond's article "Las relaciones genéricas de la ficción sentimental española" is particularly helpful in this context.

11. On the emphasis on subjective experience in the religious context, see Andrés Martín, "Alumbrados, erasmistas, 'luteranos' y místicos, y su común dominador: el riesgo de una espiritualidad más 'intimista.'"

ing the need for resolution in literature, a need which pure pastoral does not meet.[12]

Spain's sixteenth-century shepherds and shepherdesses alone embody the values set forth by Luis de Granada, who says: "Man's happiness lies neither in the body nor in the body's good but rather in the spirit and in spiritual and invisible goods" (No está, pues, la bienaventuranza del hombre, ni en el cuerpo, ni en bienes de cuerpo . . . sino en el espíritu y en bienes espirituales y invisibles, *Guía*, 318). Unlike courtly lovers, the shepherds and shepherdesses wear a costume that appears to annul the value of their nobility of blood; they are clearly courtly figures, but nevertheless they renounce the outward benefits of their social status and exterior merit to concentrate on their virtue, their inner merit.

The major characters of the *Diana* lead lives and wear clothing that symbolize their humility (clothing symbolizing humility, but not necessarily humble) as well as their having literally and metaphorically stripped themselves of worldly trappings to focus on spiritual concerns, to which they dedicate themselves entirely. The clothes they wear in the *locus amoenus* and the pastoral life they lead, for its lack of discomfort and muted elegance, is a superb transmutation of *recogido* asceticism and renunciation of the world for God into a courtly (aristocratic) humility and retreat into one's inner world after severe disillusion in the outer one. The parity before love of the characters, who come from a disparate collection of social classes, likewise exalts spiritual merit over worldliness.

Although the pastoral characters may have inherited their obsession with love from earlier literary types, theirs is not the devotion of the courtly lovers who preceded them; the norms of medieval love are centered around social experience, for which the criteria are self-conscious denial of the flesh or surreptitious surrender to it. In them, desire to attain "love" (love being the word often used to mean a strictly sexual relationship) is what prompts the action or the lyric moment, whether that desire is acted upon,

---

12. Felismena's initial and final active outbursts, both violent, are excused by the allegorical nature of her attack against the savages (the first) and the fact that she is no longer in the *locus amoenus* when she kills the knights attacking Don Felis (the second). On Felismena as the *Diana's* heroine, see Walter Davis, *A Map of Arcadia: Sidney's Romance in its Tradition*, 23–26; John de Oliveira e Silva, "Recurrent Onomastic Textures in the *Diana* of Jorge de Montemayor and the *Arcadia* of Sir Philip Sidney," 35. I dispute such readings further in chapter 3.

sublimated, or controlled by self-conscious force of will. Books like the *Diana*, on the contrary, focus predominantly on the characters' sentimental experience alone, in its own right, represented beyond the physical and moral confines of society. Importantly, they are driven by the desire to *regain* lost love, meaning primarily sentimental satisfaction, not attain it, and so progress on toward a resolution in marriage. As Keith Whinnom indicates, Spain's own cancionero lyrics, although likewise centered on the love experience, represent it in a fashion that differs greatly from that of the pastoral characters': the primary goal of the cancionero poets being formal artistry, whose priority overrides all other objectives, the expression of one's inner experience is therein inappropriate.[13]

In a context in which inner activity such as memory and emotion take precedence over physical movement and fulfillment, passivity becomes not only a necessity, but a goal, indispensable for the exploration of mental events. This constitutes another alliance between pastoral and religious meditation, since both rely on the temporary lack of physical activity to engage the spirit. When the passive moment ends, so does the pastoral; likewise, when the recogido returns to the world, the contemplative moment is lost. Clearly then, the shepherdesses' and shepherds' lack of will and characteristic abulia is what makes possible their most positive experiences, their immersion in thought alone, even if only for a time. To conclude that Montemayor's attempt at representing human experience in the *Diana* was a failure because of his characters' passivity is to deny the value of pastoral itself.[14] Pastoral characters, Montemayor's first and foremost, were spectacular successes in Spain and in much of western Europe precisely because they faithfully reflected esteemed values and represented the human condition in a way perceived as valid during the age in which

---

13. The comparisons between courtly lovers and the pastoral characters in this chapter were facilitated by Deyermond's lucid exposition of the qualities of courtly love, the first of which is the outward nobility of the lovers (*The Middle Ages*, 13). Roger Boase's "Courtly Love in Spanish Literature: A Continuing Debate" and Bernard O'Donoghue's *The Courtly Love Tradition* are also helpful in this context. On the theme of physical love in cancionero poetry, see Keith Whinnom's *La poesía amatoria de la época de los Reyes Católicos* and Ian Macpherson's "Secret Language in the Cancioneros: Some Courtly Codes."

14. Cf. Avalle-Arce: "Montemayor's attempt failed.... The shepherds are nothing more than passive spectators who witness the lively parade of these vital forces from the isolated, ideal lookout of their pastoral condition" (NPE, 95; see also page 91).

pastorals were written. Those values embodied in them demonstrate a vivid appreciation for contemplative and sentimental experience.

Because of their exclusive engagement in acts of memory, imagination, and empathy, Montemayor's shepherdesses and shepherds take part in activities akin to those religious practices prescribed for the lay population by the recogidos. Indeed, the emphasis on self-examination and recreative recollection evident in the lives of Montemayor's pastoral characters might be interpreted as an exaggerated secular version of the religious meditation recommended by recogido writers. Quoting Saint Bonaventura, Luis de Granada insists on retirement from the world for meditation and self-contemplation saying, "It is best to have some oratory or secret place that is a bit removed from family noise and turmoil, to which you may remove yourself as if to a quiet port, free from the tempests of worldly cares and affairs" (Será bien que tengas algún oratorio y lugar secreto que esté un poco apartado del ruido y estruendo de la familia, al cual te debes acoger como á un puerto quieto y libre de la tempestad de los cuidados y negocios del siglo, LdO, 307). This was a commonplace theme in recogido treatises. Juan de Ávila attributes the idea to Saint Jerome, whom he quotes as saying, "Find some appropriate place, somewhat removed from the noise of this family, to which you may go as one who finds a haven, fleeing from the great tempest of your cares; and . . . may all the worries from the rest of the day be gently recompensed with this time free of activity" (*Audi*, 142).

It is but a short step from this abandonment of the world into the recollective inactivity of *Arcadia*, and it is no surprise that Montemayor, whose alliance with the piety preached by men like Granada has been established, took that step. Garcilaso immediately comes to mind as Montemayor's precursor. Nonetheless, his eclogues, however similar in mode to the *Diana*, differ profoundly from Montemayor's book for their overt debt to classical poetry, their idyllic structure and their depiction of scenes versus a narrative that progresses from a recollected past into the moving present, and the sealed atmosphere in which they take place, lacking reference to a world impinging immediately on the *locus amoenus*. Unlike Garcilaso's eclogues, Montemayor's *Diana* shares a didactic preoccupation with contemporary religious literature, a characteristic continued in its imitations.

The passage from religious to secular application of the retreat and meditation motifs was facilitated by the prohibition of books like Luis de

Granada's *Libro de la oración* (*Book of Prayer*) and Montemayor's *Obras* by the Spanish Inquisitor General in 1559. Certainly in Montemayor's case, some of the themes that Catholic reformism taught him to appreciate in religious literature, such as disdain of worldliness and exaltation of private contemplative experience carried out by the individual beyond the structure (control) of society, found a natural outlet in pastoral fiction. In a broader sense, it is also likely that such religious themes spilled over into the secular realm spontaneously and generally.[15]

The Christian who retreats from the world to meditate or to live and the pastoral character alike are seeking unmediated love, and both depend on individual experience beyond the confines of religious and social hierarchy. Both rely on acts of memory and imagination: religious meditation uses the former to delve into the personal past in self-examination and the latter to project the imagination onto biblical stories; pastoral meditation uses memory to recall individual past experiences in love and imagination to listen sympathetically to the stories of others, to the point where another's cares are felt as those of the listener.

The pastoral characters of the *Diana* differ from the supposed sinners to whom books like the *Book of Prayer* were directed, however, in that they have not transgressed their ideals. Their self-examination thus leads them to confirmation of their status as perfect lovers who have been wronged by others, not done wrong themselves. In this, they are identical to the narrative voices of Montemayor's religious writings, none of whom are represented as repentant sinners, but rather as dignified victims or lamenters of the unworthy ways of the world. The pastoral characters' autobiographies are sinless confessions, shared with each other and not with a figure of authority, reviews born of their guiltless victimization: all have suffered a failed, pure love. In this, they mark a stage in the development from religious self-examination to autobiography (the secular, sinless confession), consistent with the passage from a theocentric society into an anthropocentric one.[16]

---

15. Jean Pierre Dedieu's research, on the general population's awareness of Catholic dogma in Spain during the era of Tridentine attempts to catechize, promises to reveal a surprisingly high level of literacy in doctrinal matters among an equally surprisingly broad sector of the populace, a component that should be considered in any account of Spanish culture as a whole during this period. See his "The Archives of the Holy Office of Toledo as a Source for Historical Anthropology."

16. Logically, then, T. C. Zimmerman refers to the birth of Renaissance autobiogra-

FORMAL VEHICLES OF IDEOLOGY   119

For their belief in themselves as faultless practitioners of an ideological code, Montemayor's characters are similar to his hermit Dileto, who is likewise represented as an authority and an experienced, faultless lover (of God), as capable as the shepherds and shepherdesses of reproducing not only his past individual experience with that love, but its doctrine as well. He displays an intellectual wisdom as much at odds with his costume as the pastoral characters' familiarity with love theory is with theirs. Although the nature of their insights into love differ greatly, the supposed source of Dileto's wisdom is identical to that of the pastoral characters': experience and the authority it confers upon those who live righteously. Like Dileto, the shepherds and shepherdesses practice only their devotion in love, beyond the confines of society. They all exhibit their author's tendency toward extremism, and their exclusive dedication to *otium* at the expense of their "real" lives liken the pastoral characters to secular versions of the illuminists. Appropriately, both were censured by moralists, who made the logical connection between an idle mind and the devils' workshop. The protagonist of Fray Bartolomé Ponce's religious adaptation of the *Diana* cries, "Oh Cupid!, how you only have power against the idle, for it is in idleness that evils are conceived, betrayals take effect, and sins are committed. Alas, as soon as I became idle I found myself enamored and lost."[17] As is true with Montemayor's religious works, parallels between the pastoral characters and the illuminists cannot consistently be maintained; they illustrate illuminist tendencies that may be found in early recogido piety.

There is a certain control over inner experience, individual and private though it may be, implied by the manuals of devotion that proposed to teach the worshipper how to pray. They are a codification of religious sentiment and prescribe the practice of a set of rules designed to guide the

---

phy as "a transmogrification of the medieval practice of confession." Zimmerman, "Confession and Autobiography in the Early Renaissance," 121.

17. *Primera parte de la Clara Diana a lo divino repartida en siete libras . . . dirigida al prudente lector,* 11v–12r. The illuminist María de Cazalla apparently conducted religious meetings in her kitchen, where the congregation consisted of those who had abandoned their professional activities: "abandoning the business of commerce and trades they had, wanted to retire in order to serve Our Lord and sought out new ways to serve Our Lord." In Milagros Ortega Costa, *Proceso de la Inquisición contra María de Cazalla,* 260–62; witness's report from 1533. Cazalla was tortured and sentenced, as an illuminist, to public penance. See Bataillon, E&E, 470–74.

Christian along the proper route of intimate experience. The libros de pastores likewise appear to deal with emotional experience beyond the controlling hand of society, yet never abandon either the attempt to control the lovers' interpretation of their "private" experiences. This codification of inner life, which dictates not the rules of love in society but the rules of love in itself, is deflected into the pastoral narrations in two ways. For one, the characters check not only their own and each other's behavior, but they evaluate each other's feelings as well. First, when Montemayor's Selvagia declares that she has come to recognize the fickle nature of love and fortune and so resigns herself to whatever may come, Sylvano reminds her of the doctrine by which they pretend to live. When he asks if she knows of any cure for their malady, she unflinchingly replies, "Stop loving" (Dexar de querer). He questions how she would do that, and she answers, "However fortune or time would have it" (Como la fortuna o el tiempo lo ordenasse). Sylvano reprehends her, reinforcing the tenets of the very doctrine that has brought them both nothing but unhappiness: "I tell you then that I would not insult you by not feeling compassion for your suffering, because love that is subject to time and to fortune cannot be so great that it brings trials to the one who endures it" (Aora te digo que no te aría agravio en no aver manzilla de tu mal porque amor que está subjecto al tiempo y a la fortuna, no puede ser tanto que dé trabajo a quien lo padece, LD, 69).

This pastoral didacticism preceded and followed the *Diana:* in Montemayor's first eclogue (1554), Tolomeo hastens to remind Lusitano that true love is a matter of the spirit, not physical beauty. Vandalina is indeed beautiful, "but the idea does not consist in that; / it is quite removed from it, for true and virtuous love / is an effect of sentiment only" (mas no consiste en eso el pensamiento; / muy fuera va de allí, que el amor fino / un solo efecto es del sentimiento, SC, 182r; GP, 87). In the *Galatea,* published twenty-six years after the *Diana,* Cervantes's Elicio likewise censures Erastro for implying too much of a relationship between beauty and love: "I want to tell you that the quality of love with which I believed you loved Galatea has been much adulterated for me, because if you only love her for her beauty, she has little for which to thank you . . ." (LG, 200). The characters devote almost all of their time to listening to and evaluating each other's behavior. They censure actions that threaten the ideological code by which they live and thereby zealously protect the integrity of their idealized existence, even while witnessing the contradictions inherent in that idealism's implementation. They are conservative in their tenacious determination to maintain a grip on idealistic love in the face of its failure. Their ironic intimacy is in keeping with the religious climate of the age, in which affective spirituality was taught and encouraged, and also closely supervised; thus Eugenio Asensio describes recogido piety as "that type of mysticism as favored by the public as distrusted by the Inquisition."[18]

The second way in which Spain's pastoral characters demonstrate a concern with ideological control is the overt forms of sermonizing in which the supposed rustics engage. Whereas Sannazaro's shepherds are self-consciously artistic, the shepherdesses and shepherds of Montemayor and his followers are self-consciously didactic. True to the circumstances surrounding their origins, an age of doctrinal definition for the Catholic church and a period of intense interest in lay piety and secular spirituality, the *pastores* of the Spanish pastoral narrations all represent ideologically correct love in a formal way.

The three most studied books of the genre, Montemayor's *Diana*, Gil Polo's *Diana enamorada* (*Diana in Love*), and Cervantes's *Galatea*, all contain sermonic sections during which the characters instruct each other, and the reader, on the nature of true love. Montemayor went so far as to copy fragments from Leone Hebreo's *Dialoghi d'amore* (*Dialogues of Love*) into book four of the *Diana*, and his main characters regularly display an offhand familiarity with the mandates of love theory. They run into difficulty not with their doctrinal knowledge, which is flawless, but with their attempts to put that idealism to work in the moving time represented by the fiction. The minor importance of the doctrine compared to their experiences interpreting it and living by its rules, highly significant in itself, keeps these books from becoming philosophical and, as mentioned in chapter 1, at the same time attests to the contemporary importance of indoctrination.

The two traits established above, the pastoral characters' total dedication to sentimental experience in its own right and their overt concern with instruction in doctrine, are distinctive features of Spain's sixteenth-century pastoral narrations. It may be that these inclusions in the pastoral anecdote, as Montemayor developed it in his prose narration, are func-

---

18. "El erasmismo y las corrientes espirituales afines," 93.

tions of the religious environment of the times, as are its exclusions. Political themes are virtually non-existent in the libros de pastores, as is any group consciousness that might challenge the individual's delight in her or his own trials and suggest the application of those experiences to a wider context; each individual undertakes a campaign to prove his or her uniquely difficult problem. This characteristic explains the genre's transformation into autobiography in the seventeenth century, documented by Avalle-Arce (NPE, 141–74). Neither the Italian models preceding the *Diana* nor the English adaptation of the same, Sidney's *Arcadia*, display such limitation of theme, and neither do they contain characters who are all not only able to reproduce love doctrine, but determined to prove that they are as well.[19]

Spanish pastoral characters are also noteworthy for their total immersion in the spiritual realm of the *locus amoenus*, a hermetically sealed environment that is free from the cares that are unrelated to emotional existence. The sincere esteem in which the physically inactive life, or part of one's life, was held constitutes a marked distinction between Spain's pastoral books and Sidney's version of them, a distinction stemming partly from the differences between Spanish and British history in general, and religious history in particular. Characters in the English *Arcadia* are, as David Kalstone notes, "apt to be brought to the bar of heroic responsibility. The participation of a king and princes in a shepherd's celebration—their nobility tarnished somewhat by retirement and disguise—sharply dramatizes Sidney's point of view."[20] The characters of Spanish pastoral books are often disguised members of noble families, but they are never princes or kings. This is the case in part because the English version of the pastoral anecdote borrowed more heavily from chivalric motifs than

---

19. As Thomas P. Harrison observes, the English version is "a work brimming with allegory of person and state" ("A Source of Sidney's *Arcadia*," 71), most unlike the *Diana* and its imitations. Peter Lindenbaum traces Sidney's changing attitudes toward pastoral, productively comparing the English text with Montemayor's, in the first two chapters of his book *Changing Landscapes: Anti-Pastoral Sentiment in the English Renaissance* (22–90).

20. "The Transformation of *Arcadia*: Sannazaro and Sir Philip Sidney," 245. Obviously, a substantial amount of time elapsed between the publication of Montemayor's *Diana* (1559) and Sidney's *Arcadia* (1590). By 1590, the relatively naïve quality of the *Diana* wouldn't have been appreciated in Spain either, and the comparisons that follow are for purposes of general contrast. Nonetheless, the fact that pastoral prose narrations emerged from the Peninsula is significant.

did the Spanish and are thus centered around the heroes' quests for their royal identity and proof of their worth as rulers, something which does not appear in the libros de pastores.

Spanish authors and readers were able to embrace the classical *otium* motif and identify with the passive pastoral characters readily. Granted, their enthusiastic immersion in the disguise was made possible because it represented an important concept of social status in Spain, that of not *having* to do anything. Is was also facilitated, however, by Spanish religious culture, which fostered a mentality that prepared the way for wholehearted acceptance of a literature representing the dedication of one's time to the development of one's inner life, even at the expense of one's "outer life" (economic and social status). Love, in the totality of secular and religious culture, was the most excellent of spiritual experiences. Therefore, in the Spanish context, developing and proving one's spiritual prowess, interpreted as one's ability to love, *was* one's "heroic responsibility." The unique circumstances of Peninsular pastoral characters were among the principal reasons for the outstanding success of the libros de pastores. They neatly capture the aristocratic yet virtuous idleness to which many aspired, and incarnate widely circulated religious ideals as well.

The undisputed significance allotted to issues of spirituality, with its concurrent formal display within the fictional context, is complemented by the unique type of society represented within the pastoral narrations by the collection of characters accumulated in the *locus amoenus*. Spanish pastoral societies represented in the libros de pastores consist of individuals of varying social classes who congregate to lament their problems in love: natives and visitors, disguised nobles and country dwellers. All are welcomed equally within the confines of the pastoral setting, all engage in basically the same activities, and all are afforded the same kind attention. Class distinctions, when they surface, do not prohibit anyone's emotional trials from being addressed in turn, and questions of social rank exclude no one from the community's goals of self-expression. Spain's pastoral narrations are peopled with shepherdesses and shepherds who are sufficiently noble in spirit to justify their inner equality with any disguised noble who intrudes on the pastoral enclosure.[21] Focus is fixed on the

---

21. The theme of nobility of spirit as a class issue had surfaced in earlier Spanish

primary characters' parity before the forces of love and fortune, regardless of their origins.

In the comparable English version of the anecdote, on the contrary, the cast of characters does not constitute an integrated whole of shepherds and shepherdesses, but rather a collection of lowly shepherds into which noble characters are thrust by fortune, with the result that they treat their humbler companions as inferiors. The readiness with which the Spanish characters diminish or erase their social status while among the pastoral corps indicates that the disguise itself implied a betterment, not a demeaning, of one's person. The fact that in Sidney's pastoral narration, "the courtier of *Arcadia* cannot join an entertainment with the innocent impunity of shepherds" proves the point by contrast.[22] In Spain, courtiers were indeed integrated into the pastoral scene because it implied no social step down for them.

The Spanish reading population was quite accepting of the pastoral character as one sufficiently noble in its humility to represent it. The English were perhaps less so; the most basic pastoral contradictions went largely uncontested in Spain, whereas in England they were not. Sidney was compelled to explain his own book's existence, saying of his shepherds, "Then was their manner ever to have one who should write up the substance of that they said; whose pen, having more leisure than their tongues, might perchance polish the rudeness of an unthought-on song." As Peter Lindenbaum observes, they "in effect have a secretary, who touches up and improves what he hears."[23] In the Spanish pastoral books, the characters speak for themselves because they are an inherently different breed of shepherds and shepherdesses whose lives are tied to spiritual idealism, not realism. They evolved in an age and a land in which illumination by grace, which included doctrinal wisdom, was not only accepted but exalted. Thus, Sidney's contrived explanation, which calls attention to the artificiality of the mode with self-conscious commentary, was unnecessary, for authors and public alike generally went along with the maneuver.[24]

literature, notably in the *Tragicomedia de Don Duardos* by Montemayor's compatriot Gil Vicente (1470?–1536?).

22. Kalstone, "The Transformation of Arcadia," 245.

23. Sir Philip Sidney, *The Countess of Pembroke's Arcadia (The Old Arcadia)*, 56; Lindenbaum, *Changing Landscapes*, 25.

24. The acceptance was not universal, although it sufficed to carry the *Diana* repeatedly into reprint. Alonso Pérez, author of one of the first continuations of Mon-

In short, the pastoral anecdote in Spain acquired a prestige that would seem to indicate a direct relationship between the country's religious history, with its concomitant alliance of Spanish readers to the values of recogido piety, and the pastoral values captured by the literary shepherds and shepherdesses. For example, never is a shepherdess or shepherd disdained by an outsider in a pastoral narration, yet Sidney's prince-in-disguise Musidorus gets nothing *but* disdain from his beloved Pamela while dressed as a shepherd, precisely because she perceives him to be beneath her, in spite of her natural attraction to him.[25] Since the Spanish shepherds and shepherdesses of the pastoral narration incarnated religious values that were consonant with the cultural values of the time, the pastoral anecdote as it was formed by Montemayor was accepted as imitable, as noble, and therefore as heroic, within its own modest proportions.

The quality that most distinguishes Montemayor's pastoral lovers from others in the European love tradition was also a fundamental feature of sixteenth-century Catholic reformism, one that was primary among the ideas of the Spanish mystics: love can be realized, and directly with the beloved by means of simple contact. The problem they all consistently lament, however, is the transitory nature of human affection, no matter how spiritual one's devotion is, and the intervention of bad fortune; this, in turn, is a natural consequence of humanity's lack of divine characteristics, and the consequences of human life's inherent imperfections. All of the shepherds and shepherdesses in the *Diana* have at one time enjoyed direct contact with their beloved, unmediated by intervening social convention and hierarchy, just as the reformist worshipper of God enjoys the potential for equally unmediated contact with the divine. The pastoral characters' love is obsessive not because it is physically or emotionally unfulfilled, or impossible in itself. Significantly, love is represented as possible; all of Montemayor's characters have known success in love before the narration begins. But, like earthly realization of the divine, it cannot endure as a happy state and thus the Spanish pastoral lament, so similar to the Psalmist's complaint of life's injustice, is born.

---

temayor's book, found fault with the original characters' behavior, inappropriate for shepherds and shepherdesses, a problem of decorum in neo-Aristotelian terms; see NPE, 107. Cervantes was perforating the hermetic seal of the pastoral narrations by 1585, in the *Galatea*.

25. *Old Arcadia*, 52, 55, 57.

This stance had serious consequences: the characters' familiarity with each other breeds a kind of contempt, or at best, misunderstanding, something that obviously did not happen in the instances in which God was the beloved. No longer working within the vassal/lord paradigm that produced the lover/beloved relationship of medieval love, with all its inherent idealism of the beloved, the shepherdesses and shepherds face their beloved as equals, with the intention of establishing a mutually satisfying relationship. Thus, human imperfection plays a significant role in the *Diana* and its imitations, since in these texts the beloved are freed from the repression of idealization and are quite fallible. Montemayor tends to overidealize the lover in exchange, who is victimized by that fallibility. Later authors, balancing out the credit and the blame, were able to arrive at what looks like a more realistic assessment of human reality by allowing for Montemayor's frank evaluation of the beloved in the lover as well.

Although the pastoral characters faithfully portray the universal pastoral lament of loss and the dominion of the inner world over the outer, they display other characteristics that tie them to a particular moment in the history of Spanish culture and Spanish spirituality. True to their ideals and attentive to their experiences and those of others like them, the shepherdesses and shepherds cannot fail to point out the difficulties inherent in living out one's beliefs. They are retreating, after all, from something. From their protected and supposedly isolated vantage point, they are most eloquent witnesses of the ways of the world at large, the very world they appear to reject. Their flight from reality, as that of Montemayor's Dileto, indicates how difficult it is for virtuous love to function in life beyond the confines of the mind and the spirit. For unlike their pastoral precursors, Spanish shepherds and shepherdesses live in time, not out of it. This important characteristic was bestowed upon them by the narrative structure of the pastoral narrations as Montemayor crafted it.

Narrative Structure

The pastoral anecdote took a daring step away from its own history when Montemayor cast the *Diana* in prose with moments of song that punctuate, rather than contain, its central material. Prose signals the reader to approach the text in a different attitude from that assumed for verse, and itself implies the presence of time, not temporal suspension as does lyric poetry. The greatest pastoral literature was appropriately written in verse, precisely because this poetic quality of suspension, temporal and mental, is fundamental to the pastoral mode.[26] Montemayor compromised the poetic nature of pastoral when he wrote the *Diana*, for although there is a substantial amount of lyric verse in his book, the plot is forwarded in the prose, which is the more important of the two in relationship to the whole. Thus, his pastoral narration moves in time and thereby allows him to communicate his message, which is not about love, but about love in life and in time itself.

In the *Diana*, a wide variety of literary presences are evoked at one time or another: there are formal elements from the books of chivalry (interrupted and episodic plots, an open ending), from sentimental fiction (allegorical episodes, letters), from lyric poetry (love poems), from narrative poetry (story-telling poems), from the *novella* (short inserted stories, one adapted from Bandello). With regard to mode, as well as pastoral there are elements of romance (peripatetic plots, assumed identities, anagnorisis) and of novel (psychological insight, the sense of alienation from the world). The physical environments in which the characters move are real in kind (with several identifiable locations) but false in degree (all are idealized). The characters themselves run the gamut from fantasy figures reminiscent of the chivalresque and mythic worlds (Felicia and her nymphs, Orpheus, the savages, the knights) to "real people" represented in pastoral fiction through its function as *roman à clef*. This hybrid quality in structure, characters, and content was something continued by all of Montemayor's successful imitators; thus, for example, Gil Polo included Turia as a counterpart to Orpheus in his *Diana in Love*, and Cervantes used Calíope in the *Galatea*.[27]

---

26. About the poetics of prose and verse, see Jonathan Culler, "Poetics of the Lyric" and "Poetics of the Novel." Montemayor's prose has a lyrical rhythm nonetheless, as López Estrada indicates (LD, LCIII). See Alpers's discussion of pastoral suspension in *Singer of the Eclogues*, 96-97.

27. Wardropper describes such blending of fictional types, typical of sixteenth-century literature, in his article "Fictional Prose, History and Drama: *Pedro de Urdemalas*." Davis describes the "hospitable" nature of pastoral in reference to its special potential to accommodate other literary forms (*Map of Arcadia*, 168). On the identification of real people in pastoral narrations, see Jean Subirats's "La 'Diana' de Montemayor, roman à clef?," López Estrada (LD, LXXXIV-LXXXVII), and Juan Bautista Avalle-Arce's introduction to Cervantes's *Galatea* (1:C-CI).

In order to make such a disparate combination tenable, Montemayor elaborated on the basic structure of universal pastoral literature: a narrative present in which the past is recalled and given a greater significance than the present in which it is remembered. By allocating to the past almost all of the physical action in the *Diana* and allowing that action to appear in the narration only through remembrance, Montemayor was able to include elaborate stories which, although decidedly not pastoral in themselves, are nested in a narrative setting that respects the precepts of pastoral decorum. Pastoral interludes were very popular in chivalric fiction and are traditionally cited as the forerunners of the *Diana*. Montemayor, however, turns the tables on his predecessors by writing pastoral fiction with a chivalric interlude, Don Felis's arrival in book seven. The difference between the two is highly significant, since the former emphasizes action over thought while the latter stresses thought over action, thereby indicating a fundamental shift in values.[28] All of his successful imitators copied this structure, and some used it more consistently than he did himself.

The narrative weave of the libros de pastores consists of two levels of plot development: one is the continuing present that takes place within the pastoral enclosure, here referred to as the first narrative plane.[29] The other is the series of autobiographical memories of events that have occurred outside the pastoral world and are recalled by the characters within it, the second narrative plane. The combination of the two allows the pastoral narrations to expand synchronically, whereas chivalric and sentimental fiction extends diachronically. Books like the *Diana* consist of multiple episodes recalled over a brief period of time, episodes told as past events which, once caught up to the narrative present by their telling, continue into it, intertwining and overlapping with each other in the first narrative plane at the books' ends. The initial vertical expansion that results from the imposition of second-plane narrative onto the first was made possible by the integral use of memory in the present tense of the fiction.

---

28. Sidney Cravens considers Montemayor's debt to his friend Feliciano de Silva to be much more substantial in his book *Feliciano de Silva y los antecedentes de la novela pastoril en sus libros de cabellerías*.

29. The two narrative planes of pastoral narration and the limitations they bring to fiction are described in greater detail in Elizabeth Rhodes, "Sixteenth-century Pastoral Books, Narrative Structure, and *La Galatea* of Cervantes."

FORMAL VEHICLES OF IDEOLOGY   129

In narrations that are truly pastoral, it is memory alone—the second narrative plane—that imports non-pastoral activities and events to the *locus amoenus,* thereby protecting the qualities of pastoral that make it the contemplative mode that it is. Appropriately, the literary shepherds and shepherdesses are endowed with phenomenal memories capable of reproducing exactly a lengthy conversation that occurred years before, including letters and poems that formed part of the event. This device, although not verisimilar, does allow the reenactment of an open spectrum of events that are related as past occurrences whose intensity appears not to have faded at all with time.

In the first narrative plane, an omniscient narrator typically conducts in silence his chorus of individual voices, allowing the characters to speak for themselves by means of dialogue. The second narrative plane is in first person and is necessarily limited to the teller's point of view. Therefore, there is very little overt narrative editorial in the pastoral books. Instead, the characters speak for themselves, thereby providing a broad panorama of perspectives, enhanced by their autobiographical nature.

Presentation of these multiple points of view is in turn made possible by a distinctive feature of Spanish pastoral narrations; the *Diana* and its imitations have a communal structure, one that allots narrative time to multiple plots rather than focusing exclusively on the tale of one person or one pair. Although this communalization is often found in pastoral literature, it was not typical of prose fiction in the sixteenth century.[30] Its presence allowed the world represented by the fiction to become problematic and contradictory, as several individuals bring their own points of view to the whole. Although this novel perspectivism is typically attributed to Cervantes (NPE, 238), it is inherent in the structure of the libros de pastores as invented by Montemayor. The fact that Cervantes's first published work, the *Galatea,* was a pastoral narration is significant, as is the fact that it directly imitates the narrative structure of Montemayor's *Diana.* The primary narrative importance allotted to memory and review of doctrine, the

---

30. Byzantine fiction also contains a multitude of characters, whose stories are related over an expanse of episodic telling. Pastoral fiction differs from it in the congregational nature of the narrative structure (compared with the Byzantine characters' tendency to drop in and out of the narrative present) and the extensive physical movement of the main characters that characterizes Byzantine tales but is lacking in the first plane of the pastoral narrations. A discussion of Byzantine fiction and the second narrative plane of the pastoral narrations follows.

testimonial nature of the *Diana*'s narrative structure, as well as the subjective focus of its content are some of the consequences that Montemayor's religiousness brought to bear on the pastoral narration as he created it.

The first narrative plane is what the sixteenth century inherited from the classical pastoral of Theocritus and Virgil and the literary tradition that developed from it. The binary structure of narrative past and present here described is latent even in Virgil's first eclogue, in which Tityrus, a native shepherd who pertains to the first narrative plane, is joined by Meliboeus, an outsider whose perspective differs from that of his pastoral friend. The bucolic half of this wistfully confrontational structure, passive, contemplative, and lyrical, constitutes the essence of the mode. Therefore, a text's acceptability as pastoral depends on successful development of the first narrative plane as the basis of the narrative whole. On this primary narrative level, time takes on peculiar dimensions, reflecting the absolute priority of remembrance and sentiment in the pastoral world. Mikhail Bakhtin describes it eloquently: "This is a dense and fragrant time, like honey, a time of intimate lovers' scenes and lyric outpouring, a time saturated with its own strictly limited, sealed-off segments of nature's space, stylized through and through."[31]

Montemayor's creative voice, contemplative, withdrawn, and disillusioned, found ample room for representation within the confines of time and space peculiar to the first narrative plane. Like his religious writings, the *Diana* approaches life with a long and sad gaze at the past, a past that has left the characters holding their memories, embittered by its proof of their dignified victimization. Montemayor's book begins, "Coming down from the mountains of León was forgotten Sireno, whom love, fortune, and time had treated in such a way that the smallest misfortune he suffered in his deplorable life led him to expect nothing less than the loss of that life" (Baxaba de las montañas de León el olvidado Sireno a quien

---

31. *The Dialogic Imagination*, 147. Bakhtin's description facilitates the observation of several interesting analogies between pastoral painting, a sub-category of landscape art, and the Spanish pastoral narrations. The power of both, for example, is based on effects of composition and description rather than on those of allegory or narrative. Pastoral art developed from religious paintings, principally accomplished by Giorgione's development of the works of the Venetian *Quattrocento* artist Giovanni Bellini. David Rosand describes Giorgione's accomplishment as revealing "a space for private, secular meditation" ("Giorgione, Venice and the Pastoral Vision," 41).

Amor, la fortuna, el tiempo, tratavan de manera que del menor mal que en tan triste vida padecía, no se esperava menos que perdella, LD, 9).

In order to respect the poetic nature of the mode, action which takes place on the first narrative plane does not extend much beyond talking and singing and participation in poetic events such as elegy or visits to monuments, plastic remembrances of the past. The environment is unchanging and unchallenging, facilitating the inward gaze rather than the outward. As Andrew Ettin observes, "First, the pastoral landscape does not call attention to itself . . . [it] exemplifies pastoral virtues. . . . Pastoral space, therefore, exists for its emotional coloration."[32] As the place and time of devotional retreat, it is withdrawn from the real world and exists as a function of the mind. The first narrative plane provides the foundation for books one through three in the *Diana*, in which the characters are congregated and ushered to Felicia's palace.

To protect the fragile bucolic world, whatever violence occurs on the first narrative plane should be allegorical, such as the intrusion of the three wild men in book two of the *Diana*, or the stag hunt and the mock naval battle in Gil Polo's *Diana in Love*.[33] For the same reason, any change that occurs on the first narrative plane is best brought about by supernatural means, such as Felicia's magic water in Montemayor's and Gil Polo's books, because it allows the pastoral characters to maintain their essential passivity, effectively lifting the responsibility for change out of their reach and consequently beyond the confines of the first narrative plane. At the moment when action intrudes into the first narrative plane, the pastoral dissipates. Thus, Cervantes ends the *Galatea* just as Elicio is about to take his destiny in his own hands and confront Galatea's father.

To the extent that the characters are made to appear self-contemplating victims without seeming self-centered or irresponsible, they are literary shepherdesses and shepherds whose representative qualities were attractive to sixteenth-century readers. With their counterparts in religious literature, the pastoral characters share the ideological assumption that contemplation is as significant as physical activity and that the practice of

---

32. *Literature and the Pastoral*, 129; 131.
33. For different interpretations of the role of violence in this context, see Mujica's two articles on the subject: "Antiutopian Elements in the Spanish Pastoral Novel"; "Violence in the Pastoral Novel from Sannazaro to Cervantes," as well as John Cull's "Further Observations on Violence in the Pastoral Novel."

virtue brings rewards, but at indeterminate intervals. Their essential passivity before their lamented situations and their introspective nature correspond perfectly to Montemayor's religious ideal of subservience to a higher order than the human, and to the fundamental importance he gives to self-examination as well as the humility that ideally follows in its wake.

Although all of the main speaking characters who appear on the first narrative plane are pastoral, they fall into two categories. One is the group of shepherds and shepherdesses native to the *locus amoenus* of the fiction; in the *Diana* these are Sireno, Sylvano, and Diana. They exemplify the pacific and melancholy personality of the pastoral character who has no other life than the one he or she lives out on the first narrative plane. Within the context of the fiction itself, the pastoral garb serves them as clothing, not as disguise. Although in his prologue, Montemayor says that his book consists of true stories disguised in pastoral attire and names (LD, 7), this claim is made from without the fiction; that is, the characters themselves make no direct reference to such roles. The only textual reference to their fictionality is Felicia's wry comment on the lack of verisimilitude of what they say and do (see *infra* 162). The stories of the native shepherds and shepherdesses are those truest to the pastoral mode and hence are those in which the least amount of activity occurs, even though they are understood to constitute the axis around which the other stories revolve. Thus, in the *Diana*, the relationship between Sireno and Diana is the one which is implicitly the most important, even though Diana does not actually appear until book five, and Sireno's love for her is never completely resolved. The other characters' love stories are variations on the problems of this pair. Likewise, in Cervantes's *Galatea*, the relationship between Elicio and Galatea is the narrative thread that unites all the others, although theirs is also the one in which the least actually happens.[34] They are the characters whose hospitality makes possible the other characters' pastoral experiences and thus the narration itself.

In accordance with pastoral tradition, the *Diana* is also peopled with characters whose pastoral masks do not fit them so tightly that they cannot be distinguished from another identity they have within the fiction.

---

34. Ruth El Saffar approaches the relationships between these two characters and the others in Cervantes's book in *Beyond Fiction: The Recovery of the Feminine in the Works of Cervantes*.

These are individuals who dress and behave as pastoral characters during their stay in the *locus amoenus*, but whose lives nevertheless are known to have functioned previously in a broader context than the pastoral life they lead on the first narrative plane. In Montemayor's book, one finds Selvagia, a Portuguese shepherdess, sent to the banks of the Ezla by her father; Felismena, a Sevillian noblewoman in search of her wandering lover Felis; and Belisa, who abandoned her nearby village for an isolated hut along the Ezla to lament the death of her lover Arsileo and his father. The non-native shepherdesses and shepherds are integrated into the narrative whole, even though they come and go from the bucolic center in which the others live. Their presence and occasional absence from the first narrative plane make it clear that the value placed in pastoral on inner experience and spiritual life represents a fundamental and universally significant *facet* of the human experience which, in literary representation, could be integrated into the totality of that experience, rather than constituting the totality itself. The combination of characters that Montemayor created, and the intimate ways in which they interact with each other, made possible the advent of literary beings who carry the mark of their inner lives with them wherever they go.

The autobiographies related by the non-native pastoral characters while in the pastoral environment constitute the second plane of the narration. As long as the interpolation centers around the love problem that brought its protagonist to the *locus amoenus*, there are no restrictions of time, place, or degree on the things she or he chooses to relate about the past. Since the events related in them occurred outside the bucolic enclosure, during a time when the teller was not under the obligations of pastoral decorum, the restrictions on place and activity which govern the modal integrity of the first narrative plane are effectively lifted. This is why the native shepherds and shepherdesses do not participate in the second narrative plane; they have presumably always lived "pastorally," and therefore what they remember is identical in kind to what they do.

Montemayor's book proves that pastoral narration is capable of encompassing such seemingly unpastoral events as death and murder for love (Celia's death, Arsenio's apparent killing of his son), deceit of the most nefarious type (the trio of Selvagia-Ismenia-Alanio), and stories that hint of homosexuality (Selvagia and Ismenia; Felismena and Celia) and incest (the triangle of Arsileo, Arsenio, and Belisa). Such strident events do not take place within the *locus amoenus*, rather they are recalled therein as events passed through the filter of memory, a double-distancing technique that buffers the pastoral enclosure from the harsher aspects of physical reality and the non-normative aspects of psychic reality.

The exaggerated level of activity in the second-plane narrations and the fact that they can be interrupted and later continued are two features of the pastoral narrations that liken them to Byzantine fiction and attest to the growing popularity of the Greek romances that influenced both fiction and literary theory in the second half of the sixteenth century. The episode about Felismena, for example, is more akin to Byzantine than chivalric fiction in that in it a pair of lovers, not just the hero, participate in the extravagant physical action of the plot. The affinity between romance and the pastoral narration, based on an emphasis on wish-fulfillment and general exaggeration, derives largely from the nature of the second-plane narrations set into the pastoral part of the narrative.[35] This combination left the fiction representing the two extremes of action and contemplation, extremes that would be balanced out in later works. Jarring though the combination may be, its presence is very significant.

The pastoral narrations differ substantially, then, from collections of stories such as Boccaccio's *Decamerone*, Juan de Timoneda's prose fiction the *Patrañuelo*, or even María de Zayas's short novels, the *Desengaños amorosos* (*Disillusions in Love*); the characters' tales are always autobiographical and, more importantly, their protagonists are subsequently observed in the present tense of the narration acting in the wake of their memories, immediately influenced by them.[36] What the *Diana* brought to

---

35. The second-plane narrations in books like Montemayor's are clearly not pastoral, yet neither are they what El Saffar calls "quest romance" because of their lack of resolution ("The Truth of the Matter: The Place of Romance in the Works of Cervantes"). The second narrative plane cannot be accounted for using either her category of quest or escape romance (pastoral belonging to the latter, she says), not by fault of her sound evaluation of the mode but by the blending of fictional types that occurs in sixteenth-century prose. Alban K. Forcione describes the emergence of Byzantine fiction's influence in his book *Cervantes, Aristotle, and the* Persiles. He traces the vogue of such literature to the rediscovery of Heliodorus's Greek romance, the *Ethiopian History*, which was translated into French by Amyot in 1547.

36. Ettin provides multiple examples of what he calls implicit and explicit pastoral inserts, but unfortunately does not refer to the Spanish pastoral narrations and their structural innovations in this light (*Literature and the Pastoral*, 75–95). In any case, the second narrative plane differs from a series of inserts for the high degree to which the material in them is integrated into the narrative whole.

prose narrative was not only tales, but tales of the people telling them and living out their consequences. Life's relationship to fiction became more intimate in the process.

The combination of the moving present and the remembered past in the *Diana* emphasizes the influence of each character's emotional experiences on her or his personality. The individual is represented as one whose participation in the present tense of the narration is deeply affected by inner experience, which is revealed through memories. Such inclusion of past and present as joint determining factors of individual character would not have been possible had Montemayor not set the first narrative plane moving in time. That movement allows the characters to display the consequences of their previous confrontations with life's disappointments in a present tense that progresses, marking a significant advance in the nature of character portrayal. Américo Castro noted this novelty, saying, "Pastoral narration becomes possible when the individual, in search of personal awareness, all lines cast off, sets out to row his or her own boat."[37]

Because the characters have proven themselves to be perfect lovers before their arrival onto the first plane of the narration, their stories do not exemplify adherence to a code of behavior, such as courtly or Neoplatonic love. Their exemplary nature as good lovers is understood from the beginning as intrinsic to their literary character and is communicated clearly by the innocent and disillusioned posture they display in the narrative present. Instead, their tales are about the conflicts that arise when their desire to live out ideological and timeless pure love is thrust into the context of their life experiences, which progress chronologically. They appear in the narration immersed in melancholic recollection of those experiences, having suffered the confrontation between their desires and reality before the narration begins. Although literary characters' exclusive devotion to memories was subdued as realism in literature became increasingly dominant, the dualism was never abandoned: one of the modern literary character's salient features is an existence that consists of a balance, or conflict, between internal and external experiences.[38]

Each of the authors of Spain's most studied pastoral narrations weighted

---

37. "Los prólogos al *Quijote*," 277.
38. Ian Watt elaborates on this dualism in the chapter "Realism and the Later Tradition: a Note" (in *The Rise of the Novel: Studies in Defoe, Richardson and Fielding*, 290–301).

differently the balance between recollection of what has happened before the narration begins and what actually happens in the narration itself, according to the different messages they used the fiction to convey. Montemayor, prone to melancholy complaint, lingers on recollections of past injustices suffered by his characters; well over half of the *Diana* is devoted to acts of memory. Gil Polo, more interested in the individual's struggle to come to grips with the past in his *Diana in Love,* increases the amount of action that takes place in his characters' "present." In the *Galatea,* Cervantes eliminates the distance between his characters and their pasts by having them appear in the narration as events are still happening in what should constitute their memories. Lope de Vega allows the present to dominate the narration in his *Arcadia,* emphasizing dramatic activity almost to the exclusion of acts of memory, in keeping with the dynamism of his works in general.

Throughout this process of juxtaposing expectations and experience, everything in the narration is subjugated to the sentimental impact it has on the characters, in keeping with their own fixation on emotional events. Like Montemayor's religious characters, they are devoted to recollection and lament of the world's evil ways. The content of the tales and what happens after they are told never strays significantly from the theme of love, which itself serves to unite the first and second narrative planes. By making their moments of past happiness seem ended and remote, the temporal and spatial distance between the lovers and their past experiences justifies the lament they voice in the first narrative plane. In the time that actually passes in the narration, they are contending with something inside themselves, not outside them: their memories. For their perception of a part of themselves as something beyond them, they are akin to the recogido authors, and Montemayor himself, who likewise tend to exteriorize the internal. As Sireno's lament in book one of the *Diana* indicates, Montemayor's characters perceive their own memories to be an extrinsic entity: in an exclamation typical of the pastoral company, he cries, "Ah, memory mine, enemy of my repose!" (¡Ay, memoria mía, enemiga de mi descanso!, LD, 11).

The unique quality of melancholy that typifies sixteenth-century peninsular pastoral is largely due to the characters' perception of the time and distance separating them from how, and in some cases, where, they used to be. The main characters of Sidney's *Arcadia* provide a bright contrast to their Spanish counterparts, for they share neither a temporal nor physical distance from their love experiences with the Spanish characters. The memories they bring to the narration are of aggressive heroic conquests, not of unhappy emotional experiences, and consequently they are less introspective and less disillusioned than their Peninsular counterparts. Surely the emphasis placed on self-examination and contemplation in Spanish Catholic reformism was influential in the development of this narrative structure, especially since Montemayor was responsible for its creation.

It was the need to represent the human experience as a constant interplay between the world without and the one within, between what one wishes and expects to happen with what indeed happens, that the pastoral narration seems to have satisfied. Both sides of the balance between desire and fact are equally vital in what modern readers find to be realistic representation of life in literature, and it is in the *Diana* that the narrative structure leads to that end. According to Américo Castro, "It is in the pastoral narrative where, for the first time, the literary character becomes a strictly human, singular being, an expression of a 'within oneself.'" Significantly, he does not accredit pastoral verse with the gain, rather "*el relato pastoril,*" pastoral narration, precisely the kind of book Cervantes wrote in the *Galatea* in imitation of the *Diana*. It is because the characters witness constant interchange between past and present, thought and deed, desires and events that what Castro finds so noteworthy can occur: "the sensitive consciousness of each one is defined as autonomous and decisive."[39]

Pastoral characters are fundamentally escapists, at least temporarily. The structure of Montemayor's pastoral narration opened wide the door of the past—the source of their problems—by greatly enlarging its presence and significance. Bigger than life in the present, the past overwhelms the shepherdesses and shepherds in the first three books of the *Diana* through Montemayor's development of the second narrative plane. It is only in the final three that the characters strive toward some sort of reconciliation between what has been and what is. By representing them thus, Montemayor captured the intrusion of inner life, of memory, desire, and disillusion, on existence. His pastoral characters are captured in the dilemmas of human experience as the recogidos, not the humanists, found them to be: subject to human fallibility, consonant with their recognition

---

39. "Los prólogos al *Quijote*," 276.

that powers greater than their own control life, in the ultimate analysis. Overcome by the sad reality of life's imperfections, the shepherds and shepherdesses' voices sing the same lament as Montemayor's religious works, as we find them retreating into recollective fantasy, into desire for harmonious union that human imperfection makes impossible. In the *locus amoenus*, the characters are unfailingly haunted by the very problems from which they seek relief: their inner lives, their illusions, and their memories of how they fared in the world. As the *Diana* ironically makes apparent, these are things from which no one can escape, for they lie within.

3
LOS SIETE LIBROS DE LA DIANA
Ideological Love
and Human Experience

"The most commonly accepted opinion now is that the success of the Diana *is due essentially, if not exclusively, to Montemayor's ability to develop two themes that corresponded to the desires and sensitivities of his readers: Platonic love and the pastoral myth. I wonder if this reduction does not lead to the mutilation of the* Diana *as a novel."*
(Maxime Chevalier, "La 'Diana' de Montemayor y su público")

The *Diana* was the first book of its kind and with it "is born, in a state of perfection, the Spanish pastoral novel" (NPE, 69). Accepting Montemayor's text as the first and perfect pastoral narration means accepting it with what now look like inconsistencies and contradictions in form and content that lend a patchwork quality to the book from a modern perspective. This was apparently no hindrance to sixteenth-century readers' enjoyment of it, for the *Diana* was the third most printed book of fiction in Spain during the Golden Age (numbers one and two were *La Celestina* and *Guzmán de Alfarache*). As Ian Watt reminds the modern reader of prenovelistic literature, "If we assume on *a priori* grounds that a coherent plan must be present, we find one, and thereby produce a complex pattern out of what are actually incongruities."[1]

Indeed, attempts to extract a linear, literary argument from Montemayor's book have proven frustrating. For example, in her refreshing study of the *Diana*, Ruth El Saffar says, "We must suppose that Montemayor hoped for a simple resolution to the complexities of love con-

---

1. Ian Watt, *The Rise of the Novel: Studies in Defoe, Richardson and Fielding*, 129. On the most printed books of Montemayor's time, see Keith Whinnom, "The Problem of the 'Best-seller' in Spanish Golden Age Literature."

ceived of as an individual experience." But must we? Her conclusion that Montemayor's material "failed to produce satisfying results" begs the question: "Satisfying for whom?"[2] Montemayor's own audience evidently delighted in the book, and modern criticism's difficulties with making sense out of that delight would seem to indicate that either inappropriate criteria are being used to evaluate the text or that literary tastes have changed absolutely since Montemayor's day, or both.

The following sections, focusing on the first possibility, propose to delineate the *Diana*'s incongruities as meaningful elements of Montemayor's text, and suggest a significance for them in keeping with his other works and the literature of his day. In the process, I will suggest that reading the *Diana* in terms of humanistic themes and modern literary criteria denies the text a meaning for which it was originally heartily appreciated. Just as Montemayor's religious writings fall comfortably within a religious tradition quite distinct from the Renaissance spirituality typically used to interpret them, so the *Diana* in many ways relates to themes and forms of that "other tradition," the one that preceded, not followed, Renaissance humanism.

Although Montemayor was the first to develop the two narrative planes described in the previous chapter, the *Diana* does not illustrate a consistent balance between them from beginning to end. This irregularity, disconcerting from a novelistic point of view, is well reconciled with the content of the chapters and where the action in them takes place. Books one through three do establish a strong and regular rhythm that alternates between first- and second-plane narrations, in keeping with those books' domination by the literary forms of pastoral and romance: introduction of Sireno and Sylvano, Selvagia's tale; the threesome's encounter with the nymphs, Felismena's tale; the seven characters' walk to Felicia's palace, Belisa's tale. After book four, however, the *locus amoenus* is abandoned as the primary narrative scene and, all the characters' pasts having been revealed and supposedly resolved, is never reestablished as the home base of the action. Books five to seven, therefore, are devoted to sporadic updates of the main characters' travails, in an attempt to keep track of all of them simultaneously as their adventures take them in a variety of directions. This structural bifurcation is indicative of the text's movement away

---

2. "Thematic Discontinuity in Montemayor's *Diana*," 197–98.

from literary convention into the realm of the mirror image characteristic of modern fiction.[3]

Critical attention to the *Diana* has been overwhelmingly dedicated to the quest for themes of mainstream scholarship in it, typically Neoplatonism; none of the many studies now existing of Montemayor's pastoral narration consider the relationship between his religious writings and that book.[4] As a consequence, many facets of the book's plot that have been identified as crucial are not necessarily so. On the other hand, an equal number of its narrative moments and fictional qualities have been silenced or extracted out of context in the interests of constructing its relationship to Renaissance humanism. This produces a distortion of the text, one that consistently emphasizes certain narrative events and passes in silence over those that obscure the humanistic vision. The only way to realign Montemayor's book with itself is to reconsider the plot as it progresses as a whole, and finally as part of the ideological entity that Montemayor's complete works form together. This chapter will deal with the text as a narrative progression, marking the relationship of its important moments to both the religious material presented in chapter 1 and the formal novelties described in chapter 2. Comments about the *Diana* as part of a distinctive corpus of works are reserved for the Conclusion.

The *Diana* itself begins with a brief plot summary, the single-page "*Argumento*," in which the narrator explains that Diana, beloved of Sireno, has married the wealthy but inferior Delio during Sireno's forced one-year absence from the country, apparently forgetting Sireno's pure love for her and her promises to wait for him. Sireno's friend Sylvano is presented as another shepherd enamored of Diana, whom she has always disdained. Book one opens, then, with Sireno's melancholy return to the banks of the Ezla in León, knowing that Diana is inaccessible to him.

In the context of Montemayor's complete works, there is nothing unique about the plot outlined in the "*Argumento*," based on a pair of lovers trying to endure separation. There are many poems in his 1558 *Segundo*

---

3. Almost all modern studies of the structure of the *Diana* follow Bruce Wardropper's important article ("The *Diana* of Montemayor: Revaluation and Interpretation") by dividing the book into three parts, as has been done here.
4. Generally following the ideas of Francisco López Estrada, principally his editorial comments in the *Diana*, and Juan Bautista Avalle-Arce (NPE), almost all studies of the *Diana* mention Neoplatonism as the informing philosophy of Montemayor's book, and those that do not, do not refute the idea.

cancionero (*Second Songbook*) that treat the same situation. For example, a new "Canción" begins "Nothing remained for the weary heart" (Ya no faltaba al corazón cansado), and tells of the narrator's learning from a friend that his beloved had married someone else during his absence. It describes his subsequent reluctance to undertake the journey home and his attempts to deny that his beloved would forget "this simple love of so many years" (este sencillo amor de tantos años, SC, 86r–89v; GP, 417–20). Indeed, the story is the same one told by Montemayor in almost all of his poetry in one form or another, a consistency of theme that makes a positive identification between Montemayor and Sireno highly likely. The fact that Sireno is something of a self-portrait of Montemayor is significant for the influence it has on what the narrator of the *Diana* is willing to reveal about Diana herself (almost nothing) and on the narrator's attitude toward Sireno's relationship with her (which is far from impersonal).[5]

The "*Argumento*" ends with this statement: "And from here begins the first book, and in the others you will find very diverse stories, about cases that have truly happened, although they are disguised under pastoral names and style" (Y de aquí comiença el primero libro y en los demás hallarán muy diversas hystorias, de casos que verdaderamente an sucedido, aunque van disfraçados debaxo de nombres y estilo pastoril, LD, 7). Such claims to historicity were standard practice in books of chivalry, where they were used to bolster the status of the text and invoke the reader's willing suspension of disbelief for a fanciful plot. What had previously been a false claim in that context, however, is partially true in Montemayor's text; following in the pastoral tradition, among the characters in the *Diana* are fictionalized versions of real people, such as Sireno and Diana, and among its settings are real geographic locations.[6]

---

5. On the identification of Montemayor with Sireno, see López Estrada, LD, 21–27, and Elizabeth Rhodes, "Introducción a la 'Historia de Alcida y Silvano' de Jorge de Montemayor," 132–33. Joseph R. Jones says of the "Argumento," "The inaccurate synopsis was a printer's addition," that, he contends, contradicts Diana's claim that she married Delio out of filial obedience ("'Human Time' in *La Diana*," 141, n.4). However, the discussion between Diana and Sireno in book six (LD, 272–74) over that point shows us that the narrator of the "*Argumento*," whose relationship to Montemayor is clear, is simply adopting Sireno's point of view, quite appropriate as a prelude to book one.

6. Marcelino Menéndez Pelayo, "La novela pastoril," 249, identifies Diana with a woman named Ana who was living in León in 1603, citing historical information and Lope de Vega's play *La Dorotea*.

In the *Diana*, the narrator's definition of his partially historical text as one related directly to historical reality contorts previous literary practice into a testimony of how self-conscious fiction was becoming; the problem culminated some fifty years later with Cervantes's publication of a translated manuscript about a certain Manchegan gentleman. Self-consciousness is the result of introspection, and would naturally be expected in an author whose religious works insist on the importance of self-examination. The *Diana* further manifests its author's concern with historicity in a sentimental context, with its constant reference to individual experience as the ultimate testing ground for love ideology. The characters do not strive toward ideal behavior in love, they personify ideal love in a markedly self-conscious fashion. Their difficulties arise when their conformity to perfect love's standards is throttled by what happens to them in time, and the narrator's awareness of how true to life the ensuing conflicts are is made manifest by the reference to the truth value of his fiction, with which he opens his tale.

Book One

Book one begins with Sireno's return to his homeland from the north. He is greeted by his friend Sylvano, who shares with him some memories of the days with Diana before Sireno left. These are poetic recollections, and they underscore Diana's intended fidelity to Sireno while affirming her previous pure love for him. Their melancholy exchange is interrupted by the arrival of Selvagia, whom Sylvano recognizes as a newcomer to the riverbank community. The three engage in a conversation that reveals Selvagia's bitterness over love, for a reason still unknown.

To justify her complaint, Selvagia tells her story, beginning the first second-plane narration. She recalls how she met and fell in love with Ysmenia, a woman. At the end of their first encounter, Ysmenia told Selvagia she was a man, Alanio. (Alanio was actually an identical cousin of Ysmenia and the object of Ysmenia's own affection.) The real Alanio subsequently fell in love with Selvagia, who believed she had loved him all along. Ysmenia attempted to win Alanio back through jealousy by feigning love for Montano, with the result that she truly fell in love with Montano and also led Alanio back to his previous affection for Ysmenia herself. In the process, Montano decided he loved Selvagia, who, of course, remained true to her original affection for the real Alanio. A tidy ring of confusion ensues into the present tense of the narration, in which Selvagia loves Alanio, who loves Ysmenia, who loves Montano, who loves Selvagia.

The symmetric artistry of such a coincidence is exaggerated, yet it is not without symbolic meaning in reference to the confusion and bitter irony that often trail along behind love. It is precisely this symbolic value, attending the extravagance of exemplarity, that assimilates Selvagia's tale to what Watt calls "the traditional conception of plot in fiction, where the author chose his story because it was in some way so neat, so amusing or so striking that it stood out from the common run of experience and asked to be told and retold."[7] The same may be said of Felismena's story, which follows in book two, as well as Belisa's, in book three. These three exaggerated events are all related by shepherdesses who are not natives of the *locus amoenus*. In keeping with their tellers' grafted relationship to the pastoral setting, these tales are allied to the oral tradition characterized by emphasis on the extraordinary. Their status as non-native shepherdesses harmonizes with the non-pastoral nature of their love experiences; the characters who are natives of the Ezla riverbanks have suffered less flamboyant difficulties, more pastoral in kind and more novelistic for their lack of neat resolution.

Sixteenth-century readers, however, were still charmed by the sort of remarkable tales told by Selvagia, Felismena, and Belisa. This taste for the exceptional, which Francisco Rico aptly describes as "a thousand leagues from the modern realistic novel," endured well into the seventeenth century in literature. Closer to Montemayor's time, Cervantes's character Don Fernando describes the pleasing nature of the Captive's peripatetic tale in *Don Quijote*, saying "It [the story] is all rare and strange and full of sudden happenings that astonish and fill the hearer with wonder" (DQ, 1:514).[8] Although twentieth-century tales as exaggerated and as coincidental as Selvagia's have fared better in the visual media than in literature, they do remain a fundamental attraction of fiction and are testimony of human nature's most perennial expectations of imaginative culture: release from the strictures of daily life. The neat tension of Selvagia's dilemma meets this need.

7. *The Rise of the Novel*, 107.
8. Rico refers to the line in Lope's *El peregrino en su patria* that says, "Things are written for their noteworthiness" (cited in his prologue to Lope de Vega y Carpio's collected stories *Las Novelas a Marcia Leonarda*, 10).

Just when the confusion among the four young lovers reached its peak, Selvagia's father sent her away to an aunt's house on the Ezla, where she received news from home that Montano had abruptly wed Ysmenia, and Alanio was to marry Ysmenia's sister. This sudden and seemingly arbitrary turn of events, about which she had virtually nothing to say, shut Selvagia out of the former quadrangle for good, abruptly ending her relationship with Alanio. She thus shares with Sireno the bitter experience of having learned about a beloved one's marriage to someone else during an absence. Like him, she has been victimized by events that transpired beyond her control. Already, the *Diana* is acquiring the tones of self-righteous complaint and the emphasis on the virtues of innocent suffering that dominate its author's religious works. Selvagia joins the shepherds in songs of lamentation, and book one ends much like a self-sufficient eclogue, with the unhappy trio singing as they return to the village at the day's end.

Montemayor has written Selvagia into a corner, similar to the bind in which Sireno finds himself. Although Alanio's wedding had not actually taken place when Selvagia was exiled from her homeland, she assumes it has happened when she tells her tale. She and Sireno are confronted with true love that has failed, leaving them in love with married partners. Were their love truly selfless and disinterested, these situations would be bearable. But they are not for Montemayor's characters, who wrestle with the dilemma of whether to remain faithful themselves in a hopeless situation or get on with life, thereby compromising their ideals. What the first narrative plane captures is their period of indecision and their disillusion. Sireno and Selvagia's circumstances differ greatly from those described in the courtly tradition of impossible, often illicit loves, for theirs have only become impossible; they were not initially so and were never illicit. In this context, love in itself is attainable. Its durability as a happy state, however, is repeatedly questioned.

The temporal point at which the narrator joins his characters in book one is the one used throughout the other books and is significant: their stories do not begin until they appear to be over. By the time Sireno appears on the scene, he has successfully courted, won, and lost his beloved Diana. The reasons for their relationship's disintegration are debated throughout the seven books of the *Diana*, producing a tension between the two characters that runs through the book like a taut cord from which the other stories are hung. Selvagia's difficulties are revealed in close proximity to those of Sireno, for the two have much in common.

By beginning his narration not only *in medias res* but after all the essential narrative action has occurred, Montemayor opens the characters' stories at a temporal juncture that justifies their lament as much as possible. Knowing himself betrayed, Sireno can do nothing but bemoan his situation and at the same time affirm his own superiority to Diana as a lover. He was true to her, while she betrayed him. This is the same disillusioned stance adopted by all the lovers in the book, who carry their memories around with them like photographs to be shown, images from the past that prove their status as the better of the two in their relationships. They are all paragons of behavior in love who got what they did not deserve. The nature of the opening interchanges between Sireno, Sylvano, and Selvagia typifies the essential tone and temporal perspective of Montemayor's works as a whole, particularly his 1558 religious verse. The voice is one of self-righteous indignation, adopted by the faultless first-person voice sadly revealing the ways of an imperfect world and her or his disillusioning experience in it. As in all of his writings, that voice's lament sounds repeatedly *after* disillusionment has struck its final blow.

The first book is unlike the others in that it is an artistic whole unto itself, balanced between the Sireno-Sylvano lyric component and Selvagia's story, which relates a flurry of emotional activity. The melancholy quality of the first narrative plane is firmly established by Sireno and Sylvano's poetic interchange before they happen upon Selvagia, whose second-plane narration removes the text from the *locus amoenus* physically and temporally. After her troubles are revealed, the first narrative plane is reestablished and the balance between meditation and activity is set to continue. Her earlier disillusion justified, Selvagia is integrated into the company of her companions, whom she joins without hesitation on their excursions to isolated corners of the pastoral environment. Appropriately, the book closes with the self-conscious sentence, "And here ends the first book of the lovely Diana" (Y aquí haze fin el primero libro de la hermosa Diana, LD, 62).

Book Two

The second book opens on Selvagia's long and silent imaginings and her lament against Alanio's inconstancy, after which she sings a song about the destructive effects of time and fortune on love. Fortuitously, Sylvano is himself enmeshed in his own amorous contemplations nearby. He hears her singing and, in a foreshadowing of their eventual union, "wakes as from a dream and was very attentive to the lines she was singing" (despierta como de un sueño y muy atento estubo a los versos que cantava, LD, 66). In their subsequent conversation, Selvagia denies love's eternal nature using arguments based on her experience, and thereby reaffirms its subjection to time and fortune. Sylvano begrudgingly allows for the possibility, but denies that his own affection could ever falter, his haughty certitude foreshadowing his impending change. The couple is joined by Sireno and together the three happen upon, and hide to listen to, three nymphs, who are singing about the transitory nature of love.

The nymphs' song underscores, in a lyric context, what the main protagonists' experience has indicated in a narrative context: the instability of human emotions, the absence of the eternal in the sentiments of men and women (LD, 72). This theme, which will be a constant in all of the forthcoming lovers' stories, will also be approached again from a theoretical angle in book four and its early apparition serves as proof of its importance. True to the recogidos' understanding of life on earth as one fraught with imperfections, and true to his own tendency to interpret it from the vantage point of the innocent victim, Montemayor immediately grasps his narrative from the perspective of guiltless witnesses of those imperfections. With the nymphs' appearance, the narration takes on a quality of fantasy, emphasizing the subjective nature of love itself and drawing attention to the priority of mental experience over the physical in the narration.

The nymphs Cinthia, Polydora, and Dórida review what has become part of the communal memory of the *locus amoenus* during Sireno's absence from it: his final conversation with Diana, set into verse and sung as if it were a work of art. Sireno, a native shepherd of the Ezla riverbanks, neither tells his own story nor witnesses its full revelation by anyone else. Its most important elements, Diana's previous love for him, her promise of fidelity and breaking of that promise, are revealed and repeated by Sireno and others in a circular movement, locking both Sireno and Diana within the boundaries of melancholy lament. At the song's end, the narrator remarks on the nymphs' wondering admission that time did indeed seem to cure Diana's "pain of love" (*mal de amor*) for Sireno (LD, 81), sowing another seed for the theme of separation that will also be explained theoretically in book four. Their comments serve to validate Sireno's and Selvagia's insistence that people's feelings change over time, and unpredictably so.

Suddenly three savages break onto the quiet scene and tie up the nymphs in hopes of capturing their affections through force, a clearly allegorical interlude representing the destructive side of passion unleashed against chastity. Their violence also exemplifies desire's unreasonable nature in good as well as bad love, a theme that surfaces again during the theoretical discussion in book four.[9] Sireno, Sylvano, and Selvagia demonstrate their good intentions and basic helplessness by throwing rocks at the brutes with limited success. Fortunately, a brave "shepherdess," Felismena, emerges from the forest in time to club and arrow the savages to death, representing allegorically what the pastoral characters represent more realistically, the dominion of control over physical desire necessary for pure love.

Felismena's ties to the ideals of romance are immediately apparent. Unlike the native shepherds and shepherdesses, she has superior outer qualities, as is made clear by her control of her environment. Unlike them, she enters the narration in pursuit of a specific goal. As she joins the pastoral company, however, her aggressive qualities subside and she proves herself adaptable to the pastoral mode. As Felismena and the others leave the remains of the savages behind, she sheds her allegorical role and acquires a vulnerability more in keeping with the pastoral disguise she wears: she, like the others, explains immediately that she suffers due to another's inconstancy in love.

While the three pastoral characters return to the village for food, Felismena joins the nymphs beside a fountain to rest. She there tells her complete story, the second of the second-plane narrations. Prefacing it in the same way as her companions have theirs, she affirms what experience, not theory, tells her:

> Love is not such that the one who feels it can respect reason, nor does reason enable the enamored heart to depart from whatever path along which its fierce destinies may guide it. And as proof, we have at hand what experience shows us.

9. As Avalle-Arce indicates, Montemayor's savages are similar to the figure of Desire in Diego de San Pedro's *Cárcel de amor* (NPE, 87). Such creatures, and the violence they bring with them, have been studied in detail. On the savage, see Richard Bernheimer, *Wild Men in the Middle Ages: A Study in Art, Sentiment, and Demonology;* Alan Deyermond, "El hombre salvaje en la novela sentimental"; and John D. Williams, "The Savage in Sixteenth-century Spanish Prose Fiction." Although Montemayor borrowed little from Sannazaro's *Arcadia*, these savages may be descendents of the satyrs which attack the nymphs in the *"Prosa terza"* of that book.

(No es el amor de manera . . . que puede el que lo tiene, tener respecto a la razón, ni la razón es parte para que un enamorado coraçón dexe el camino por do sus fieros destinos le guiaren. Y que esto sea verdad, en la mano tenemos la experiencia.) (LD, 94)

She thereby posits another idea that will be validated at Felicia's palace, love's unreasonable nature, and reiterates Sireno's and Selvagia's feelings of victimization at the hands of fortune and their recognition of experience's priority over idealism.

Felismena's tale carries the text well beyond the limits of pastoral decorum in kind and degree, appropriate for material recollected within the *locus amoenus:* born under a curse of Venus and a blessing of Minerva, she grew up in Seville as a noblewoman. The effects of these goddesses' intervention in her life were evident from the moment Felismena appeared in her Diana-like disguise, lamenting her misfortunes in love. The control over her destiny exercised by supernatural intervention in her life before her birth is symptomatic of Montemayor's notions about humanity's helplessness in the hands of greater, undeniable forces. This is the same concept Felismena and the other characters display in their vulnerability to fortune and time, the same concept of submission before a higher power expressed by Montemayor's religious poetry in strictly Christian terms. Unable to escape her destiny, Felismena must find a way to live with it.

She continues her narration, telling how Don Felis courted her for a year, at the end of which she acknowledged their mutual devotion. News of their secret affection reached Felis's father, who sent his son off to court immediately. The theme of parental intervention, which will prove to be the ultimate source of the problems between Sireno and Diana, emerges for the second time. Like the exile imposed on Selvagia by her father, the whisking away of don Felis by his father is presented as sudden and arbitrary from Felismena's point of view. Such parental mandates constitute further control over them from an authority they cannot contest and, indeed, are bound by the laws of social behavior to respect.[10]

---

10. Montemayor's poetic version of the Pyramus and Thisbe story, included in editions of the *Diana* after 1561, contains a long diatribe of Thisbe's against her father, quite remarkable in itself and interesting in the light of Diana's situation and Sireno's probable representation of Montemayor. See B. W. Ife's edition of Montemayor's

Sireno and Selvagia were permanently cut off from their beloveds by the inviolable rite of marriage, leaving them the disquieting options of eternal unhappiness or the abandonment of their original loves and, consequently, the loss of their status as perfect lovers themselves. Felismena, however, still has time to do something about her situation before it is too late, since both she and Felis are still unmarried when she commits herself to action. After contemplating the detrimental effects of separation on their relationship, she disguised herself as a man and took off after him. Upon arriving at court, she discovered that he was pursuing Celia, who disdained him. Desperate, Felismena became his page, thereby acquiring the job of serving as the intermediary between her own lover Felis and her rival, Celia. Celia fell in love with Felismena, believing her to be a man, and died of that unrequited love.[11] Upon learning of her death, Felis ran off to parts unknown, and Felismena undertook the two-year search for him that led her to the forest beside which the savages attacked the nymphs.

Felismena's second-plane narration is typical of romance fiction for its relative extravagance, peripatetic plot and emphasis on wish-fulfillment.[12] Unlike Sireno, Sylvano, and Selvagia, she is passing through the *locus amoenus* on her way to somewhere else, and in this she is unique among the characters. Unlike her companions, Felismena has a goal to pursue and is therefore much more active than they. Modern readers unfailingly sympathize with her because her initiative is imitable in the context of modern values. However, it is her situation, not her character, that makes her exceptional.

---

poem, 12–14. The only father figure presented in a sympathetic light by Montemayor is Alcida's, and his humanity derives from his grief over his daughter's death ("Historia de Alcida y Silvano," vv. 1085–1143).

11. Exactly how Celia dies is ambiguous in the *Diana*, although an air of suicide lingers therein. Interestingly, when Barnabe Googe wrote his eclogue adaptation of this episode, published in 1563, she plainly kills herself: "And strake herself with cruel knife / and bloody down doth fall" ("Egloga quinta" in his *Eclogues, Epitaphs and Sonnets*, 91–92).

12. Although Felismena's story is an adaptation of one of Bandello's *novelle*, these qualities were written into the story by Montemayor as he adopted it from the original. On Bandello as a source, see López Estrada, LD, 94–96. Montemayor's version had notable success in British literature, described in Thomas P. Harrison's "Concerning 'Two Gentlemen of Verona' and Montemayor's *Diana*" and Dale B. J. Randall's "*The Troublesome and Hard Adventures in Love:* an English Addition to the Bibliography of *Diana*." It also provided the basic plot for Ana Caro Mallén de Soto's 1653 drama "Valor, agravio, y mujer."

Felismena's determination to get the man she wants is typical of all of Montemayor's female characters *except* Diana, for whom they serve as obvious contrasts; it is worth pointing out that Selvagia and Belisa as well go to extremes to secure the affections of their beloveds, and they are successful. By the time they appear in the narration, however, that success has been swept away by the accumulated effects of parental intervention, human fallibility, time, and fortune. When Felismena appears, on the contrary, her efforts to regain Felis are not hopelessly pitted against his marriage to someone else or his death, and she is thus able to continue acting on her desires, whereas her fellow shepherdesses are not. Had Felis married Celia, Felismena's activity would have been as severely curtailed as Selvagia's.

Felismena's melancholy posture before her victimization at the hands of fortune made her representative and admirable in the sixteenth century, and this is something she shares with her pastoral companions. This determinism, in which a character's behavior is dictated by her or his circumstance (and not vice versa) is precisely what allies the *Diana* to Montemayor's religious works and the literary tradition that preceded, not followed, him. The *industria*, or ingeniousness to outsmart one's own bad luck that Cervantes was to bestow on some of his characters, does not appear in the *Diana*.[13]

At the conclusion of Felismena's tale, the nymphs are astounded not by her having dressed up as a man to pursue her beloved, but that she would dress up as a shepherdess and abandon her "accustomed attire" (hábito natural) because of love (LD, 125); the violation of one's sexual identity seems to have been less serious than that of one's social identity.[14] The fact that Felismena was willing to do both indicates the power of love, the

---

13. The word *industria* is used by Felismena in reference to the skill with which she obtained the men's clothing she needed to follow Felis (LD, 105). In truth, not all of Cervantes's characters display that *industria* for which they are generally admired. Cardenio, for example, passively stands by and watches as his beloved is betrothed to another (DQ, 1, ch. 24). Basilio's story, in which the word *industria* is fundamental, appears after that of Cardenio as a more satisfying solution to the same problem, although it is not the only one represented by Cervantes (DQ, 2, ch. 20). The relative powers of the individual and fate, or God, were far from clear during the Golden Age, in spite of humanism's optimistic exaltation of the former.

14. The case of Cervantes's character Dorotea provides further evidence, for upon realizing she is a woman, the Priest comments on her "unworthy attire" (hábito tan indigno) rather than on her disguise as a man (DQ, 1:346).

irrational and levelling force that rules equally over all within the *locus amoenus*, the same power that led Selvagia to fall in love with someone she believed to be a woman. The nymphs join Felismena in her lament about fortune's whims and invite her to accompany them to Felicia's palace, where her troubles will surely be solved by the hostess's special curing powers. Importantly, Felismena agrees only out of courtesy, for she doubts that anyone except Felis himself can solve her problems: "I don't know who could remedy such a grave malady except the one who caused it himself" (No sé . . . quien a tan grave mal pueda dar remedio, sino fuesse el propio que lo causó, LD, 126). This remark foresees the eventual resolution of her problems by the wayward Felis's return to her, and is another example of the main characters' level-headed awareness of their situations.

When the nymphs express their wonder over why don Felis failed to recognize Felismena while she posed as his page, Felismena observes that Felis's memory of her was well worn by the time she arrived at court and was so focused on Celia that he never thought of her at all (LD, 127). Her story thereby provides a "real-life" illustration of lovers' natural tendency to grow away from each other during separation due to memory's progressive weakness, something that becomes a theoretical issue in book four. The fallibility of memory is reaffirmed as the final note of the *Diana* when Felis himself confesses that he had not recognized Felismena because "his understanding was so distracted" (de puro divertido en el entendimiento, LD, 299). By calling attention to the imperfections inherent in memory through multiple narrative vehicles in his book, Montemayor displays how precarious the life of his characters—and of the human beings they represent—really is, for they depend on memory for their spiritual sustenance. Their inconstant ability to remember the past is an extension of the human imperfections to which all ideals, such as the impeccable functioning of the soul's three faculties, are subject. Significantly, by describing Felis's memory and understanding as something beside, not within, him, Montemayor again casts a problem of human nature that lies within the human character into a mold representing it as something external to the characters themselves.

These repeated rationalizations of lovers' forgetfulness and subjection to distracting thoughts (at the expense of their first loves) are allowed for some, but are never applied to Diana and her "forgetfulness" of Sireno, even though her actions are identical to those of others who are forgiven.

Montemayor thus protects the forgotten lover without exculpating the woman who forgot him. Felismena's helplessness in the hands of *ausencia* (separation or absence) joins her to the great majority of Montemayor's characters, and allies her directly with Sireno, who suffers from the same problem. They are both the victims of unfaithful lovers who were unable to remain constant during a separation.

Sireno, Sylvano, and Selvagia rejoin their company, and after a brief repast the nymphs extend to them their invitation to visit the wise Felicia, whose name reveals the happiness they can expect in recompense for their efforts against the savages. Polydora says, "There is no other way for you all to receive the reward for your trials" (no de otra manera podéis recibir el premio de vuestro trabajo, LD, 129), thereby indicating that their efforts on behalf of chaste love deserve compensation; the shepherdess and shepherds are to be rewarded for their behavior just as knights of chivalry receive recompense for their deeds, which acquire heroic proportions.[15] Their reward, however, will consist of an emotional prize, in keeping with Montemayor's exaltation of spiritual values rather than political or material standards.

Sireno repeats Felismena's courteous acceptance of the nymphs' offer, but asserts that only time and fortune can cure his troubles. He observes that all the paths leading to a solution are closed to him and speaks with empathetic sadness of Diana's union with someone below her, revealing already the temperate attitude he will try to adopt toward her after Felicia's magical intervention in his life (LD, 130). Selvagia and Sylvano agree to join them, and the book ends with four main characters accumulated, following three nymphs on a path that will lead them out of the *locus amoenus*. The second book does not close self-consciously as did the first, indicating the narration's departure from the idyll- or eclogue-type structure, to form instead a whole with interwoven plots.

Book Three

In book three the seven characters come upon a hut on a river island where they hope to spend the night. At this moment, among the company

---

15. Gustavo Correa observes the heroic nature of sentimental feats in the *Diana* in his article about Felicia's temple, "El templo de *Diana* en la novela de Jorge de Montemayor."

are two single men and two single women, whose enjoyment of such circumstances would be completely compromising in any other context. Their freedom to participate in these activities without censure depends absolutely on their status as literary shepherds and shepherdesses who display the "innocent intimacy" with which Wardropper characterizes their interaction.[16] Protected by the nobility of intention with which Montemayor endowed them, they are freed from the need for social supervision beyond that of the nymphs, whose association with chastity accompanies them. The nature of Montemayor's characters, who commit no misdeeds but rather suffer the misdeeds of others, repeats one of the primary qualities of the narrators of his religious works, likewise innocent, likewise vulnerable.

In the hut they discover a sleeping shepherdess, whom they awaken with their arrival. They lead their new companion, Belisa, outside to a fountain, a more appropriately poetic locale for her recollections. With little coaxing, she begins the third second-plane narration, insisting all along that she only does so on the condition that it not lessen the pain she feels, which she has no interest in losing for fear of tarnishing its perfect nature: "The great reason I have to live as shrouded in sadness as I do has put enmity between me and the consolation for my pain. So that if I ever thought I would attain that consolation, I would kill myself" (la gran razón . . . que tengo de vivir tan embuelta en tristezas, como vivo, a puesto enemistad entre mí y el consuelo de mi mal. De manera que si pensasse en algún tiempo tenello, yo misma me daría la muerte, LD, 132). Belisa is not only an example of extreme suffering for love, she is also a living example of the chaste lovers of dead men who are later commemorated in monuments inside Felicia's palace.

The newcomer to the group tells of being courted as a young girl by the wealthy widower Arsenio, whose son Arsileo was a student in Salamanca when her troubles began. His studies completed, Arsileo returned home an expert poet and was commissioned by his father to write poems for Belisa on his father's behalf, pretending they were for a friend. Belisa saw through the ruse and fell in love not with the father but with the son. She thus found herself respectfully affectionate to the elder Arsenio at the same time she was amorously attracted toward the younger Arsileo, who in turn fell in love with her. As her involvement with Arsileo increased, so

16. "The *Diana* of Montemayor," 128.

grew her affection for his father, and she found herself unable to abandon one or the other.

For the third time in as many second-plane narrations, the father figure brings an abrupt halt to love's idyllic moment. Arsileo and Belisa met one night at her window; at the same time Arsileo's father was conducting his usual rounds up and down Belisa's street, hoping for a sign of favor from her. He saw a man beneath her window and, in a fit of jealousy, killed him. Upon realizing he had killed his son, he drew his sword and impaled himself. Belisa immediately fled from her home and took refuge on her solitary island, whose disconnection from land symbolizes the self-imposed isolation in which she spent the six months prior to the group's happening upon her.

Belisa, like Sylvano, refuses to acknowledge love's flawed nature. Both are self-righteous about their devotion; she says, "Pain that is cured with time can be endured with little difficulty" (mal que con el tiempo se cura, con poca dificultad puede sufrirse, LD, 159–60). She thereafter refers repeatedly to time as the insurmountable barrier to the solution of her problems, a certitude like that of Sylvano's which will be proven wrong: time, it turns out, is the solution to her problem, not its cause. Like the rest of her companions, she accepts out of courtesy the nymphs' suggestion that she accompany them. They do not even tell her where they are headed, nor does it seem to matter to her. Beneath her exquisite manners, there seems to lie a desire to turn her will over to someone else, quite in keeping with Montemayor's positive attitude about submission: "but since your will is that I accompany you, I shall not depart the smallest bit from it; and from here on you may, lovely nymphs, make use of my will however yours may see fit" (mas ya que tu voluntad es essa [que las acompañe], no determino salir della en un solo punto; y de oy más podéis, hermosas ninfas, usar de la mía, según a las vuestras les pareciere, LD, 161).

Belisa, like Sireno, Sylvano, and Selvagia, is faced with a situation in which happiness is truly impossible without a breach in the fidelity she proudly practices. The fact that she, who faces death as her problem, is treated comparably to the others, who face marriage as theirs, indicates a curious equality in suffering between the two situations. The very picture of the true lover according to the standards exalted by Montemayor, Belisa faces the rest of her life determined literally to suffer through it until it ends, ever faithful to her original love. The contrast with Diana, whose loyalty could not withstand even a temporary separation, is clear.

Importantly, the possibility of happiness is extended to the characters as the result of their having undergone trials involving both physical and emotional suffering. They have all proven faithful in times of adversity, enduring exaggerated hardships that have made them wise through experience. In their disposition to undergo these trials and in their enlightened state resulting from them, the characters—particularly the retreating Belisa—are fundamentally akin to Montemayor's hermit Dileto. Further, the nymphs' intention is that happiness be awarded from a force outside the characters themselves; Felicia is initially portrayed as a superior being who intervenes in the normal course of human affairs, one who is expected to right the wrongs unjustly committed against the righteous. Compensation for the lovers' trials is to be granted following successful proof of worth and is to be rewarded by a being above human limitations, a process identical to that of attaining religious grace and the arbitrary way in which it is awarded as described in Montemayor's religious works.

At this point in the narration, the process of earning one's just reward is similar to the way in which a knight such as Amadís of Gaul is saved from the clutches of evil by his patron magician Urganda, who repeatedly steps in at just the moment when the knight's limits are about to be surpassed. The shepherds and shepherdesses are likewise in untenable situations, and at the limits of their idealism (an idealism that Amadís embodies himself as a character). Their heroic proportions, like Amadís's, have been overcome by situations which have been represented, like the knight's, as beyond their control, when the supernatural intervenes.

The fact that the popularity of the *Diana* overlapped with that of the books of chivalry indicates an important relationship between Montemayor's recourse to romance and Garci Rodríguez de Montalvo's fundamental reliance on the same. However, there are significant distinctions: the pastoral characters are devoted to emotional, spiritual heroics, which naturally lends them to comparison with religious experience, also emotional and spiritual. They have been done wrong by others and thus are victims, not saviors. For this, they are similar to Amadís only during his penance, for a sin he did not commit, in the Peña Pobre, an episode with religious connotations in itself. Except for Felismena, the pastoral characters are essentially passive at the point when the narrator joins them. Like those aspiring to grace, they must sit by, maintain their virtuous positions, and wait. This is the posture for which the pastoral mode is best suited.

By the end of book three, all the main characters have been brought together, and the appropriate autobiographies have been told. Having arrived at the present of all concerned, the narration can carry all of them along into the future without the need for interrupting backward glances. The objective of the pastoral impulse having been realized, the *locus amoenus* can be abandoned. Although the second narrative plane is invoked in the last books for purposes of updating characters and the reader about past events, it is never used to the unrealistic extent it is in books one to three. Instead, recollected material is brief and to the point of the issue at stake in the first narrative plane. Having experimented with extensive autobiographical sections through expansion of the pastoral mode's potential for such material, Montemayor retains the concept of the individual as one whose character is shaped by her or his past, but abandons the purely literary fashion in which that past is revealed.

Appropriately, book three closes almost at dawn, signalling the arrival of a new day for the characters. Unlike the first book, which ends at sunset as a self-enclosed unit, and the second, which ends during the late afternoon of the second day with the trip to Felicia's palace only begun, the third finds all the characters on the verge of arriving at the palace and in a state of suspension, awaiting something that appears to be just beyond their reach. Ideologically, they are identical to the righteous described in Montemayor's religious writings: having suffered innocently the injustices of an imperfect world, there is nothing they can do themselves to relieve their emotional anguish but remember it, thereby affirming their own virtue. They spend the hours of remaining darkness in contemplative solitude, enclosed within the limits of the same memories that they have just shared: "Each one chose that place most agreeable to him or her to spend what remained of the night. Those in love spent the time more in tears than in sleep, and those not in love recovered from the day's fatigue" (Cada uno escogió el lugar de que más se contentó, para passar lo que de la noche les quedava. La qual, los enamorados passaron con más lágrimas que sueño, y los que no lo eran, reposaron del cansancio del día, LD, 161). Having passed through the darkness of book three, which tells of a journey, describes an encounter with death, and occurs during the night, they are able to find that day that follows it. The time appears to have arrived for all of these unfortunate people's fortunes to change.

The characters' movement together toward Felicia's territory is typically interpreted as a pilgrimage or quest, one that takes place in the first three books. Juan Bautista Avalle-Arce relates the journey to the folk motif of the type used in "The Wizard of Oz" (NPE, 85), and Amadeu Solé-Leris builds on that idea.[17] The assignment of this type of structure to the overall action of the seven books is based on the notion that in them the five lovers accumulate, undertake a journey as a group to a temple, where they are supposedly enlightened and supposedly renewed, and subsequently go on with their lives the better for it all. Montemayor's commitment to religious matters and the spiritual concerns of the *Diana* make such an interpretation particularly alluring.

However, the quest and pilgrimage motifs themselves imply an activism that goes against the grain of virtually everything Montemayor wrote. Further, the motivations and forms necessary for a narrative to be considered representative of a pilgrimage, the primary requisite of which is a search, are decidedly missing from his book.[18] Imposing such motives on the lovers in the *Diana* denies not only its author's predilection for depicting reactions to events rather than the events themselves or solutions to them, but also contradicts the positive attributes of suffering and lament that do indeed find constant expression. Such enterprise would have been at odds with Montemayor's devoted attention to contemplative, not active, values, the very qualities that attracted him to the pastoral mode in the first place, and those that most characterize his religious works. Significantly, the trip to Felicia's temple is offered as a reward for Sireno, Sylvano, Selvagia, and Felismena's defense of the nymphs against the savages. Felismena's appearance on that scene was as fortuitous as is the resulting visit to the temple, and represents the intervention of a force beyond the human—fortune—in the lives of human beings. Montemayor repeatedly interpreted such forces as overpowering any events forthcoming from merely human actions. Belisa is encountered along the way purely by chance, immediately proves herself to be a worthy companion, and joins the others in an act of compliance, not determination. The "journey" to the palace takes

---

17. Amadeu Solé-Leris, *The Spanish Pastoral Novel*, 34. The pilgrimage motif is the most convenient, common, and erroneous approach to the structure of the *Diana*: I used it in my article "Sixteenth-century Pastoral Books, Narrative Structure, and *La Galatea* of Cervantes"; Mujica refers repeatedly to the pilgrimage theme in the chapter on Montemayor in her book *Iberian Pastoral Characters*; Bruno Damiani builds an entire chapter on it in his La Diana *of Montemayor as Social and Religious Teaching*.

18. Juergen Hahn's book *The Origins of the Baroque Concept of Peregrinatio*, defines the pilgrimage thoroughly, in contrast with other quest motifs and narrative structures.

less than one day and is not proposed until the end of book two, and even then is it suggested by the nymphs, not the human characters.

Unlike pilgrims or those on a quest, Sireno, Sylvano, Selvagia, and Belisa do not seek out either Felicia or the solution to their problems she supposedly represents, for their role as pastoral characters prohibits them from such action. Like Montemayor's hermit Dileto, they have realized the futility of pursuing perfect love in the world and live withdrawn from it in contemplative suffering. Like Dileto, they have dedicated themselves to recollection of things they have learned, not to action. When the narration finds them, they are not seeking anything; their only goal is their lament, and this is perfectly in keeping with the dominion of the pastoral mode in the first three books. Although they feel they are victims of love's imperfections, they are fond enough of their own fidelity and self-righteous suffering to prefer enduring their loss to remedying it by abandoning their first loves. It is precisely this fidelity that both prohibits them from taking any action that would compromise that same loyalty and enables them to enter Felicia's palace through the arch of the faithful lovers.

Of all the main characters, only Felismena is "questing" after anything: she seeks Felis literally and Felicia only metaphorically. Appropriately, the nymphs offer the visit to Felicia first to her, while alone with her, since it was she who saved them from the savages. Her appearance on the pastoral scene brings narrative action to the book, and her actions produce the consequences that lead the other characters to abandon the pastoral scene. Therefore, as will be observed, the trip to Felicia's palace brings an ambiguous happiness to the truly pastoral characters. Felismena has the strongest alliance of all to the world beyond the *locus amoenus;* although it is she who carries the first narrative plane forward in time, she is the exception, not the rule, and her final "happiness" is fraught with imperfections.

The lovers are initially ambivalent about the visit proposed by the nymphs and have to be led there and, as has been indicated, they are skeptical about Felicia's ability to do anything for them. Appropriately, they do not assimilate any serious changes in their lives as a result of her intervention; all of the endings to their respective stories have been prepared well in advance of their arrival at her abode and may be interpreted as resulting from their characters and the vision of the life experience presented by Montemayor: as T. Anthony Perry says, "It is to Montemayor's credit, however, that the love problems (and their solutions) are not extraneous but arise from the depths of the characters themselves."[19] Montemayor's vision, as mentioned, attends to humanity's need to endure the bad moments of life (to enjoy them, in fact, for the proof of worth they imply) and hold out for the change in events which is bound to come as a result of the instability of life in general. The characters have already expressed repeatedly the irrevocable subjection of pure love to time and fortune, which results in changes in people's affections. Knowing this to be true, they must pass through time in order to witness its effects on themselves.

All five of the lovers are totally free of any attitude that would convincingly liken them to penitents or traditional pilgrims. They have done nothing wrong and thus do not seek a purifying experience or forgiveness, nor have they witnessed anything remarkable for which to give thanks. Instead, they have been wronged themselves. What they lack is the power to forgive others, not forgiveness for themselves. Their attitude is not one that anticipates the help such a trip will produce, rather it is one that assumes it cannot hurt. Just as Montemayor's worshipper can only suffer hardships in anticipation of the touch of divine grace, just as his captive Israelites can only voice their sad lament and await divine salvation, so his human lovers' lot is to suffer along until providence intervenes, or the wheel of fortune turns (both being depicted as the same type of event). In either case, the individual will *be led* along the proper path. The pilgrimage motif in the *Diana* can only be applied, with some imaginative interpretation, to Felismena's pursuit of Felis, and even that is a consequence of the wish-fulfillment quality of romance, similar to the quest or pilgrimage but much broader in scope.

Book Four

Book four, which describes the first of two days spent at Felicia's palace, is the epiphany of the seven books, meaning "the point at which the undisplaced apocalyptic world and the cyclical world of nature come into alignment."[20] It stands in the middle of the seven chapters and marks a

---

19. *Erotic Spirituality: The Integrative Tradition from Leone Hebreo to John Donne*, 84.
20. Northrup Frye, "Archetypal Criticism: Theory of Myths," 203; see also 204–6. Wardropper was the first to point out the fourth book's central role in the structure of the *Diana* ("The *Diana* of Montemayor").

turning point for everyone, superficially signaling abrupt changes, but also formally acknowledging the emotional adjustments that the characters have been making all along. Their stay provides a time and space removed from both the *locus amoenus*, dominated by the past, and the world beyond it, which signifies the future. It removes them to a place out of time, providing an escape into the psychological realms of fantasy and allegory in which the lovers can realize the adaptations that time itself has been effecting within them, changes that would have come about in their lives if time had been allowed to run its normal course.

The fourth book opens by the light of the morning star, Venus, symbolizing love's continued dominion over the characters' lives: "The morning star was already beginning to cast its usual splendor" (Ya la estrella del alva començava a dar su acostumbrado resplandor, LD, 162). Leaving the island, the characters share their stories with the newcomer Belisa and are subsequently led by the nymphs through a dark and wild forest. The dark forest and the characters' guidance through it by three nymphs borders temptingly on religious symbolism, in which the three nymphs might symbolize the three faculties of the soul or faith, hope, and charity. No such interpretation is justified by the text, however. The characters' being led through the woods does reinforce the motif presented in the preceding books of their being led out of metaphorical and literal darkness or overgrowth (symbolizing exaggeration), suffering and the night, before arriving at happiness, Felicia. Further, it emphasizes their passage from real time to fantastic time, culminating in their arrival at the palace and underscoring the magical aura about the wise woman they meet there.

The first-plane narration is here drawn out of the natural world and toward that of fantasy. As it wavers between the two, a sixteenth-century version of what has since been classified as the fantastic emerges, a narrative cosmos in which the real and unreal coexist.[21] Felicia's equivocal nature points to the unstable ways of the happiness she symbolizes. Appearing to be both human and superhuman, she is a stately duenna with a regal presence who greets the company saying, "For I, without having been told by anyone, know who you are and where your thoughts are taking you, as well as everything that has happened to you until now" (Pues yo, sin estar informada de nadie, sé quien sóis y adonde os llevan

---

21. Tzvetan Todorov, *The Fantastic: A Structural Approach to a Literary Genre*, 25.

vuestros pensamientos, con todo lo que hasta aora os a sucedido, LD, 163). That evening, however, she denies having any supernatural power, replying to Sireno's question about true love with a show of humility: "Just as that question is more than a shepherd might ask, so it should be that she answering it be more than a woman" (Assí como esa pregunta es más que de pastor, assí era necesario que fuesse más que muger la que a ella respondiesse, LD, 95).[22]

Felicia's wavering authority is underscored by the fact that she later imparts only one of the three bits of wisdom about theoretical desire that follow and indicates that, although she is an authority on love doctrine, she is not the only one. Sylvano picks up the topic where she leaves it off, and his authoritative words are followed by those of the nymph Cinthia, who proposes her own ideas about the effects of separation on love. Felicia has supernatural powers, but the other characters are as well informed about the nature of desire as she, and whereas she and Cinthia speak theoretically, they have their experience to support what they say. The parity of the characters' wisdom with that of Felicia recalls the way in which Montemayor, imitating the Catholic reformists in his religious works, allots authority to those who have witnessed the truth in their lives, an authority equal to that of any other.

Again, there is nothing in the text that overtly suggests a religious interpretation of Felicia's role in the *Diana*. Nonetheless, Montemayor's religious writings do support reformist ideals that challenge the supremacy of the intermediary's (priest's) acquired knowledge over the infused wisdom acquired by the worshipper alone. His staunch support of personal, sentimental experience in faith and of enlightening divine love could reasonably produce the ambiguous authority of a figure like Felicia. The supposed intermediary between fortune, a superhuman power, and the characters, she is not any wiser than they, rather she possesses a prescience that they do not. This is a divine quality: in Montemayor's "Diálogo spiritual" ("Spiritual Dialogue"), Dileto distinguishes between God and the devil by the former's knowledge of the future, which Satan does not have (DS, 9r). Further, the results Felicia's hocus-pocus brings about are subtly presented as what the characters would have accomplished themselves with time, if left

---

22. The narrator's wink at the reader is accomplished here by Felicia's reminder that she and the pastoral characters alike are fictional characters playing roles within that very fiction.

alone. The result is a striking parallel between Catholic reformist respect for and simultaneous ascendance beyond Church hierarchy, replete with riches and ceremony, and the characters' reverence toward Felicia, her unstable status between the human and superhuman, and the questionable worth of her interventionist authority, likewise replete with material and ceremonial splendor.

The text's alliance with the realm of fantasy in book four is apparent in the structure and materials of Felicia's palace. Her abode is an urbanized version of Apolidón's grove, described in the episode of the True Lover's Arch in *Amadís de Gaula* (*Amadís of Gaul*). Entrance to both is attained by passing under an arch, after which the characters progress through four chambers: "Apolidón made an arch at the entrance to the grove, in which there were all kinds of trees; and there at the entrance were four rich chambers of unusual workmanship as well" (Hizo [Apolidón] un arco a la entrada de una huerta, en que árboles de todas naturas hauía; y otrosí hauía en ella quatro cámaras ricas de straña lauor, AG, 2:358). The jasper of Felicia's palace echoes the clear jasper of Apolidon's creation (LD, 165; "piedra jaspe muy clara," AG, 2:358). Felicia's bronze column repeats Apolidon's iron one (LD, 173; "padrón de fiero," AG, 2:358).[23]

The messages on the arches above the entrances are fundamentally identical, and their similarity, which Avalle-Arce has noted in passing, deserves close attention.[24] The one in *Amadís* says, "Beyond this point no man or woman shall pass who has failed his or her first love" (De aquí adelante no pasará ningún hombre ni mujer si hobieren errado a aquellos que primero comenzaron a amar, AG, 2:358). To the faithful lovers who enter, Apolidón promised perpetual fame: "those [faithful lovers] will see our images and their names written in the jasper" (éstos verán las nuestras imágenes e sus nombres escriptos en el jaspe, AG, 2:358). Later, Montemayor's characters do indeed read the inscribed names of women who were faithful to their dead lovers (LD, 177).

The entrance to Felicia's palace is guarded by two silver nymphs holding a tablet that bears this inscription:

---

23. Subirats finds the materials in Felicia's palace to be identical to those of an actual palace at Binche ("La 'Diana' de Montemayor, roman à clef?"). Such materials seem to have constituted a pat "palace description," too common to assign to any one building. In any case, the more extensive similarity with the *Amadís* text is undeniable.

24. Avalle-Arce, "El arco de los leales amadores en el *Amadís*," 155.

> Whoever enters, look well how s/he has lived
> and look whether s/he has kept the prize of chastity
> and she who loves well or has wanted to
> let her look to see if, because of another, she has changed.
> And if that first faith s/he has not lost
> and that first love has conserved
> s/he may enter into the temple of Diana
> whose virtue and grace are superhuman.[25]
>
> (Quien entra, mira bien cómo a bivido
> y el don de castidad, si le a guardado
> y la que quiere bien o lo a querido
> mire si a causa de otro se a mudado.
> Y si la fe primera no a perdido
> y aquel primer amor a conservado
> entrar puede en el templo de Diana
> cuya virtud y gracia es sobrehumana.)
> (LD, 165)

Montemayor transformed Apolidón's authoritative statement into an echo of the call to self-examination so typical of his own religious writings:

> Recollect yourself my soul, and turn your memory
> upon itself, let not the night find it,
> and it will follow the victory with Christ.
>
> (Recógete alma mía, y tu memoria
> revuelva sobre sí, no le anochezca,
> y seguirá con Cristo la victoria.)
> (SCS, 203r; not in GP)

Of course, all of Montemayor's characters are so pure at heart that they pass the test and gain entrance to the palace; only readers of *Amadís* know that the unpure are thrown from the arch by its supernatural powers. The arch above Felicia's palace, then, insists on a proving process

---

25. Spanish uses the third person singular of the verb, without a personal pronoun, to indicate a masculine or feminine subject, an ambiguity of which this inscription takes advantage. The awkward "s/he" in the translation is used to indicate that ambiguity, since the first two lines of the tablet may refer to men or women, as may lines five through eight. Lines three and four, however, refer to a woman and are clearly directed at Diana who, as Sireno notes immediately, could not pass under that arch.

based on contemplation ("look well . . . let her or him look well" [mira bien . . . mire]), after which it offers to a select few access to a temple wherein their righteousness will be confirmed. The same procedure of entrance designed to winnow out the select from the many is a motif Montemayor had taken up in his adaptation of Climacus's *Scala paradisi*. Just as the motif in the *Diana* is derived from a non-humanistic literary tradition (the chivalric), so in the "Spiritual Dialogue" it is derived from the ascetic, not the Christian humanist, spiritual tradition (a work by one of the Desert Fathers). Indeed, there are several references to triumphal arches, symbolic of the acquisition of Christian virtues, in Montemayor's religious verse, and the frequency with which he used the image therein probably facilitated the transfer to a secular context. For example, he describes the doors of Jerusalem in his "Exposición moral sobre el salmo 86" ("Moral Exposition on Psalm 86"): "it had two royal doors: / one arch was of humility / and another of virginity" (tuuo dos puertas reales / un arco fué de humildad / y otro de virginidad).[26]

As noted in chapter 1, removing Climacus's metaphor of the biblical Jacob's ladder, Montemayor built his "Dialogue" text on that of the twelve gates of Jerusalem. Severo describes salvation as the earning of passage through each gate by sufficient practice of the ascetic virtues he and Climacus describe at length.[27] Dileto says, "Know, Severo, that in order to enter into the celestial Jerusalem, which is heavenly glory, you must enter through one of seven doors. And if you should enter by the merit of all seven, it would be much easier for you to reach God" (Sabe, Severo, que para entrar en la celestial Jerusalén, que es la gloria celestial, has de entrar por una de siete puertas. Y si por el mérito de todas siete pudieses entrar, muy más fácil te sería alcanzar a Dios, DS, 84r). To get into Jerusalem, or heaven, one must pass through at least one of these gates, as the

---

26. In the edition by López Estrada, 514.

27. The importance of Montemayor's alteration of the basic metaphor of Climacus's *Scala* from a ladder, or vertical ascent, to doorways, or horizontal progression, was discussed in chapter 1 (*supra* 90–91). It is worth mentioning again here that such a change protects the distance between the human and the divine by graphically eliminating all direct contact, even metaphorical, between the two, leaving God as the agent of grace who descends to humanity rather than humanity as the noble race that ascends to the divine. Although Climacus's text is not Neoplatonic, Montemayor nonetheless removed the very metaphor that implied a human ascent to the divine, the ladder.

human lovers must test their love by passing through the arch at Felicia's palace. Just as his pastoral characters have suffered innocently to enter that palace, so his Christian must likewise undergo similar trials to attain heavenly glory. At no point in either text are the realms of the superhuman and the human mixed; after their practice of suffering and self-examination before entry, there follows a mystery involving a superhuman force that cannot be attained by human understanding. Further, just as in his "Spiritual Dialogue," Montemayor begins with the assumption that the worshipper is free of sin by the time he or she is confirmed as a member of the select few, so the *Diana* deals only with lovers who are likewise free from imperfections in their practice of love as they approach Felicia's test.[28]

The company of perfect lovers passes under the arch and the characters begin their visit of the palace. Upon entering, the group is led into Felicia's chambers, where they are served a sumptuous meal, after which three nymphs serenade them on elegant instruments, leaving the lovers "as if beside themselves" (como fuera de sí, LD, 167) and inspiring them to join the nymphs in a song. The musical interchange subsequently performed by the nymphs and the pastoral characters has a message that might serve as the Portuguese author's motto, one that indicates agreement by natural and supernatural beings about the nature of love and humanity's experience with it:

> *Nymphs*
> Love and fortune,
> sources of trials and injustices,
> higher than the moon
> will carry one's affections
> and to that same extreme one's passion.
>
> *Shepherds and shepherdesses*
> No less unfortunate is the one
> who never suffered pain of love
> than the most enamored one
> who lacks favor,
> *for those who suffer the most are the best.*

---

28. Therefore, contrary to Damiani's thesis, the characters do not seek forgiveness in Felicia's temple, because they have not erred or "sinned" in their love; see Rhodes, "Review of La Diana *of Montemayor as Social and Religious Teaching.*"

(*Ninfas*
Amor y la fortuna
autores de trabajo y sinrazones,
más altas que la luna
pornán las aficiones
y en esse mismo extremo las passiones.)

(*Pastores*
No es menos desdichado
aquel que jamás tuvo mal de amores
que el más enamorado
faltándole favores
pues los que sufren más, son los mejores.)
(LD, 167, emphasis added)

Likewise, his secular verse is saturated with the same notion and its implications. In a 1554 poem republished in 1558, the proportional relationship between suffering and merit is expounded in a lexicon purposefully resonant with religious overtones that exalt the perfection awarded to the one who obeys divine mandate. The poet gathers his readers, calling:

Come then, lovers, you who subjects
are to what love orders and wishes,
and in me you will see that the one who suffers most
will have the best place among the perfect.

(Venid, pues amadores, que sujetos
estáis a lo que amor ordena y quiere,
y en mí veréis que aquel que más sufriere
mejor lugar tendrá entre los perfectos.)
(SC, 122r–v; GP, 39)

There is a parallel between this idealized, innocent suffering, on one hand, and the suffering of Christ and the true Christian, as represented in Montemayor's religious works, on the other. The positive value Montemayor attributes to guiltless and willing submission to pain is as fundamental to his vision of love as it is to that of the recogidos. It is alien to the dignified sentiments of the Neoplatonists and the humanists alike. Montemayor's exaltation of suffering comes straight from sources like Luis de Granada, who reminds his reader that the measure of one's worth corresponds to the measure of one's hardships, such that "the most privileged is the most pained and afflicted" (el más privado sea más afligido y atribulado, LdO, 86). Montemayor returns to this idea repeatedly in both the religious and the secular contexts. It is a positive sentiment: of the captive Israelites, the narrator of his exposition of the "Super flumina" Psalm says,

> Now their grief brings them pleasure
> and makes more glorious their victory,
> which came not from them but from heaven.
>
> (Ahora les da placer su desconsuelo
> y su victoria hace más gloriosa,
> la cual no vino de ellos mas del cielo.)
> (SCS, 181v; not in GP)

Further, Montemayor's lovers, like the worshipper depicted by Granada, are doubly worthy since they suffer unjustly in a secular context just as the righteous Christian suffers innocently in a religious context and thereby imitates Christ the better: "If you suffer without sin and without blame, you should be so much the more consoled, for that is suffering upon the cross of the Savior" (si padesces sin pecados y sin culpa, por eso te debrías más de consolar, porque eso es padescer en la cruz del Salvador, LdO, 87). This is a profoundly Christian, ascetic ideal, one that dominates the *Diana* as well as Montemayor's other works, making possible the vital dilemmas his characters express. For, as will be seen, when willing suffering for the ideal fails to produce the deserved results, conflict ensues.

Felicia's palace is significantly removed from the *locus amoenus* and is full of amazing things to look at, wonder over, eat, and talk about. It provides an oasis in the characters' trials, where emotional accounts are tallied and rewards prepared, in a process not too far removed from Dileto's formula for purgatory (see *supra* 99). Upon arriving there, they abandon their obsession with themselves as they are given other things to see and do. The activities in which Felicia engages them allow them to view love from a more objective distance, inspiring the ideological discussions that follow the entertainment.

The characters' simple distraction from their obsessions is obviously part of their change of heart that follows. Although Felicia's first step in healing the lovers' wounds is more discreetly administered than the one Lope de Vega's enchantress Polinesta provides for Anfriso, it is nonetheless identical to it. Polinesta says to the disillusioned lover, "I will take you to the temple of exercise and liberal arts, the honest entertainment of which may distract your fatigued memory so that you will not recall if you ever saw Belisarda in your life."[29] Occupation and distraction, in contrast with the *acedia* or "sloth" upon which the pastoral *otio,* "leisure," borders precariously, were recommended in Golden Age medical treatises as the cure for love melancholy. Although Montemayor's characters display some of the symptoms of this obsessive malady, and although what happens to his characters at the palace follows part of the remedy typically prescribed for sufferers of the disease, their changes of perspective derive more from common sense. Further, love melancholy as a pathological state is at odds with the natural quality Montemayor bestows on the love lament, excessive though it may seem today. He provides no specific reference to the particular infirmity of melancholy, and, although the lovers are subtly led along the path to overcoming their sadness, it is never overtly stated that they can or should take any steps to "cure" themselves of anything considered an illness.[30] On the contrary, the characters' abulia is clearly a positive part of their nature. Montemayor's solution for his characters, which removes them from the static *locus amoenus* and offers them a slightly veiled symbol as the answer to their problems (time), is fundamentally the same as the one prescribed for Anfriso. What becomes a central issue in later pastoral books, that love's pains can actually be cured naturally with time and distraction, is present, if subtly proffered, in the *Diana*.

After their song about suffering in love, the first conflict over love's nature arises. Felicia proposes a relationship between virtuous love and good fortune that offends the shepherdesses and shepherds, observing:

> In these cases of love I have a rule that I have always found to be true, and it is that the one possessing a generous soul and a fine understanding has a tremendous advantage in the business of love over the one who does not. Because, given that love is virtue, and virtue always settles itself into the best place, it is clear that individuals of fortune will be much better lovers than those who lack it.
>
> (En estos casos de amor tengo yo una regla que siempre la e hallado muy verdadera y es que el ánimo generoso y el entendimiento delicado, en esto del

---

29. *Arcadia,* 359.
30. Teresa Scott Soufas's book, *Melancholy and the Secular Mind in Spanish Golden Age Literature,* examines the symptoms of love as a physiological malady.

querer bien lleva grandíssima ventaja al que no lo es. Porque como el amor sea virtud y la virtud siempre haga assiento en el mejor lugar, está claro que las personas de suerte serán muy mejor enamorados que aquellas en quien ésta falta.) (LD, 170)

Sylvano, representing those whose fortunes are clearly of an inner, individual nature, asks just what that generous soul and fine understanding entail, to which Felicia replies, "It is in nothing else than man's own virtue, such as having a lively discernment, thoughts inclined toward higher things, and other virtues that are born with the individuals themselves" (No está en otra cosa sino en la propria virtud del hombre, como es en tener el juyzio vivo, el pensamiento inclinado a cosas altas y otras virtudes que nacen con ellos mismos). Sylvano declares his satisfaction that she does not find valor and virtue's origins to have their roots beyond the individual, "because the one who goes to find them in his ancestors is greatly lacking the benefits of nature" (porque assaz desfavorecido de los bienes de naturaleza está el que los va a buscar en sus passados, LD, 170). "Bienes de naturaleza" were those admirable qualities with which one was born; "bienes de fortuna" were those goods and qualities acquired during life. Sylvano posits that nobility is something with which one is born, but does not inherit.

This passage is perhaps Montemayor's response to the difference of opinion expressed by Cesare Gonzaga and Gaspar Pallavicino in Castiglione's *Il libro del cortegiano* (*The Book of the Courtier*). The former contends that the ideal courtier must be born noble and of a noble family ("nato nobile e di generosa ['nobile'] famiglia") to which the latter responds by saying that such nobility is not necessary ("a me non par cosí necessaria questa nobilità"). Pallavicino voices an opinion that surely caught Montemayor's attention:

> But of our diversity and degrees of nobility and ignobility, I believe that there are many other causes, among which I hold fortune to be foremost, because in all worldly things we see it dominate and almost persist in the game of raising often to the heights of heaven whomever it pleases without any merit, and burying in the abyss those most worthy of exaltation.... Often one sees supreme gifts of nature in very lowborn people.

Pallavicino considers such qualities as "intelligence, beauty of countenance, proportion of one's person, and that grace that appeals to everyone at first glance" (IC, 49) to be more important than noble birth. Gonzaga prevails, maintaining that for the perfect courtier, nobility of blood is desirable, if for nothing else than the immediate respect and attention it demands from others. Sylvano and his friends, however, clearly side with Pallavicino, and it is reasonable to assume that Montemayor, lacking nobility of blood but fond of representing himself as being inherently noble by nature, did also.

In spite of the social liberalism it implies, this brief interchange provides a good example of how the pastoral characters can appear to support social reformist values such as disdain of familial nobility, yet never abandon the status quo. Such a posture would be perfectly in keeping with Montemayor's religious values, which seem to support reformist theology but are nonetheless basically conservative. Felicia acknowledges Sylvano's opinion and has the grace to state it herself (LD, 170), but immediately thereafter she sends Felismena off with the nymphs to dress in courtly finery and elegant jewels, clearly in homage to her social status.[31] The shepherds and shepherdesses are astounded at her transformation, and she is thereafter treated with the deference due one of her rank (LD, 179, 194, 222–23).

After she dresses, Felismena rejoins her friends and they begin their tour of the three remaining chambers in Felicia's palace which they visit. These include a patio containing a column carved with figures of war heroes, a room of alabaster walls carved with figures of chaste women, and the interior hall. This last room, the inner sanctum, has golden walls, a floor of precious stones, and is decorated with statues of virtuous ladies and a life-size one of the goddess Diana. To one side is a silver fountain beside which an enchanted Orpheus is perched to deliver his song in praise of living virtuous women.

In the innermost chamber, the lovers sit and listen to Orpheus, who first plays a harp so beautifully "that those who heard him were so beside themselves that no one recalled anything than might have happened to him"

---

31. On Felismena's jewels, see Francisco Márquez Villanueva's interesting article "Los joyeles de Felismena." Márquez indicates that Montemayor's attention to Felismena's jewelry supports Juan de Alcalá's accusation that Montemayor's father was a silversmith, i.e., a Jew or a converso. Another telling detail may be the narrator's curious observation that the candle holders on Doña Catalina's monument were "of fine and well wrought silver" (de fina plata, muy bien labrados, LD, 191).

(que los que le oyan, estavan tan agenos de sí que a nadie se le acordava de cosa que por él uviesse passado, LD, 179). Orpheus's song is a traditional panegyric suited to the courtly setting in which it is performed, and constitutes something of a social register of 1559. It was so pleasing to his listeners "that they were so amazed, it was [as] if none of them had experienced anything except what they had before them" (que assí los tenía suspensos, como si por ninguno dellos uviera passado más de lo que presente tenían, LD, 191). This is the third experience with musical rapture that the characters have at the palace, and the narrator is careful to state how well such interludes distract them from their problems. The fact that music plays a primary role in the process of characters' emotional development is not surprising in a book written by a professional singer.

Leaving the inner sanctum, the characters visit the sepulchers of "nymphs and ladies who had, with great purity, maintained the chastity owed to the most chaste goddess" (nimphas y damas, las quales avían, con gran limpieza, conservado la castidad devida a la castíssima Diosa, LD, 191). This is a stinging, ironic contrast between the goddess Diana, whose name and image appear repeatedly throughout book four, and the woman for whom the *Diana* was named; as Perry has stated, "Each mention of the name is a disturbing reminder of the tension between mythical perfection and reality."[32] The alliance Montemayor makes between physical chastity and emotional constancy, spelled out in the inscription over the entrance to Felicia's palace, was typical of his day. Although Diana has not violated the code of physical chastity, her sentimental infidelity has branded her as morally unchaste, or inconstant. This extended meaning of *"castidad"* is invoked by Juan Boscán, who describes his married life saying, "Now *chaste* love attends, and orders / that all be enjoyable to me" (agora el *casto* amor acude y manda / que todo se me haga muy sabroso)(emphasis added). This "chaste" love is the same of which he continues to say,

> Now I am thinking, being in my chamber,
> how I will be able to enjoy myself with my wife,
> having her in bed or out of it.

---

32. *Erotic Spirituality*, 80.

(Ya estoy pensando, stando en mi posada,
cómo podré con mi muger holgarme,
teniéndola en la cama o levantada.)[33]

For Montemayor, always interested more in the emotional impact of events than in their physical consequences, Diana is unchaste in the worst sense, for she has broken her word and violated the ideal. The extent to which she is excluded from the company of true lovers in the *Diana* is emphasized by Montemayor's decision to center his entire book around the temple of Diana's superhuman counterpart of the same name, the very goddess of chastity.

The distant, plastic representation of death in book four, true to the elegiac tradition of pastoral, is finally personalized when the vision of Catherine of Aragon's tomb moves Belisa to lament untimely demise. Her outcry, in turn, restores the characters' control of the narration after its focus on their lessons in how to earn earthly fame and glory from examples of the dead. As has been the case with love and relationships until this point, death is presented in strictly human, mortal terms; any reference to a world beyond that of the suffering characters is decidedly missing in the *Diana*. What is more, Montemayor scrupulously avoids explicit reference to God in the *Diana;* the one mention of the divinity in it, an indirect reference, is among the sentences he copied from Hebreo in book four. Likewise in his religious works, description of the rewards attained by the righteous from God are conspicuously missing. Far from meaning that Montemayor questioned the existence of heaven or God's mercy and justice, it provides further evidence of his preference to dwell on the moments of suffering that precede those rewards, already mentioned as a fundamental trait of his works.

Leaving the palace, the characters rejoin Felismena for some conversa-

---

33. *Obras*, 531. The three men in the *Diana* who are as emotionally unfaithful to their first loves as Diana was to hers are described as inconstant by the women but not as unchaste. A woman's sexual integrity in the sixteenth century included more than her physical condition, since her virginity could be blemished or lost altogether. Juan Luis Vives, supposed prince of the humanists, pauses in his long tirade about the need for women to lose their lives before their virtue to support St Jerome's notion "that a woman should kill herself before she allows her virginity to be stained or lost." He had previously contended that women would be better off blind than be allowed to read the "wrong" books, *Instrucción de la mujer cristiana*, 115, 34.

tion in the meadow surrounding the garden, a physical positioning that represents the integration of courtly and pastoral themes and characters. Divided into three groups, they are seated within speaking distance of each other: Felicia, Felismena, and Sireno; Sylvano and the nymph Dórida; Selvagia and Belisa with the nymphs Cinthia and Polydora. For their physical arrangement, the company resembles a sixteenth-century social gathering of a literary academy or salon, transferred outdoors. Conversation in such a setting may be expected to reflect the codes of elegant dialogue in vogue during Montemayor's day, and the content likewise to reflect the interests of courtiers, not philosophers.

The conversation held by the characters in book four of the *Diana* constitutes a short manual for talking about philosophy, not for philosophy itself. It is generally considered to be the authoritative statement about love in the *Diana* and in Montemayor's works as a whole, and is likewise typically believed to support a "Neoplatonic frame" for the entire book.[34] In spite of the importance that scholars attribute to this section, it has not yet been closely examined. Its examination, however, dissociates Montemayor's text from that Neoplatonic frame and so dissociates from Montemayor's texts any critical approach that proposes it. Since this implies a radical departure from long accepted and repeated ideas about the *Diana*, the following is undertaken in some detail.

The narrator initiates the tripartite conversation that follows by casting an air of protocol, not sincerity, about it. Sireno begins to speak, "desiring to see the talk and conversation conform to the time and place as well as the person with whom he was speaking" (queriendo que la plática y conversación se conformasse con el tiempo y lugar, y también con la persona a quien hablava, LD, 194). Each of the three groups then takes up a topic about the nature of love. Two-thirds of what they say is adapted from a passage at the end of book one of Leone Hebreo's *Dialoghi d'amore* (Dialogues of Love), a treatise published in Italian in 1535.[35]

---

34. NPE, 88, and Mujica (*Iberian Pastoral Characters*, 118). Since Avalle-Arce's ideas about the *Diana* in *La novela pastoril española* are the most well known, I cite them primarily. As indicated in note 4, the notion that the *Diana* is related to Neoplatonism in one way or another constitutes the standard ideological approach to the text.

35. The *Dialogues* were mentioned in chapter 1 as an ideological contrast to Montemayor's religious works (*supra* 72, 78). Leone Hebreo [Jehuda Abarbanel] had probably finished his dialogues by 1503, but not until 1568 were they published in

Taking into account the exclusive focus on human love in the *Diana* and Montemayor's talent at copying popular ideas from the works of others that do not really harmonize ideologically with his own, one would expect to see a secularized and generally popularized version of Hebreo's Neoplatonism emerge, fragmented, in the pastoral narration, in keeping with "the time, the place, and the people speaking." At this juncture, it is also worth keeping in mind that Montemayor's most constant patron, the extravagant and rather childish Duke of Sessa, belonged to the Accademia degli Affidati di Pavia, founded during the era of the Italian literary academies characterized by less serious treatment of philosophical matters. This section of the *Diana* was surely written with people like the Duke in mind, not Hebreo or Ficino or Plato.[36]

Sireno begins by asking Felicia why, if love is born of reason, its effects are unreasonable. She responds saying that although indeed born of reason, thereafter it is not governed by it, rather by the extremism inherent in every experience of virtuous love (LD, 194–98). Second, Sylvano elaborates on the exaggerated effects of love on lovers in a discussion with Polydora. As she plays the role of the skeptic (Sophia in Hebreo's dialogue), he underscores the need to be in love in order to understand it and clarifies the fact that true love endures beyond the attainment of desire, unlike dishonest love, which ends with the satisfaction of appetite (LD, 199–201). At the conclusion of the exchange between Sylvano and Polydora, Montemayor abandons Hebreo's text.

In the third conversation, Belisa wonders how a lover could ever forget her or his living beloved, implicitly contrasting Sireno's and Selvagia's inconstant lovers with her own continued fidelity to the dead Arsileo.

Spanish, by the Jewish cabalist Gedalich ibn Jachjah (Venice). A 1584 translation by Hernando de Montesa was reprinted in 1593 (Zaragoza). The third, by Garcilaso de la Vega el Inca, was published in 1590 (Madrid) and has been the most widely reedited; see pp. 53–56 of José María Reyes Cano's edition of Hebreo's text. López Estrada transcribes from Garcilaso's translation (LD, 194–201). I use the photostat copy of the first Italian edition, Rome 1535, since it is likely the one to which Montemayor had access.

36. On the Duke's capricious personality and general irresponsibility, see Eugenio Mele and Narciso Alonso Cortés, *Sobre los amores de Gutierre de Cetina y su famoso madrigal*, 15–16. The Accademia to which he belonged is among those described in Willard F. King, *Prosa novelística y academias literarias en el siglo 17* and Michele Maylender, *Storia delle Accademie d'Italia*.

Cinthia responds, offering a very rational explanation of why people forget each other due to memory's limited capacity to endure across time. Hers is an elegant exposition that continues in Hebreo's tone and style exactly. Nonetheless, it flatly contradicts the definition of love as eternal found in the *Dialogues* (DA, 34r) and all truly Neoplatonic texts, a definition Montemayor eliminated as he borrowed from Hebreo's book. Cinthia's ideas were likely made up by Montemayor, since they rationally explain the very difficulties encountered by the lovers in the *Diana*. Thus, they confirm Felismena's earlier observation that Felis did not recognize her while she served as his page because his mind was elsewhere and his memory of her was worn. The natural tendency of lovers' constancy to waver during separation had also been observed by Selvagia, who said of Alanio, "and since being apart from me caused him to forget me, and Ysmenia's presence caused him to love her, he returned to his first love, leaving me tricked by mine" (y como el estar ausente de mí, le causasse olvido y la presencia de la su Ysmenia, grandíssimo amor, él bolvió a su pensamiento primero, y yo quedé burlada del mío, LD, 518). Montemayor is trying to explain, in an oblique and stylish fashion, how Diana could possibly have forgotten Sireno during his prolonged absence.

The matters confirmed by the company, then, are the extreme effects of love's unreasonable nature and the tendency of lovers to forget their beloveds during periods of separation. There is nothing exotic or philosophical about their remarks. Felicia is not an authority figure in this scene, nor are these expositions "her doctrine";[37] everyone except Selvagia and Felismena contributes something to the conversation, for the characters, like Montemayor's hermit Dileto, have already been enlightened by their experience and need no lessons in love. Any goal of love beyond reciprocal love itself is never discussed, nor are love's merits themselves presented. In a similar fashion, Montemayor's religious works never dwell on the benefits of Christ for humanity, before or after death, and never consider the reason why religious devotion is so important. As in the *Diana*, emphasis is on description of devotion's rules and how those rules are played out in human experience. There is virtually no mention of the value of love as an experience leading to awareness of an order beyond the mortal, in this or any of Montemayor's works, or of love as the contemplation of beauty that

---

37. Perry holds that it is, *Erotic Spirituality*, 82.

signals a higher ideal, the most basic of the Neoplatonic concepts. On the contrary, the material is limited to descriptive commentary about lovers' irrational behavior and the limited potential of human memory to endure across time. These are all themes that have been well established in the narration prior to their theoretical exposition in book four; nothing revealed about the nature of love here contradicts what the characters' own experience with it has proven.

The conspicuous presence of Hebreo's treatise in the *Diana* has beguiled scholars into defining Montemayor's book as "a presentation of love stories ruled by Neoplatonic principles" (una presentación de casos de amor regidos por principios neoplatónicos, NPE, 88). In this context, four issues take on substantial significance: the nature of Hebreo's treatise as a whole, the nature of the passage taken from it by Montemayor, the ways in which he modified it as he wrote it into his book, and the relationship of the borrowed material to the rest of the narration. Consideration of these problems reveals the questionable value of using Montemayor's recourse to Hebreo as evidence of the text's alliance to currents of humanistic thought, currents that are alien to the ideas expressed by its author in all his other writings and ultimately alien to what the text itself—including the quotations from Hebreo—says.

Leone Hebreo's dialogues are among the *trattati d'amore*, a wave of treatises written in positive response to the Florentine Academy's attempts to integrate the classical, Christian, and the medieval philosophical traditions. Although highly successful in Italy, the *Dialogues* were published only three times in Spain during the entire sixteenth century.[38] Chevalier contends that among the many readers of the *Diana*, there were very few who also read Hebreo's text with enthusiasm; the majority, he says, were interested in popular Neoplatonism. This popular Neoplatonism would have been the type set forth by the poet Pietro Bembo in book four of *The Courtier*, a nonphilosophical transmutation closely allied to medieval Neoplatonism and one which overlapped well with the cultural tradition of love that preceded humanism. For the smattering of philosophy that is indeed

---

38. In the introduction to his edition of the *Dialoghi*, Reyes lists thirteen Italian editions, published between 1535 and 1587 (52). The Spanish editions were mentioned in note 35. Treatises about love had a long-standing tradition in Italy well before the advent of the Florentine Academy. See Nesca A. Robb, *Neoplatonism of the Italian Renaissance*, chapter 6.

in it, Montemayor's book is more important as a manual of how to display familiarity with the philosophical concepts then in vogue than as a philosophical treatise, a characteristic it shares with Castiglione's treatise.[39]

Hebreo's ideas are fundamentally Neoplatonic, and thus "the central concern of the *Dialoghi d'amore* and of all its descendants" is "the refutation of dualism and the justification of universal unity." Further, "Leone identified man's highest goal as intellectual contemplation, withdrawal from the world, and delight in God's eternal ideas."[40] For his interest in contemplative experience and his use of the theme of withdrawal from the world, it is likely that Hebreo was an attractive source to a writer of Montemayor's inclinations. For his vision of the cosmos as an ordered, harmonious whole directed by a familiar and benevolent deity, for his consistent expression of the invaluable nature of knowledge acquired through purely intellectual pursuit, and for his delight in God's eternal ideas, he is at odds with the themes expressed by the Portuguese author in both his secular and religious works. In their common concern with the human spirit within the human body, they are kindred. The themes shared by Hebreo and Montemayor are also evident in the literature of Spanish Catholic reformist spirituality of the last quarter of the fifteenth century and the first half of the sixteenth: exaltation of the contemplative experience, interest in the workings of love, treatment of desire as a force operative on the soul in the temporal human condition, and withdrawal from the world.

In the final analysis, however, the philosopher and the fiction writer are radically distinct. Whereas Montemayor's focus is ever inward, dwelling on the self and the justification of one's ideas by one's own experiences, Hebreo's attention progresses inward, outward, and upward, rising to the

---

39. Chevalier, who does not mention Castiglione, thus calls the *Diana* a "courtly novel," apparently in reference to the social rank of its readers ("'La Diana' de Montemayor y su público en la España del siglo 16," 41–42).

40. Perry, *Erotic Spirituality,* 5–6. He describes Hebreo's enthusiasm for intellectual growth on p. 12; as indicated in chapter 1, Montemayor rejected intellectualism in favor of infused wisdom. Recourse to secondary sources is the most efficacious way to avoid extensive description of Hebreo's ideology, inappropriate here. Other insightful treatment of Hebreo's book is in Marcelino Menéndez Pelayo's *Historia de las ideas estéticas en España* (2:10–42), John Charles Nelson's *Renaissance Theory of Love: The Context of Giordano Bruno's Eroici Furori,* Robb's *Neoplatonism,* and Andrés Soria Olmedo's *Los* Dialoghi d'amore *de León Hebreo: Aspectos literarios y culturales.*

essential experience of transcendence beyond the self. Without this transcendence, scholars' so-called "Neoplatonism" is simply one form or another of spiritual love that happened to be represented in a text composed after the advent of Marcilio Ficino.

Aside from common spiritual themes, another, more unexpected alliance exists between Hebreo's text and a writer of Montemayor's tendencies: there is a large measure of courtly love incorporated into the *Dialogues* which too often goes unattended. Filone is the humble lover seeking to please the *belle dame sans merci*, Sophia, by suffering for her. He returns with marked insistence to his plan to see his desire gratified; Sophia aptly evades him. This interest in fulfillment in time, or in human history, is also present in the *Diana*, for the characters are moving toward a rewarding relationship with another person.[41]

As Perry and others point out, Hebreo's dialogues are part of an integrative tradition that encompasses and strives to reconcile philosophical currents from the Bible and classical times through Hebreo's age, as well as express his own ideas about the subject. Montemayor found in the passage he chose from the *Dialogues* an eloquent confirmation of some of his own long-standing beliefs about the ways of love, in a source it was becoming fashionable to quote as he wrote the *Diana;* what has been referred to as the "snob appeal" of Hebreo's text should not be ignored.[42] Such appeal would be particularly enticing to a writer like Montemayor, whose anxiety to feel himself accepted by the type of people for whom he wrote was apparently substantial. A talented interpreter of his readers' tastes, Montemayor was also quite adept at copying others' ideas without ever really integrating them into his own system of thought. One might recall, for example, his extensive use of Climacus ("Spiritual Dialogue"), his adaptations of Savonarola ("Devota exposición del salmo '*Miserere mei, Deus*'") and his "Pater Noster," and what Asensio calls his plagiarism of Lorenço de Cáceres ("Los trabajos de los

---

41. See "Sofia and Filone as Courtly Lovers," Perry, 29–31, and Soria Olmedo, "El marco de los *Dialoghi* y la conversación amorosa" in his *Los* Dialoghi d'amore *de León Hebreo*, 63–96. It should be noted that the concept of fulfillment in history, versus beyond it, is profoundly Judaic. Hebreo was a prominent Jew exiled from Spain after their expulsion in 1492; Montemayor's possible Jewish heritage has been mentioned. A general explanation of the concept of history in the context of Judaism may be found in Juston Smith, "Judaism."

42. The term is Nelson's (*Renaissance Theory of Love*, 74).

reyes").⁴³ All of these provide evidence of Montemayor's ability to try on the perspectives of others with great success, a trait also evident in the convincing nature of his female characters.

The passage cited from Hebreo's text in the *Diana* is a confirmation of the characters' experiences in ideological terms, proving that love is a virtuous, spiritual experience that induces people to irrational behavior. There is not another passage in the entire *Dialogues* more squarely aligned with prehumanistic attitudes about the topic. Montemayor picks up Hebreo's text just after the statement of its author's basic thesis: love is the desire for union with that which is held to be good, a definition nowhere to be found in the *Diana*. Further, he stopped copying just before Hebreo made a rational process out of love's unreasonable effects by subjecting them to a force he termed extraordinary reason.⁴⁴ Montemayor's care to avoid mentioning both love's transcendental nature and its reasonableness is perfectly consonant with his traditionalism, his fixation on human, earthly experiences, and his failure to perceive any open route of human access to the divine in his religious works. His selection from the *Dialogues* protects his belief in the irresolvable difference and distance between the human and the superhuman, and harmonizes with the limitation of human potential to strictly human problems observable in his writings as a whole.

Montemayor not only carefully selected from the *Dialogues* those few folios he used in the *Diana*, he also made changes in what text of Hebreo's he did use, modifying it to produce a passage faithful to his own vision of love as expressed in his pastoral narration.⁴⁵ Among the most significant alterations in the *Dialogues* text effected by Montemayor are those designed to contradict, not merely eliminate, the notion of human love as eternal, mentioned briefly above. Whereas Hebreo calls the wound of

---

43. Eugenio Asensio, "Lourenço de Cáceres y su tratado *Dos trabalhos do Rei* (con una nota sobre Jorge de Montemayor plagiario)."

44. Perry's insistence that pp. 195–98 of the *Diana* are about the theory of extraordinary reason (*Erotic Spirituality*, 81; 127 n.8) seems to have arisen from a hasty reading of the text, the same that gave rise to several inaccuracies in his otherwise perceptive reading (Coimbra is confused with Montemôr-o-Velho, 79, Belisa with Felismena, 83).

45. A complete comparison between the two texts is too lengthy to elaborate here. A careful comparison between the text of the *Diana*, 194–201, and Garcilaso's translation of Hebreo's *Dialoghi* provided by López Estrada in notes there, will reveal a series of changes, the most important of which are highlighted in what follows.

love's arrow "difficult to cure and very burdensome to heal" (difficile á curarsi & molto graue á sanare, DA, 33v), Felicia calls it "hard to cure and *very slow* to heal" (mala de curar y *muy tardía* en el sanar, LD, 196-97; this and following emphases added). Gone is Hebreo's next sentence describing love's wound: "To the one who observes it from the outside, it seems little, but considered from within it is very dangerous, and most of the time it becomes an *incurable tumor*" (Chi mira quel di fuore gli pare poco, ma secondo l'intrinseco è pericolosissima, & il piu de le uolte si conuerte in *fistola incurabile*, DA, 33v-34r). Hebreo's love is a profoundly Neoplatonic experience because it makes manifest a divine quality—eternalness—in human life. Montemayor's, on the contrary, does not. Hebreo goes on to explain, and Montemayor continues to eliminate, the metaphor of love as an arrow wound, impervious to the unstringing of the bow or the death of the archer.

These changes accomplish two ends. First, they prepare the way for Cinthia's convincing exposition on memory's fallibility, referred to above, which is set forth in Christian terms of the soul's three faculties (LD, 200-201).[46] Cinthia, unlike the others and unlike Hebreo, is not concerned with love itself rather with the effects of human nature on ideologically perfect desire. This is also Montemayor's central concern in the *Diana*. Like the quotation from Hebreo, her observations confirm what the characters' experiences with fallible lovers have made clear: love should indeed be well-intentioned, pure, and noble. That is no guarantee, however, that things will work out.

Love is not an isolated force in human experience, but one which must contend with the human condition, *fallax* or imperfect as it is.[47] In that

---

46. The concept of memory, will, and understanding as the three faculties of the soul originated in Augustine's *De trinitate*, to which Montemayor refers repeatedly in the first part of his "Diálogo spiritual" in that context (perhaps through Lombard's *Sententiae*, which often paraphrases Augustine's text). Cinthia's mention of them here is curious because she uses theological principles to explain an experience in human love and she, like Augustine, refers to the temporary nature of human memory. On the history of Augustine's ideas about the three faculties, see John K. Walsh, *El Coloquio de la Memoria, la Voluntad y el Entendimiento (Biblioteca Universitaria de Salamanca ms 1.763) y otras manifestaciones del tema en la literatura española*.

47. The word *fallax* was used by Melchor Cano to describe human experience in his censure of Bartolomé Carranza's 1558 *Comentarios sobre el Catechismo christiano*; see *supra*, 73.

condition, ideologically sound love is dependent on memory's power during periods of separation, a power that fades with distance from its source like a river (LD, 202). Unlike Hebreo, Montemayor deals with constancy in love, not eternalness, and they are two different principles. Eternal love is necessarily one that extends beyond the temporal limits of human life and must, therefore, be linked in some way to an extra-human force, the divine or nature, for example. In cannot be played out in human beings, whose lives on earth must necessarily come to an end.

The radical substitution of eternalness by constancy in love made by Montemayor is perfectly in keeping with his consistent focus on and limitation to human experience, as well as his conception of human nature as being relatively untouched by divine qualities. The fundamental Neoplatonic transcendence from the human to the divine is not only missing in this ideological exposition, it is replaced with Montemayor's poignant concern with human experience itself, untouched by the divine in any immediate way, imperfect, and problematic. His careful description of love in the world, not beyond it but subject to its ways, lays what looks like a philosophical foundation for what happens to several of the characters in the wake of their visit to Felicia's palace: they change their minds, or hearts.

Editing Hebreo's text for inclusion in his own, Montemayor systematically eliminated other divine qualities of human love on which the Neoplatonists founded their vision of universal harmony. One such trait is the identification of love with charity. Hebreo says, and Montemayor eliminates: "For loving is charity and should begin from love of oneself, which we do not do since we love others more than ourselves, nor is it a little" (Che l'amare è carità & da se medesimo debbe principiare, il che non facciamo, che amiamo piu altri che noi medesimi, ne questo è poco, DA, 33v). A concept as allied as this one is to Christian *charitas*, declared outright as *"Deus charitas est"* (1 John 4:8), would not have been eliminated by an Erasmist (or an illuminist). Montemayor may well have been reluctant to repeat it for that reason. Regardless, he avoids the religious connotations of the love-charity equation, precisely what Hebreo invokes, by leaving out the entire phrase and once again curtailing any transcendental quality of love for his characters, to insist on the human nature of their plights.[48] Not an Erasmist in any case, Montemayor may have found

48. Extremely curious in this light is Montemayor's parallel elimination of the

Hebreo's notion, that love of self should be the foundation for love of another ("da se medissimo debbe principiare"), was inconsistent with his own emphasis on love as a process of suffering and self-denial. He did include Hebreo's preceding sentence, which confirms this suffering quality in human desire: "for the one who loves well does not love himself, which is against all reason and equitableness" (per che quel che bene ama, se medisimo disama, il che è contra ogni ragione & deuere, DA, 33v).

Related to the disappearance of Hebreo's charitable love is a further deletion that removes yet another divine quality from human love, underscoring the immediacy of the experience Montemayor is describing and shortchanging the philosophical depth of the *Dialogues* as a source of the *Diana*. Hebreo says of love, represented by Cupid: "Because his mother Venus has beautiful eyes, he nonetheless desires what is beautiful [i.e., in spite of his blindness], and *reason judges a person to be beautiful, good, and kind, and from here love is born*" (Perche la madre Venere ha gl'occhi belli, però desidera il bello, *& la ragione guidica la persona bella, buona e amabile & di qui nasce l'amore*, 33v).[49] Felicia, however, says only: "And as his mother Venus has beautiful eyes, so he always desires what is the most beautiful" (Y como su madre Venus tiene los ojos hermosos, assí él dessea siempre lo *más* hermoso, LD, 196). This elimination, as well as the addition of the superlative, harmonizes with Montemayor's vision of love, which tends toward exaggeration and away from rational explanation of the mysterious.

Whereas the humanists made a moral experience out of affection in which goodness meant kindness, generosity, or uprightness, all of which they considered to be evidence of divine qualities in the human being, their predecessors in the European love tradition described it instead as a proving ground for feudal values such as fidelity, endurance, and valor on

---

phrase "God is charity" from his adaptation of Climacus's *Scala paradisi* in his "Diálogo spiritual." The 1540 Latin translation of the Greek text states "Charitas Deus Est" (CXCVIIIv), but in his "Diálogo," Montemayor begins his Spanish version of that section just *after* this declaration, thereby skirting the issue (178r). His reluctance to identify God with charity is in keeping with his tendency to describe the deity as awe-inspiring rather than loving and generous. His failure to include the phrase was not due to any potential danger of such an expression, for Luis de Granada's 1562 (post-*Index*) translation of Climacus's book reads "Dios es caridad" (*Escala*, 377b).

49. On blind Cupid in "Renaissance" iconography, see Edgar Wind, "Orpheus in Praise of Blind Love," in *Pagan Mysteries in the Renaissance*, 57–77.

the part of the lover, who appropriately cried for favor and mercy from the beloved. Hebreo departs from the medieval tradition by stressing moral over social values, and at the same time from Plato for his emphasis on goodness and beauty, not beauty alone, as the axis of the love experience. In the *Dialogues*, love is defined as the desire for union with what is held to be good; goodness is the essence of the spirit that links humanity with the divinity, which in turn is often made manifest through earthly beauty. The incorporeal dimensions of this theoretical love deserve attention in literary criticism: in study of love in general and of the Neoplatonic exaltation of beauty in particular, focus is all too often limited to the physical attributes of woman as the necessary vehicle that inspires the lover to contemplation of "greater" things, or to the erotic elements of the love experience, implied or stated.[50] As Fray Luis de León's poetry proves so well, Neoplatonism is founded on the idea that certain earthly spiritual, fundamentally sentimental, experiences reflect the divine, experiences by no means limited by or even related to feminine beauty. Further, Neoplatonic beauty reaches well beyond the confines of physical events and must transcend the physical state to be Neoplatonic, thereby surpassing mere spiritual love. Montemayor's book proves that human love need not be directed toward the divine to be spiritual, and neither must it necessarily be erotic to be human. The profundities of love as a sentimental experience, meaning a nonerotic spiritual one, must be contended with, at least in texts like his.

Whereas Hebreo is obsessed with the nature of Beauty and its relation to the divine, Montemayor does not deal with the problem of beauty at all.[51] The physical attributes of his fictional world, including his female characters, lack the philosophical depth of the Neoplatonic tradition and quietly echo the more absolute ideals of the medieval tradition. When beauty is observable, it is a constant in the natural world and in some women, and in both cases, it is extreme; thus he changed Hebreo's "persona bella" to "la más hermosa" in the passage just described. In the exaggerated and fixed characteristics attributed to beautiful things and people, Montemayor is true to the mode of romance, not to Neoplatonism, not to

---

50. Alexander Parker exemplifies the former; see *The Philosophy of Love in Spanish Literature, 1480–1680*, 42, 112, 133. For examples of the latter, see Whinnom, *La poesía amatoria de la época de los Reyes Católicos*, 25, and Ian Macpherson, "Secret Language in the Cancioneros: Some Courtly Codes."

51. On Hebreo, see Perry, *Erotic Spirituality*, 22–23.

Leone Hebreo, and certainly not to Plato.[52] Diana, Felismena, and Belisa are beautiful in the same way as is Amadís's beloved Oriana, stated but not described. Diana, for example, is she "whose beauty was most extremely above that of all the other women of her time" (cuya hermosura fué extremadíssima sobre todas las de su tiempo, LD, 7). In the *Diana*, beauty is unrelated to anything except the inexplicable behavior it inspires in those who are attracted by it.

The differences between Montemayor and Hebreo become increasingly stark as the meadow conversation continues. Hebreo's Filone expresses frankly that love between men and women, born of true knowledge and true judgment, is irreproachable and is no less virtuous than it is enjoyable: "I also think that the burning love and uncontrolled affection of man for woman is no less irreproachable than that of woman for man, provided it is born of true knowledge and a sincere judgment that find her worthy of being loved; this love is no less virtuous than it is pleasurable" (Dipoi non manco penso essere inreprensibile l'imfiammato amore & la sfrenata affettione de l'huomo à la donna che a quella de l'huomo, pur che nasca da uero conoscimento & uero giuditio che la giudichi essere degna d'essere amata, qual amore tiene non manco de l'honesto che del dilettabile, DA, 34v). Felicia, for her part, does not say that love is enjoyable at all, even in its purity. Instead, she adds that the beloved must be judged worthy "por solo sus virtudes," meaning for her virtues alone, that is, not for social or physical reasons. This repeats Sylvano's earlier preoccupation with honor as a quality dependent only on individual merit. Not allowing that love is enjoyable, she does find that it is neither illicit nor impure because it ideally seeks nothing but the privilege of loving: "It seeks no other end except to love the other person for her or himself, without expecting other payment or reward for loving" (no tira a otro fin, sino querer la persona por ella misma, sin esperar otro interesse ni galardón de sus amores, LD, 198). Such idealism comes directly from the medieval secular and religious tradition of love, with its accompanying lexicon. In a similar fashion, Luis de Granada describes one of the supreme Christian virtues as: "doing all that we may do purely for the love of God, without

---

52. In the introduction to his edition of the *Diana*, Enrique Moreno Báez elaborates at length on Platonism itself as preparation to read Montemayor's book. David H. Darst considers the text in light of what he calls "Renaissance Platonism and the Spanish Pastoral Novel."

mixing in any interest or condition" (haciendo todo lo que hiciéremos puramente por amor de Dios, sin mezcla de otro interese ni respecto, LdO, 14).

Selflessness was one of the fundamental qualities of love for those who proposed to imitate Christ, and it was likewise one of the most exalted virtues of the Catholic reformists, an ideal whose literary expression culminated in the beautiful, anonymous sonnet "No me mueve, mi Dios, para quererte" (Heaven moves me not to love you, Lord).[53] The history of the relationship between selfless love as it appeared in the context of courtly love and in the *imitatio Christi* religious movements is an extremely complex issue. Without straying from the problem at hand, it can be affirmed that Montemayor inherited the notion of love as a suffering experience of self-denial from both traditions, and the two found a context for simultaneous expression here in the *Diana*. Equally certain is that the humanists and the Neoplatonists approached the love experience from a much more positive point of view, as Hebreo's text indicates.

There is no doubt that Montemayor was attracted to the selfless ideal; it is supremely Christian and represents perfectly the attitude of submission and denial to which his works demonstrate a constant attraction. Further, selfless love may not have precluded the desire to see one's love returned. Luis de Granada describes Christ's love for humanity and concludes, "Nothing declares more the presence of love than the desire to be loved" (No hay cosa que más declare el amor, que el desear ser amado, LdO, 28). In a similar passage, Selvagia had recognized the same natural tendency of lovers toward fulfillment when she declared in book one: "there is no greater sign that a person loves all she can than to want to be loved by the one to whom her freedom has been surrendered" (no ay mayor señal de una persona, querer todo lo que puede, que dessear ser querida de aquel a quien a entregado su libertad, LD, 45). It would seem that selfless love as it was understood by Montemayor allowed for desire to be loved in return, provided that reciprocality was not a requisite for the giving of love itself, as Christ desired to be loved, but loved others unconditionally.

Whether this is the case or not, it is with the concept of love's being human and truly selfless at the same time that the characters of the *Diana*

---

53. On the poem, see Marcel Bataillon's article "El anónimo del soneto 'No me mueve, mi Dios, para quererte.'"

run into difficulties. Although "disinterested," meaning that sexual or social compensation is not expected as part of the courtship process, they are not selfless in the broad or divine sense of the word: all of them expect to see their love returned, however spiritually, because if they did not, none of them would be in the state of distress they are in when they appear or the narration finds them.[54] At the time they join Felicia, all of them are still confirmed selfless lovers, in that they have not made return of their love a condition for that love's existence. However, most of them have observed that love in the world tends to give way to time and fortune and are tottering on the limits of their selflessness just when they arrive at the palace. Their desire for a mutually satisfying relationship with another person challenges their love for those married to someone else or otherwise absent. That same desire, so true to human nature and so untrue to ideal love, distinguishes them from both courtly lovers and Christ the lover. It is their need to find happiness with another person that constitutes their stories, which develop in time and not out of it; it is also what draws their desires to earth, not to heaven.

Montemayor's careful selection from Hebreo's text and his adaptation of it outlines clearly his ideology of love. Like religious experience, human affection consists of a series of trials which the individual must endure in order to proceed to happiness or grace, and, in all cases, emphasis is on the trials, not on what they earn. Virtually every love experience presented in the *Diana* is described as *"trabajos"* (trials) and is referred to as *"mi mal"* (my malady or what is bad for me), typically in antithesis to *"mi bien"* (what is good for me). Thus Sireno says of his love's beginnings, "for the good I experienced then was the beginning of the bad which I suffer now" (pues el bien que entonces passé, fué principio del mal que ahora padesco, LD, 12); Felismena says of Felis, "I began to love him well and at the expense of my pain I did begin it, since it was to be the cause of so much misfortune" (yo comencé a querelle bien y por mi mal lo comencé pues avía de ser causa de tanta desventura, LD, 103).[55] Felicia emphasizes the

---

54. The argument put forth here that the *Diana* represents a conflict between the characters' selfless ideal and less than selfless actions is at odds with López Estrada's belief: "they love love itself, without any hope of favor" (LD, LXXVIII).

55. For a sampling of Montemayor's constant use of the words "trabajos" and "mal" referent to love in the *Diana*, see pp. 19, 50, 129, 171, 222, 224, 261, 280, 284; 12, 20, 100, 137, 155, 225, 262.

indisputable need to bear love's difficulties when she encourages Felismena to be of good cheer, since although she may have undergone some trials, nothing can be attained without them ("no ay cosa que sin ellos alcançar se pueda," LD, 163). Granada recognizes the same nature of human existence, saying, "Since this life is a journey, its trials cannot be avoided until such time as we go to the place of rest" (Pues como esta vida sea camino, no se puede en ella excusar trabajos, hasta que vamos al lugar de los descansos, *Guía*, 295).

This suffering is undertaken gladly and selflessly, but however spiritual the goal of reciprocal love may be, fulfillment is still the end to which the trials would lead, if the system functioned perfectly. What the characters have found, however, is what the narrative voice of Montemayor's religious works laments as well: life does not always bring just rewards to those who deserve them. They are all in this position, the ideological soundness of their love proven by their discussion of love's ideals, when they are turned over to Felicia for a remedy to the injustice, not of love, but of life. At the conclusion of their meadow conversation, the company listens to Felicia's promise to speed up time for them and hasten the day when their fortunes would have changed regardless: "It would not be little cruelty to leave the remedy of one so in need of it to such a slow means as time" (No sería pequeña crueldad poner yo el remedio de quien tanto lo a menester, en manos de medio tan espacioso como es el tiempo, LD, 203). This reinforces Cinthia's previous direct association between Felicia and time when she said to Belisa: "And to think, lovely shepherdess, that time would not cure your pain if you were to leave its remedy in the hands of the wise Felicia, would be a great mistake" (Y pensar tú, hermosa pastora, que el tiempo no curaría tu mal, si dexasses el remedio dél en manos de la sabia Felicia, será muy gran engaño, LD, 202).

The tale of "El Abencerraje" was inserted at the end of book four in many editions of the *Diana* printed after 1561, the final year in which Montemayor made changes in the text before his death. Given his proclivity to adapt materials of other writers to his own style and taste, it is not far-fetched to posit the thesis that the version, if not the story itself, was his own, as was the idea to include it in his book.[56] The regular appearance in

---

56. Jarifa does dwell on the fact that she is acting against the will of her father in loving Abindaráez, which would be in keeping with Montemayor's persistent expression of that theme (LD, 216). José Navarro Gómez presents evidence to support his

the *Diana* of themes from romance fiction and chivalry, as well as its structure designed to incorporate interpolated materials, accommodated the addition comfortably. The "Abencerraje" was surely an attractive addition to an already pleasantly varied book for sixteenth-century readers. The story is told by Felismena just before the characters retire to their rooms for the evening, providing a further distraction for the lovers.

Book Five

Book five, unlike those preceding it, contains four separate parts and marks the disintegration of the two narrative planes that had been balanced throughout the first three books. The restructuring of the narration is indicative of the restructuring of the characters' lives as they go forth from the palace and begin to interact with each other and with new characters. The first narrative plane splits as the characters leave Felicia's domain, following three dispersed sets of characters, not one group that is gathered. After the initial scene of magical resolution, the modal sequence alternates between scenes of romance and of pastoral: first comes Felismena's happening upon Arsileo; then the life of Sireno, Sylvano, and Selvagia in the old *locus amoenus*, where Diana appears; finally, the reunion of Arsileo and Belisa, who return to Felicia's palace. Book five thus narrates a circle that tells of the characters' departure from the palace and the return of two of them to it, introducing the theme of the cycle structurally, as a complement to the way it is presented thematically.

Time, as if befuddled by Felicia's meddling, takes on repetitive and irregular dimensions and is set back twice as the narrator attempts to keep track of everyone simultaneously, even though they are in different places. Appropriately, only those characters who return to the *locus amoenus* engage in contemplative remembrance; Belisa and Felismena never return there and are not recycled into its suspended time. To manipulate the greatly augmented amount of action retold in the final three books, the narrator steps out of his invisible omnipotence and begins to overtly manipulate what is told, when, and how.

---

belief that the author was Montemayor himself ("El autor de la versión del *Abencerraje* contenido en la *Diana*, ¿era Montemayor?"). Eugenia Fosalba Vela provides further proof in *El Abencerraje pastoril: estudio y edición crítica*; see also Francisco López Estrada's *El Abencerraje y la hermosa Jarifa: Cuatro textos y su estudio.*

The book begins the morning after book four ended, with Felicia acting in accordance with her wisdom and dispensing the appropriate cures to those lovers whose situations leave them no alternatives. She administers magic water to Sireno, Sylvano, and Selvagia (the ones whose beloveds are married) putting them into a profound sleep that will last as long as she desires ("todo el tiempo que yo quisiere," LD, 224). As she awakens each one with a tap on the head with a book, symbolizing intelligence, it becomes apparent that they have accomplished the changes in their sentimental lives that they would have experienced over a prolonged period of time: Sireno claims to have forgotten Diana and speaks of his indifference to her, Sylvano and Selvagia are madly in love with each other. Critics tend to find that Felicia's intervention restores reasoning power to the characters, without directly referring to the book used to arouse them from their slumber.[57] At no time in the text is reference made to that restored reason, however, and the delight in unreasonable love found in Montemayor's works as a whole calls such a conclusion into question. At most a douse of the common sense or intellect to which Felicia refers directly later, the book complements her actions, which simply speed up time.

Felicia's potion, Montemayor's *deux ex machina*, is true to the mode of romance, for it is a material manifestation of the characters' desires. Having earned access to it by overcoming trials, they are given what they want in liquid form by a character whose power over time is greater than theirs. Felicia's magic water lowers mythical powers to earth in a well-established fashion; as López Estrada has indicated, the waters of forgetfulness were a popular concept of medieval science (LD). Rather than refer to this curing process as "Montemayor's mistake" (NPE, 90), one might affirm instead sixteenth-century readers' delight with just such direct intervention of the supernatural in the human world, especially blended as this one is with motifs of romance and literary chivalry, charged with non-literal meaning. (Twentieth-century gusto for the same ruses takes different forms, but does not alter the basic romance mechanism.)[58] One need not

---

57. For example, J. Jones, "'Human Time' in the *Diana*," 146.
58. Ruth El Saffar and Edwin C. Riley eloquently defend the charm of romance in Western civilization, successfully pointing to our own susceptibility to contemporary versions of just such subterfuges as Felicia and her potion were in the sixteenth century ("The Truth of the Matter" and "'Romance' y novela en Cervantes," respectively).

assume that Montemayor's original readers were so naïve as to not recognize either the symbolic value of the water and the book or the suggestions in Montemayor's text indicating that Felicia's elixir only makes manifest the changes toward which the characters had been moving all along.

The remarkable thing about Felicia's potion is exactly what it does to the three characters who take it, which is allow them to step outside the dictates of constancy in love necessary to enter the palace. What Frederick de Armas says is true; Felicia is indeed "intent on rewarding constancy and chastity," since this is prescriptive fiction, after all.[59] Further analysis of the point, however, reveals a fundamental irony in Montemayor's book: how she does the rewarding is by encouraging the lovers to pair with those whom they can marry, which in the end is a break with the ideal of chastity, as well as constancy, in the cases of some. In a return visit, none of those whom Felicia has helped could pass under the Arch of the Faithful (one supposes they enter through the back door when they return for their weddings in book seven). This would seem to put the narrator's tongue firmly in his cheek when he observes that Selvagia and Sylvano confirmed their love "so great between them that only death was enough to end it" (tan grande entre sí que sola la muerte bastó para acaballe, LD, 228). Both of them had previously sworn to love someone else until they died (Selvagia, 43, 45; Sylvano, 70).

Given this undeniable evidence of love's unstable nature and the unfavorable light in which marriage is described in the text, one cannot but wonder if Felicia, that is, Montemayor, is making a joke when she insists "El fin de vuestros amores será quando por matrimonio, cada uno se ajunte con quien dessea" (LD, 229), since "fin" means both "goal" and "end"; thus, "The goal (the end) of your loves will be when each of you is joined with your beloved in matrimony." In any case, the effect of Felicia's potion confirms what the characters have been saying about time since book one; even the obstinate Sylvano had stated there, "I knew that time was a proven physician for the pain that separation usually causes" (Yo

---

Further, what were perceived as verisimilar events in the sixteenth century are far removed from our own: Luis de Granada talks about dragons with all seriousness in the *Introducción al símbolo de la fe*, ed. Barcells, 139, 151. Antonio de Torquemada's *Jardín de flores curiosas* is replete with similar distinctions.

59. "Las tres Dianas de Montemayor," 350.

sabía ser el tiempo un médico muy aprovado para el mal que la ausencia suele causar, LD, 23).

The manner in which Felicia dispenses her magic is inconsistent, however, and as such, disappointing to the reader expecting a tidy resolution to be doled out to all. For those characters whose original lovers are inaccessible because of marriage to someone else (Sireno, Sylvano, and Selvagia), she alters the dimension of time. The others (Felismena and Belisa) are offered no assistance whatsoever beyond a few consoling remarks, and instead are directed away from the supernatural, back into the normal course of life, in the context of which their problems will indeed be worked out, in time itself. None of these solutions are interventionist in essence and, although they appear to be magical, there is nothing extraordinary about them beyond the fantastic environment in which they are offered. The characters, at this point proven lovers worthy of entrance into the realm beyond the human, are not allowed to transgress the essential limits of their humanity, but instead are recycled back into it. This is fundamentally the same process described in Montemayor's "Spiritual Dialogue," where the deserving righteous attain the gates of heaven but are not permitted contact with the divine because of the limitations imposed on them by the human condition, which only death can overcome (*supra* 98). Thus the entire structure of Montemayor's pastoral narration reflects the ideological foundation revealed in his religious works, in which the human and the divine operate in two distinct realms: the characters' problems are described, they are led toward supernatural resolution but denied it, and then returned to their earthly reality for whatever time might bring.

By 1605, Cervantes's character Pero Pérez was censuring "all that business about the wise Felicia and the enchanted water" (DQ, 1:118). Still, Cervantes presents his characters Cardenio, Dorotea, Fernando, and Luscinda with much the same problems that Montemayor's had, and orchestrates a solution for them that is structurally similar to Montemayor's. Rather than at a splendid allegorical palace, however, Cervantes's men and women meet at an uncomfortable roadside inn; rather than listen to the song of an enchanted Orpheus there, they listen to the reading of a story manuscript (DQ, 1, chs. 33–35). The herding of all the appropriate characters to the same inn on the same day is accomplished by a careful narrator and "heaven, by way of unusual paths unknown to us" (DQ, 1:374). It constitutes a resolution almost as unlikely as the apparition of Felicia and her spells, if much less self-conscious. Nonetheless, Cervantes's solution is an impossibility of degree, whereas Montemayor's is one of kind, and hence the priest's criticism of it in *Don Quijote*.

At Felicia's palace, the day of the cures passes quickly and without further event, indicative of the faster general pace of time outside the pastoral environment in the final books. The next morning, Selvagia accompanies her betrothed and Sireno back to the riverbanks of the Ezla, signalling her incorporation into a time and space to which she did not originally belong. Appropriately, Selvagia will be accommodated with some discomfort therein. The *locus amoenus*, suspended in time, adapts badly to changes such as permanent modifications in its list of inhabitants. Although she adjusts with relative ease, having been a shepherdess somewhere else, she and her story are from a time and place beyond its limits, and it is impossible for her to be integrated into the past ruling over it like another magic spell, a past in which she had no role.

Felismena, dressed again as a shepherdess, sets off to continue the further trials ordered for her by Felicia, and the narration follows her as she goes. Since her adventures take place in the first narrative plane, involve considerable action, and represent an aggressive pursuit of a goal, she cannot return to the *locus amoenus* and so heads west. On her way, she happens upon Belisa's beloved Arsileo, alive, recounting his story to the shepherdess Amarílida, who has joined him inside his hut.

Arsileo's abode is a mirror image of Belisa's lonely isolation after she thought she had lost him; he has taken up residence there after an unsuccessful search for her. Protesting against Amarílida's attempts to have him retell his story, he repeats the exaggerated terms that Belisa had used with her visitors. In the song Amarílida convinces him to sing, there appears the motif with which the *Diana* is to end, the cyclical nature of life, and with it, love: "A calm usually follows the storm," he sings (Venir suele bonança tras fortuna, LD, 233).[60] He asks, "Is it possible that . . . after so many trials I had to realize such supreme repose?" (¿es posible que . . . después de tantos trabajos me avía de suceder tan soberano descanso? LD, 237).

---

60. Cf. Garcilaso's Soneto 4, v. 8: "for a calm usually follows the storm" (que tras fortuna suele haber bonanza). See Herrera's commentary for other versions of the cyclic nature of fortune (Gallego Morell, *Garcilaso de la Vega y sus comentaristas*, 324). J. Jones observes of the *Diana*, "Time is the destroyer of happiness, but it is also the healer of wounds" (145).

Arsileo's role as a speaking character indicates his status as one of Montemayor's noble lovers who, having been unjustly wronged, has undergone considerable torment for the sake of his pure affection. Those lovers who commit wrong themselves, Selvagia's Alanio and Felismena's Felis, are never given the chance to voice their experiences or opinions. The one exception, as she is the exception to many regularities in the book, is Diana. By telling the tale that follows, Arsileo exemplifies what Diana does not: a lover who can provide another version of a story already told, one in which he exculpates himself from all blame for the misfortunes of which that story tells.

Felismena listens as Arsileo recalls how the evil magician Alfeo, jealous over Belisa's devotion to her young lover, conjured up two spirits who acted out the deaths of Arsenio and his son in hopes of making Belisa kill herself in despair or flee, which she did. Alfeo is Felicia's counterpart and, whereas she embodies benevolent reinforcement of life and moving time, he represents the malevolent intervention of destruction and death. Felismena joins the pair, identifies herself, and tells Arsileo where to find Belisa. This constitutes her helpful intervention in others' love problems, part of the mission with which Felicia had charged her when she left the palace; she had departed "advised about what she was supposed to do in great detail" (muy particularmente avisada de lo que avía de hazer, LD, 229).[61] Her gregarious behavior is typical of the interaction between the characters that began with the pairing of Selvagia and Sylvano. The narrator leaves the two shepherdesses together and Arsileo on his way to find Belisa at Felicia's palace, and moves abruptly back to the *locus amoenus*.

Appropriately for their environment, Sireno, Sylvano, and Selvagia are rejoined in the narrative present doing exactly the same things they did before their visit with Felicia, with minor modifications; the *locus amoenus* does not serve for passing time, rather for its suspension, and thus they are contemplating their situations. Sylvano observes that to be loveless, as is Sireno, is worse than suffering anything else. In a literary sense he could

---

61. It was perhaps Felismena's minimal role in the solution of two love dilemmas that led de Armas to propose that she actually represents the goddess Diana in the narration ("Las tres Dianas"). However, she never directly intervenes in anyone's relationship. Her determined pursuit of a man, moreover, is at odds with this thesis, and her skill at arms, versus hunting, would seem to ally her more with Minerva, her patron goddess.

not be more right, for Sireno, were he truly indifferent, would be without any interest as a character. Sireno observes that their perspectives have changed, and that this in itself is reason for caution. Consequently, he warns the new couple against indiscriminate happiness: "I assure you that fortune is not neglecting to temper the happiness you are enjoying with your loves" (yo te asseguro que la fortuna no se descuyde de templaros el contento que recebís con vuestros amores, LD, 239). Having once been in love as they are, Sireno is especially sensitive to its dangers. He repeats his warning, in the poignant tone that remains constant throughout the final three books of the *Diana:* "Oh Selvagia! I too have seen myself loved as much as anyone can be and as much without thought of seeing the end of my love as you both are now. But let no one tally an account without reckoning in fortune, nor lay a foundation without considering the changes of the times" (¡Ay Selvagia! que yo me he visto también querido quanto nadie puede verse y tan sin pensamiento de ver fin a mis amores, como vosotros lo estáis aora. Mas nadie haga cuenta sin la fortuna, ni fundamento sin considerar las mudanças de los tiempos, LD, 239). In Montemayor's world, the one in which experience is the best teacher, Sireno has learned the right lesson, that life is constant change, and in it love is subject to time and fortune. That lesson is underscored by the pair to whom he delivers his reminder, since they both exemplify human love's mutability.

As the sun sets, Diana appears for the first time in the narration, singing of her unlucky birth, life, and marriage. She reveals her version of what happened with Sireno, which differs from his: forced by her father to marry Delio, she put him out of her mind ("puse a Sireno en olvido," LD, 241), in accordance with her obligations.

What seems like a narrative inconsistency, or contradictory points of view, dissipates into human disagreement in light of information presented in Montemayor's third eclogue. This narrative poem would make an excellent appendix to the *Diana,* for in it the central themes of his pastoral narration are developed in some detail. For that eclogue, three pairs of lovers simultaneously represent the three stages of Sireno's relationship with Diana: Marfida and Lusitano are new lovers suffering the first pains of separation; Diana and Sireno portray the long-separated couple whose confidence begins to falter; Floriano and Felisa are those whose relationship was destroyed by Felisa's father marrying her to another shepherd, who is described as wealthier than Floriano but less worthy of Felisa (as the *Diana*'s namesake has a rich but inferior husband). Importantly, Diana in the eclogue, anxiously awaiting Sireno's return from a prolonged absence, reveals that he is long overdue, and she has no explanation for his delay (vv. 406-12; SC, 211v; GP, 471). The splintering of one relationship into three parts accomplished in the poem allows a more complete understanding of the situation's problematic nature, which is only partially revealed in the *Diana*. The eclogue's highlighting of the subtler misunderstandings in the Diana-Sireno relationship is lightly reinforced in the pastoral narration, because therein the narrator does not allow Diana's version to stand on her testimony alone: Selvagia had introduced and supported the same story before Diana joined her friends (LD, 244). The difference of opinion between the two main characters is never resolved, an unsatisfying lack of ending that is untrue to the mode of romance, but faithfully representative of human relationships and true to pastoral suspension.

This occasion in book five is the first time Diana sees Sireno after his return to the *locus amoenus* and after her unhappy marriage. The two immediately begin to quibble over which one of them loved the other less. Their disquieting exchange, uncharacteristic of the literary modes of romance and pastoral alike, ends with Sireno rather spitefully wishing Diana all the happiness she took from him, after which the four return to their village.[62] Sireno's supposed indifference wears thin as soon as Diana reappears and his melancholy loneliness—a literary posture—sharpens into an angry resentment that is truer to nonliterary reality. Although some of the content of this section is unpoetic, it is in eclogue form, closing at sunset with the pastoral complaints suspended until the narrator should find the characters again.

"Well, getting back to Arsileo" (Pues volviendo a Arsileo) begins the fourth and final section of book five, snatching the reader away from the

---

62. Again, there is considerable redundancy between the *Diana* and Montemayor's 1558 *Segundo cancionero*. The sonnet "Dejóme mi temor y en tal estado" (My fear left me in and in such a state) describes the narrator's experiencing the sad confirmation of the betrayal he had long feared would happen during his absence. The tercets begin, "may your new company give you the happiness / that you have robbed from me" (La nueva compañía os dé el contento / que vos me habéis robado, SC, 80v-81r; GP, 410). In the *Diana*, Sireno says, "May God ever grant you as much happiness, lovely Diana, as you once took away from me" (plega a Dios, hermosa Diana, que siempre te dé tanto contento, quanto en algún tiempo me quitaste, LD, 246).

locus amoenus and back in time. This last episode of the book proceeds quickly through Arsileo's approach to Felicia's palace, his meeting with Polydora, and his review with her of what the narrator smartly calls "everything else that had happened to their love up until then, as I have said above" (todo lo demás que destos amores hasta entonces avía sucedido de la manera que atrás lo he contado, LD, 249). As the nymph scampers off to find Belisa, Arsileo sings as he waits, voicing more strongly than the last time the theme of fortune's inevitable movement, the same idea Sireno had used to warn Sylvano and Selvagia not to overindulge in their happiness. Arsileo sings, "Now love and fortune take a turn" (Ya dan buelta el amor y la fortuna, LD, 250). His second song continues with the theme:

> What times, what movements
> what very strange roads,
> what illusions, what disillusions,
> what great happiness
> were born of so many pains!
> . . . .
> You tend, fortune, to move
> with swift movement
> . . . .
> come, fortune, come and stay.
>
> (¡Qué tiempos, qué movimientos,
> qué caminos tan extraños,
> qué engaños, qué desengaños,
> qué grandes contentamientos
> nacieron de tantos daños!
> . . . .
> Sueles, ventura, moverte
> con ligero movimiento
> . . . .
> ven, ventura, ven y tura.)
> (LD, 255–56)

His repeated references to bad fortune's eventual turning over to good foreshadow the happy endings to which he, Belisa, and Felismena are headed.

Belisa arrives with Polydora and, upon seeing Arsileo, is left as speechless as the narrator ("It would be impossible to know how to say it" [sería imposible sabello dezir] LD, 256). Arsileo continues his addresses to fortune, giving thanks for the happy resolution of their love and, in tones again reminiscent of Sireno's warning of caution to Sylvano and Selvagia, asks that his happiness be tempered so as not to tempt fortune to strike a compensating blow with a vengeance (LD, 257). He is doing what Sireno advised, "reckoning with fortune as he tallies his account" in life.

The same day that had ended earlier with the shepherds' and shepherdesses' return to their village ends again as the threesome return to Felicia's palace. On the way, Arsileo relates how his father had retreated from the world, leaving the reunited couple's problems solved. Importantly, Belisa and Arsileo return to the world of fantasy, not to the *locus amoenus;* the former draws them back to it by its association with resolution, whereas the latter served them for descriptive recollection of the problem that no longer exists, and is therefore no longer an appropriate place for them.

Book Six

The sixth book opens with a second temporal regression to the afternoon of the day that had ended twice in book five, returning to Felismena and Amarílida. No longer enclosed within the *locus amoenus* or the fantasy world of Felicia's palace, the characters display personalities truer to life than they had in either literary environment. Accordingly, they take on a more matter-of-fact attitude toward love and life. Whereas the natural setting of books one to three was an idealized locale described with some minor references to Spanish geography, in books five to seven the scenes occur in specific places that are wistfully described by the narrator. Likewise, whereas in the early books the characters were rigidly controlled by pastoral decorum, in the latter ones they are decidedly less idealized representations of human beings. Freed from form and yet positively affected by their immersion in the pastoral, the major characters become more human in their approaches to emotional trauma. As new characters are introduced, they outline sections of their pasts briefly, in a manner more in keeping with realistic conversational limits than with narrative for its own sake. The second narrative plane never recovers the extension it had in the first three books, for storytelling has ceased to be an isolated activity with literary ends and has moved toward integration into the narrative whole which more closely resembles the life experience.[63]

63. The similarity between this structural difference and the changes Cervantes

Book six begins with Felismena and Amarílida chatting when they are found by Filemón, whom Amarílida has rejected after an initial period of mutual affection. Felismena listens as the lover explains his dilemma to Amarílida: believing she loved Arsileo, he committed the ultimate indiscretion in love, publicizing what he thought was her affection for the stranger and unfaithfulness to her own relationship with him. Consequently, he damaged her reputation as a flawless lover, and this, she says, "is the cause for my love toward Filemón having grown cold" (es la causa de yo me aver resfriado del amor que a Filemón tenía, LD, 263). In keeping with Montemayor's focus on love as a question of constancy, Filemón refers twice to Amarílida's goodness as that which he offended by not believing in her, clearly using the word to mean her fidelity (LD, 263, 264). Without Felismena's intervening directly in their conversation, the two are reconciled, and she goes on her way.

The problems between this pair, presented simply and resolved rapidly, mark Amarílida and Filemón as two lovers reacting to strictly emotional problems that occur in normal relationships between people. Nothing stands in the way of their happiness except their own mistaken perceptions of other people's actions and motives, fallible perceptions subject to multiple interpretations (as were Diana's and Belisa's, as would be those of Gil Polo's shepherdess Alcida and Lope's shepherd Anfriso). No economic or social factors intervene between these two, no physical distance nor ideological need for disdain or adoration. Only the problematic nature of humanity hinders their affection, in this case Filemón's jealousy. These two are pastoral characters relieved of the excess baggage of pastoral form, leaving sensitive, believable human beings whose personalities are defined by their inner lives and past experiences.

This is a pastoral-like episode that takes place outside the *locus amoenus*. It presents a love problem that emerged in the past, which is explained by one of the lovers to a sympathetic listener. However, the moment at which the problem is addressed allows the characters to resolve their difficulties before it is too late, before each of them is reduced to melancholy recollection of what once was between them. Since there is no temporal distance

---

self-consciously made in the second part of *Don Quijote* is noteworthy. The narrator (or the translator, for it could be either) comments that therein Cide Hamete inserted no stories as in Part One, but instead included only episodes, "born of the very events that the truth offers" (nacidos de los mesmos sucesos que la verdad ofrece, DQ, 2:366).

between their conflict and the narrative present, there is no need for extensive lament or contemplation, only brief recollection followed by description of their positions, on the basis of which their reconciliation is made.

With the episode between Amarílida and Filemón, the pastoral concept is successfully integrated into the world beyond the pastoral enclosure, taking its positive values with it (attention to inner experience, the stopping of activity to remember and talk about feelings), leaving its temporal and geographical suspension behind with its self-conscious didacticism. As Felismena encounters disagreeing lovers in her travels, it becomes apparent that the *locus amoenus* around the banks of the Ezla is not the only place where people have love problems in need of resolution. Further, it is made clear that a visit to Felicia's palace is not necessary to resolve them. Likewise, the literary environments of the pastoral episodes and the palace are replaced with more realistic geographical space, so Felismena takes the place of Felicia in witnessing lovers' frank assessment of their situations. She observes them as they accept the past and move on rather than remaining locked within it, a lesson that will serve her well when she again sees Felis.

As the *Diana* reaches its final books, the pastoral anecdote, which provides a time and place for lovers to confront one another and express desire, is depicted as a multiple entity, a state of mind that pertains to people rather than a single, idealized place. It has become a function of the non-native pastoral characters' mentality and activities, not their environment. Indeed, the idea is strongly implied here that one must leave the *locus amoenus* in order to escape permanent residence in the past; that idea is confirmed by the inability of the native shepherdesses and shepherds to ever overcome the dilemmas they faced when the *Diana* began.[64]

Book six ends with one parting and highly significant glance at the main characters who have returned to the *locus amoenus*. In true pastoral fashion, they are found there, living in a world in which time is indefinite ("they were spending their lives," the narrator says of them [pasavan la vida], LD, 265). The pastoral existence of Sireno, Sylvano, Selvagia, and

---

64. This broadened application of the pastoral anecdote opened the door for Cervantes to pick up the development where Montemayor left it. One of the conclusions reached in the *Galatea* is that the pastoral impulse, the need to reflect on desire for happiness and the difficulties in carrying it out, is something that the human spirit carries within itself and pertains intimately to that spirit, not to a specific, isolated place. See Rhodes, "Sixteenth-century Pastoral Books, Narrative Structure, and *La Galatea* of Cervantes."

Diana provides a sharp contrast to the other characters carrying on their lives outside it, for the latter's temporal existence is quicker and more defined. On one of those undefined days around the riverbanks, Diana joins Sylvano and Selvagia for an afternoon rest. There, it is obvious that Sylvano cannot break the association he makes between Sireno and Diana, for upon her arrival he immediately asks her why she does not ask where her former lover is, and immediately after he refers to "your Sireno" (el tu Sireno) speaking to her (LD, 266, 272). Diana repeats what has now become the central issue of the book named after her: "Time cures infinite things that, to the individual, appear to have no remedy" (el tiempo cura infinitas cosas que a la persona le parecen sin remedio, LD, 266). A typical pastoral character, she refers to her need to wait out her problems in hopes of better days, her good days having past.

It is in this episode that the narrator's malice toward Diana, latent in the entire book until this point, becomes apparent, as does the overriding affection she provokes in her former lover. This inconsistency is neither surprising nor inappropriate; Montemayor's eclogues and poetry tell the same story time and time again, and his ability to distance himself from the situation was apparently limited. The ambiguous sentiment toward Diana felt by the author is expressed by the characters as well, who refer to her beauty and change of heart from various points of view. When speaking for herself, she defends her position eloquently and provokes sympathy, but when the narrator speaks about her, it is with a vengeance. Montemayor's talents at adapting various points of view are nowhere more apparent than here. The narrator explains, for example, that Diana resented Sylvano's falling in love with Selvagia more than Sireno's forgetting her (LD, 267) because whereas the latter meant only omission, the former meant rejection, thereby accusing her of a pettiness that is not supported by anything she says herself.[65]

Once Diana appears, Sylvano is drawn irrevocably toward the past and his own former love for her; he confesses that he will never forget her, even

---

65. This same pettiness, however, is indeed demonstrated by the poetic voice of Montemayor's 1558 "*Canción*," in which the lover abandoned during a period of absence hopes, "may the novelty be only that you forgot me; / may forgetfulness enter your mind / rather than a new love, if possible" (sea la novedad sólo olvidarme; / antes en tu memoria entre un olvido / que un nuevo pensamiento, si es posible, SC, 86v; GP, 418).

though his love is now directed toward a more appropriate and rewarding end, Selvagia. Sireno joins them and, as he approaches, is moved to tears as Diana's sheep and sheepdog recognize him joyfully (LD, 269). So the past closes in on them ever more strongly the longer they stay in the *locus amoenus*. Indeed, it was only by getting out of it that they were able to vary their perspectives at all.

The company sits beside a spring, "as they used to" (como otras veces solían), and Sireno joins Sylvano for some talk about their flocks, which provokes Diana to chide the latter for not devoting himself to praising his beloved (LD, 271). He acknowledges her as his teacher in love, and concludes by observing Sireno's obvious discomfort in her presence. Sireno, it seems, is not so indifferent after all. As Perry says, "Sireno's so-called serenity toward the woman who betrayed him is a shaky resentment, and it was Racine who reminded us that hatred is closer to love than to indifference."[66] The two former lovers immediately launch into their second spat in as many meetings, each of them defending hotly, and in a decidedly unpoetic fashion, his or her point of view. Diana insists that she was forced to marry; Sireno maintains that she could have avoided it. Sireno finally defines his love as the self-interested and quite human prospect it has been all along when, immediately after reminding Diana that she did not have to forget him just because she had married, he changes his mind, concluding that it is better that she did indeed forget him. In so doing, he reveals how irreconcilable human nature and ideal love are:

> Because there is no worse state than a shepherd's loving a married shepherdess, nor anything that will drive the one who truly loves her any crazier. And the reason is that, as we all know, the main passion that torments a lover, after his desire for his lady, is jealousy. What then do you suppose it will be like for the unlucky one who loves well to find out that his shepherdess is in the arms of her husband, and he is crying over his misfortune there in the street? And the trial does not end there, but in being a pain about which you cannot complain, because if you do, people will think you are crazy or foolish. There is nothing more contrary to repose. . . .

---

66. *Erotic Spirituality*, 85. His observation is exceptional; critics have almost universally chosen to impose a closure upon the Sireno-Diana story by supposing, as does Lindenbaum, that "Sireno's draught frees him from his past passion for Diana," leaving him "with no remembrance of his past pain" (*Changing Landscapes: Anti-Pastoral Sentiment in the English Renaissance*, 33).

(Porque no hay peor estado que es querer un pastor a una pastora casada; ni cosa que más haga perder el seso al que verdadero amor le tiene. Y la razón dello es que, como todos sabemos, la principal passión que a un amador atormenta, después del desseo de su dama, son los celos. ¿Pues, qué te parece que será para un desdichado que quiere bien, saber que está en braços de su velado y él llorando en la calle su desventura? Y no para aquí, el trabajo; mas en ser un mal que no os podéis quexar dél, porque en la hora que os quexárades os ternán por loco o desatinado. Cosa la más contraria al descanso....) (LD, 273-74)[67]

Sireno wants nothing to do with unconditional or selfless devotion, for it brings only the frustration he bitterly expresses here. This is not ideologically sound love, or literary tradition speaking, it is human emotion expressing the ultimate folly of trying to live out either one: selfless, blindly constant love, of the kind only Christ could enact, is revealed as an impossibility in the context of human experience. Montemayor here confirms, at a critical juncture in his most important text, the absence of divine qualities from human reality. Constancy, a correlative of timelessness, and selfless devotion are incongruous with the ways of human sentiment. Sireno distressfully discloses his realization that he is unable to uphold the ideals so dear to him, and so distant from the confounding disappointments he faces. He must account for time, which means change, and the other, represented as less virtuous than he. Simultaneously, he rejects the literary tradition that upholds his worn ideals as well, for he berates his situation in terms not only inappropriate for pastoral discourse (anger, not melancholy), but in reference to urban, not rural experience (he mentions the street and public opinion).[68]

---

67. Cf. this verse from a poem published in Montemayor's 1558 *Segundo cancionero:* "Since my pain is without remedy, / let them not blame me if I am silent about it / because I find, lady, / that pain that has no way out, / it is folly to make public" (Pues mi mal es sin remedio, no me culpen si lo callo, / porque yo, Señora, hallo / que mal que no tiene medio, / es locura publicallo, SC, 10v–11r; GP, 368).

68. This thesis differs from Parker's, who finds that the breaking of boundaries established by literary—and false—codes does not occur until Gil Polo's *Diana enamorada* (1564): "This is something new; the rejection of the basic positions of both Courtly Love and Neoplatonism, it marks the beginning of the attempt to bring love down to reality from the clouds of idealization" (*The Philosophy of Love*, 110). It also differs from that of Avalle-Arce, who does not interpret the end of the *Diana* as problematic, but finds instead that the characters either seek solutions to their difficulties (referring to Felismena) or "they dedicate themselves to living tranquilly, their vital problem then resolved" (NPE, 85).

Sireno breaks through his pastoral disguise in his final lament, rejecting idealism and facing reality. Ironically, it is his denial of selfless love that opens a door to realizing the ideal of constant love, for it indicates that he still feels something for Diana, in spite of the time that has passed, in spite of her marriage to Delio, in spite of Felicia's potion, and in spite of his own attempts to convince himself otherwise. There could be no truer representation of human nature in its moments of disappointment in others and in life, and Montemayor captures expressively what was surely his own difficulty in forgetting not only the woman Diana represents, but his heartfelt illusions about mutual love at the same time.

The irony of the book's end builds when Sylvano and Sireno, both supposedly cured of their love for Diana, decide to pretend they still love her: "Let us pretend that we are the way this shepherdess had us when we used to scatter our complaints throughout this field" (Hagamos cuenta que estamos los dos de la manera que esta pastora nos traya al tiempo que por este prado esparzíamos nuestras quexas, LD, 274). So they end their participation in the *Diana*, overcome by the limiting powers of the *locus amoenus* and the call of the past that so effectively haunts it. Pretending as they do, they willfully hurt Selvagia, who the narrator says is sensitive to what is happening, and Diana as well, whom their song provokes to tears (LD, 267, 274). Artistically, they regress to the self-centered, self-contemplating individuals of pastoral literature. For the pastoral characters, the escapade outside their home territory could not bring any solution to their problems, for their literary lives depend on those problems for existence in the timeless zone of the *locus amoenus*. This would seem to imply that the imposition of supernatural qualities upon the human condition, as happens in the pretended timelessness of the pastoral enclosure, produces an unsatisfactory and inherently false circumstance in which the resolution of problems is impossible.

The native shepherds and shepherdesses thus conclude their roles in the *Diana* evoking a past even more distant than the one whose passage they were lamenting when the narration began in book one. Physical regression to the pastoral enclosure inevitably signifies a temporal regression as well, a search for a sameness and a fixation that cannot be found without it. This tendency is directly related to the function of nature in the pastoral anecdote as a backdrop of stability against which the past can be mentally evoked. For, as Anthony Cascardi observes, "Nature engenders only likeness; the 'natural' is the principle by which the world is a self-generating succession of sameness."[69] Mirroring not the characters' thoughts and feelings but the impossible, idealized continuity they seek, the natural world of the pastoral retreat entraps them within itself, within their desire for what cannot be. Ending within the *locus amoenus*, book six concludes as pastoral episodes do, with the sadness of all as they turn to collect their sheep scattered in the meadow.

Book Seven

Felismena's story being the only one left to conclude, hers is the one to which most of book seven is dedicated. It tells of her adventures in the valley between Coimbra and Montemôr-o-velho in Portugal. Although described in specific geographical terms contrary to the stylized idealism typically used for the *locus amoenus*, the beauty around her moves Felismena to melancholy, typical of pastoral. Her wistful remembrance of Seville, inspired by the rural setting of the Portuguese countryside, provides evidence that as she left the pastoral enclosure, she took the pastoral impulse with her.

Felismena comes across two shepherdesses who are disputing whether one of them, Duarda, should return to her former lover, Danteo. Danteo had married Andresa in accordance with his father's will and in contradiction to the promise of fidelity he had given to Duarda. As a result, the shepherdess now wants nothing to do with him.[70]

Andresa now being dead, Armia tries to convince the hard-hearted Duarda to relinquish her independence and return to her former lover. After they welcome Felismena, Danteo appears singing in Portuguese of his constancy to Duarda, a contradictory position for him to take since he had, after all, married someone else. He then converses with Duarda in the same language, each of them defending a distinct point of view. Danteo,

---

69. "Genre Definition and Multiplicity in *Don Quijote*," 40. Cf. the narrator of the Prologue to *Don Quijote*, who says of nature, "for in it, everything engenders its own likeness" (que en ella cada cosa engendra su semejante, 1:50).

70. Parker attributes to Lope de Vega the abandoning of courtly codes to represent women as if it marked some sort of progress: "Lope transformed the image of the cruel lady, implying that the rigorous inflexibility of chastity does not exist in reality. What does exist is woman, mutable and unpredictable, and mutability is the hallmark of Nature" (*The Philosophy of Love*, 128–29). Selvagia had eloquently defended women from just the type of stereotype that Parker says Lope cast upon them (LD, 38–39), as does Duarda here.

it turns out, had wanted to marry Duarda before his father had arranged his union with someone else, and Duarda had refused to marry in secret (LD, 286). Once again, Montemayor's able use of dialogue makes it clear that individuals bring varied perspectives to the same situation. Whereas Duarda's mind is fixed on Danteo's having abandoned her, Danteo's point of view is focused on her previous refusal to marry him.

The variety of opinions brought to situations in the *Diana* deeply colors the stark discrepancy implied by Montemayor between ideology and experience in marriage. On one hand, marriage is the culmination of a happy relationship, as described by Felicia. No such unions actually occur in the *Diana*. On the contrary, three of the four that have taken place (those of Diana, Danteo, and Alanio) are marriages in which the wishes of the partners did not figure at all, much less their emotional fulfillment. Danteo seems to have emerged emotionally untouched from his marriage to Andresa, for he sings to Duarda as if it had never taken place.

Duarda and Danteo engage in much the same battle as Sireno and Diana, since they have essentially the same problem, with the sexes reversed: the sudden and inexplicable marriage of the beloved, which leaves the lover alone and embittered. The terms in which Danteo describes the change in his situation are identical to those used by the narrator in the "Argumento" to present Diana's marriage to Delio: Danteo says, "The times changed" (Os tempos se mudarao, LD, 285); the narrator says, "the times and Diana's heart changed" (los tiempos y el coraçón de Diana se mudaron, LD, 7). For Duarda and Sireno alike, parental influence is an unacceptable reason to abandon a successful relationship. For Danteo and Diana, it remains the only reason. Danteo's status as a widower allows him to voice what Diana's honor presumably keeps her from saying: that his original love remained in his heart, in spite of his social circumstances that prohibited its expression. This could understandably be what the narrator/author would like to imply about Diana.

Unlike Sireno, Duarda vehemently insists she has lost all interest in continuing with her former lover. Her exaggerated refusal to reconsider Danteo as a suitor suggests that, should she loosen her relentless grip on her pride, she could return to her love for him. Unlike Sireno, who is faced with a married beloved to the end of the *Diana*, Duarda confronts only her own psychological barrier to happiness.[71]

71. In his 1563 continuation of Montemayor's text, Alonso Pérez claims that Mon-

Felismena is about to speak to the couple when the noise from a fight between four knights is heard. Discerning that three men are fighting against one, she immediately sets to equalizing the conflict. As the defending knight overcomes one of his attackers, she dispenses with the other two with the same efficiency she used on the savages. The lone knight profusely declares his infinite debt to her just before removing his helmet. It turns out to be the inconstant Felis, whose sudden appearance leaves Felismena speechless. After collecting her thoughts, she presents her wayward lover with the list of emotional and social debts he owes her and says she cannot give him any more than she already has except her life, which she then offers him.

During her argument, Felismena does not hesitate to call Felis's attention to her selflessness, which only looked out for his desires: "If this fails to make you recognize what you owe me, remember that I served you as page for one year . . . and even as intermediary against myself . . . only to relieve the pain that your own pain of love was making you feel" (Si esto no te trae a concocimiento de lo que me deves, acuérdate que un año te estuve sirviendo de page . . . y aún de tercero contra mí misma . . . por sólo dar remedio al mal que el tuyo te hazía sentir, LD, 295). That same selflessness and willingness to suffer, an attitude she shares with the other main characters, is what merits her reward in Montemayor's system of love. Since she is up against the will of another person, one which experience has shown her can be changed, and not an insurmountable barrier like marriage, Felismena's attempts at attaining compensation are successful.[72]

Overcome by surprise and his wounds, Felis collapses into a faint, but not before the narrator insists that he had recognized both Felismena and

---

temayor himself declared his intention to marry Diana and Sireno, after the death of her husband, in the promised second part of his book (NPE, 105). Montemayor seems to have tested this possibility in the Danteo/Duarda relationship and rejected it, leaving only these stories unfinished at the book's end. It is unlikely that Montemayor would have allowed Sireno to marry Diana in a continuation, as Pérez claims, since Danteo and Duarda's relationship remains unresolved and Sireno's problems are somewhat autobiographical.

72. Cervantes's delightful character Dorotea (DQ, 1, ch. 28–46) has many traits in common with Montemayor's Felismena, one of which was mentioned in n. 14. Of particular interest are the similarities between the sermons they deliver to their unfaithful lovers, both of which achieve the goal of winning the men back to their original relationships.

the wrong he had done her (LD, 296). This admission makes somewhat redundant but nonetheless reassuring the immediate appearance of Dórida, Felicia's nymph, who douses Felis's face with water. Having revived him, she then gives him a drink from a golden cup that heals both his wounds and his love for Celia, one hopes better than the last one did Sireno's love for Diana. Unlike the pastoral characters, Felis does not sleep but only pauses briefly before declaring his renewed affection for Felismena and his dependence on her goodness and clemency for forgiveness.[73] He offers to suffer forever in recompense for the wrongs he has done her, in the exaggerated style of a courtly lover: "Never will I raise my eyes to look upon you that I will not feel in my soul all the wrong I have done you" (ninguna vez alçaré los ojos a mirarte que no me lleguen al alma los agravios que de mí as recebido, LD, 298). This seems to be a satisfactory resolution for such a relationship in Montemayor's eyes: the constancy of the faithful partner is rewarded and the inconstancy of the other will provoke eternal repentance in that partner, thereby exalting the faithful lover's superiority.

Unlike Duarda, Felismena is not at all perturbed about winning Felis back after he had loved someone else. Not a pastoral character, she is capable of accommodating change and imperfection across the diachronic axis of time; she joyfully forgives her errant beloved and they return to Felicia's palace where they are to be married, as are Belisa and Arsileo, Selvagia and Sylvano. The narrator ends his tale promising a second part, as many sixteenth-century narrators do, one in which the story of what happened to Sireno at the wedding festivities will be recounted, as well as the conclusion to the conflict between Danteo and Duarda.

The *Diana*, the first pastoral narration, thus ends in a magical palace, celebrating the characters' entrance into another stage of life, one with scarce novelistic interest for male authors in the sixteenth century. Although he promised to continue his book, it is likely that Montemayor had said all he had to say about love in the world in the *Diana* as it stands today, for all of the characters but two were married and their stories thereby ended. One exception is Sireno, singled out by Montemayor to hold true to his love against all odds, for obvious reasons. The other is Duarda, Sireno's alter-ego, whose story ends, like his, without ending,

---

73. Felis, like Dorotea's Fernando in *Don Quijote*, is a foil for the woman who loves him and is a relatively inconsistent character.

true to the pastoral mode of suspended, melancholy complaint focused on the unhappy self.

The *Diana:* A Recollection

As the above indicates, the structure of the *Diana* is tripartite, similar to the worshipper's approach to God as described completely in Montemayor's "Spiritual Dialogue" and in fragments throughout his religious verse: a period of recollection, including self-examination and review of trials exalting the innocent suffering of the virtuous; approach of the worthy to the gates of happiness; final return to the world for reassimilation into it, perpetual happiness having been determined to be impossible in the human condition.

Just as the shepherds and shepherdesses are led to Felicia's palace by fortuitous events, so Montemayor's worshipper may actively only practice virtue and eradicate vice as preparation for grace, after which the divine hand may or may not descend to intervene. There is an interesting parallel between the recogidos' attainment of happiness, which can occur only through death, and the happiness attained by those literary characters whose stories are resolved, who likewise "die" or disappear from the narration. That is, just as permanent happiness cannot exist in the human state, neither can it be sustained by narrative literature, which cannot make a story out of perfect felicity. This calls Scholes to mind, who says: "We humans are the animals who know that we shall die. We know that our lives are shaped like stories, with a beginning, a middle, and an end, and that the end is inevitable. Reading, I am contending, consists, among other things, in recognizing and facing the signs of this pattern, too."[74]

The inward glance, taking place at the portals of the superhuman realm, does not reveal sin or error in these pastoral characters' performance or beliefs, rather confirms their righteousness as it does that of the narrative voice in Montemayor's religious prose and verse. All are consistently portrayed as flawless practitioners of correct behavior and knowers of doctrine whose intellectual abilities conflict with the literary masks they wear.

---

74. *Protocols of Reading,* 18. This type of relationship between the patterns of literature and those of human existence is often and unfortunately shunted by literary critics (the works of Ruth El Saffar being a notable exception).

Those who enter the palace, like the Christian at the twelve gates of heavenly Jerusalem, have endured trials for their love. More importantly, all have suffered innocently, the supreme glory of imitating Christ in recogido piety, something that Montemayor uniquely has his pastoral characters and nymphs alike exalt in the same proportionate equation: they are the best who suffer the most.

Contact with the superhuman makes manifest only what lies within the characters themselves and leads them back into the world, not beyond it. Although they do not worship anything in the palace, the lovers do review doctrine with each other there and experience rapture through music within its walls. After a period of fellowship, their visit concludes individually, reflecting the healthy balance between a sense of community and of individuality recommended by the recogidos. Through contact with water and a book, some of them are able to reach within themselves and realize where their own desires are taking them. The others receive inspiration to persevere in their ongoing difficulties. Felicia brings to the surface what is locked with the characters, their destinies, what fortune or God wills for them in their humanity, which means in time. In the end, although some of the characters' difficulties are resolved, in one way or another they are all also left with the understanding that solutions, like problems, exist in a temporal dimension, which threatens to unravel the present in the face of the same flux that once brought them happiness. Their experience has shown them, and the reader, that this lack of permanent resolution is the norm of human life. Like Montemayor's religious works and those of his sources, it implicitly teaches the importance of accepting human life as an experience of inconstancies and imperfections, which stand out all the more for having been revealed in a literary environment that is stable and false.

Further similarities between what happens at Felicia's palace and Montemayor's ideas about human attainment of the divine are emphasized by the names of both the palace's patron and its keeper. Diana, the goddess of chastity (moral chastity more than physical, as described in above) is a divine being who demands trials, humility, and constancy in human love. That constancy is the virtue necessary to enter the "holy" gates or doors of the palace, access to which is preceded by self-examination. Within its confines Felicia—happiness—rules. The inconsistencies in her nature, which wavers between the human and the superhuman, unveils the problematic nature of happiness itself. She incarnates the characters' acceptance of the ways of life and their roles in it; appropriately, the lovers cannot stay there, for permanent happiness is represented as impossible, pertaining to a realm other than the human. It is in her palace where Montemayor's lovers ironically prove that even constancy is not an absolute virtue, for therein some of them are led to abandon it.

At no point in the process of "reward" bestowed upon the five main characters are the secrets of the divine mysteries revealed overtly, since those who drink Felicia's water are unconscious under its effects. Although they experience a change in proportion of earthly order under its spell, they do not transcend human experience; the hastening of their futures alters time's dimensions but does not change the events of time itself, nor fortune's workings through it. Further, all of the characters are not so "blessed." Although they are as worthy as Sireno, Sylvano, and Selvagia, Felismena and Belisa are likewise turned away from heaven's last gate, in that they are compelled to face their human experience unaltered, since their situations are not dire enough to require abandoning their first loves. Just as Dileto hears the angelical voice declaring that death alone brings resolution to life and escape from its irregularities, so the shepherdesses and shepherds are processed back into the context from which they originated, to continue living.

The open-ended conclusion of the *Diana* allowed Montemayor to make a strong statement about the relative value of ideology and experience in human love. The variety of ways in which the characters' stories are resolved and not resolved underscores how broad the category of experience is in comparison to doctrinal absolutism. Significantly, each of the lovers arrives at a solution appropriate for her or his own state and character. Sireno and Diana remain at odds, their problem unsolved; the same it true of their counterparts, Danteo and Duarda. Selvagia and Sylvano, having both undergone unsuccessful relationships with others, are paired, and although Sylvano remains stained by his former love for Diana, Selvagia is willing to overlook that in exchange for the love between them. Felismena is likewise willing to forgive Felis his infidelity and they are reunited; Amarílida forgives Filemón his indiscretion as well. Belisa's enduring faithfulness to Arsileo is rewarded as her misinterpretation of her own situation is corrected. In a similar but more realistic way, Amarílida and Filemón's differences based on misunderstanding are likewise corrected and followed by reconciliation. Significantly, three out of five of the women among the characters are willing to forgive and as many of the men are in need of forgiveness. The important exception is Sireno (and Duarda, a female version of him).

The only theme common to all the lovers' stories in the *Diana* is sentimental fidelity.[75] The message is made clear, however, that there are times when fidelity is a function of greater concerns, the getting on in life: Felicia offered Sylvano "another remedy so as not to want what is impossible" (otro remedio para no dessear cosa que es imposible alcançalla, LD, 223). Not longing for the impossible is probably the axiom symbolized by the book of wisdom with which she tapped the lovers on the head in book four. The marriage of one's beloved to another is reason to accommodate within oneself the change one has been forced to acknowledge without, adapting to the effects of passing time. The only character unable to accomplish this acceptance is Sireno.

Sireno's posture in the *Diana* harmonizes well with both Montemayor's religious works and his secular poetry, for it captures the disillusion of one who finds only an imperfect world, with an imperfect beloved in it, in which to carry out his ideologically sound desires. Although Sireno casts the blame for his misfortune on Diana herself, other characters' opinions dispel that blame, and in the end Sireno too has resigned himself to the idea that life and its movement are bigger than he and more absolute than his perfect love. He has witnessed the immersion of ideological desire into time, into life, and most importantly, into the problematic arena of another's desire, something with which any lover, if loving another individual and not love itself, must reckon. With his companions, he has learned that love means change in time, in acceptance of one's circumstances and the flux of life, and he is the most eloquent spokesperson of that lesson. Nonetheless, he is the least able to put his own bitter wisdom to positive use, and instead renders a painful homage to constancy and faithfulness to the unchanging ideal, at the expense of his happiness.

The other characters' experiences and words would seem to confirm that Sireno's conclusions constitute Montemayor's theme in the *Diana*. Virtuous love is an understood standard of behavior. That love, which

---

75. Unrequited love is typically mentioned as the theme of the *Diana*, which overlooks the fact that virtually all of the lovers except Sylvano have enjoyed reciprocal affection before they appear in the narration. Davis finds that the central theme is infidelity, in turn overlooking the three out of five cases in which the main characters are faithful, and constancy's exaltation at Felicia's palace (*A Map of Arcadia*, 33).

moves naturally toward resolution in a satisfying and permanent relationship, promises only temporary happiness if and when it its realized. Montemayor seems to observe, ever bitterly, that although suffering on behalf of one's ideal is a valuable prelude to recognition and fulfillment, impossible love is no delight and in its shadow human nature tends to forget the past and move on to a more satisfying circumstance.

The case is made particularly well by Sylvano, who swears he wants nothing that Diana does not want in book one (LD, 19), but after an extended period of unrewarded suffering, transfers his affections to Selvagia, largely because she loves him in return. He recognizes the same need for reciprocal affection as Sireno eventually does when he says to Diana, "I belong to my Selvagia, not only because of the many things about her that oblige me to do so, but also because she did not disdain her luck in being loved by the one whom you held in such little esteem" (Yo soy de la mi Selvagia, porque demás de aver en ella muchas partes que hacello me obligan, no tuvo en menos su suerte por ser amada de aquel a quien tú en tan poco tuviste, LD, 267). It also reveals his earlier exaggerated proclamation of selflessness to be exactly that: exaggerated, merely literary, and ultimately hollow: "I would not want my lady to undergo just one hour of sadness, although from that same hour I might have a hundred thousand of happiness" (una sola hora de tristeza no quisiera yo que por mi señora passara, aunque della se me siguieran a mí cien mil de alegría, LD, 23). As indicated, the last thing Sylvano does to Diana is hurt her.

The final message is clear: whether the virtuous lover is constant against all odds (Felismena, Belisa, and Sireno) or not (Diana, Sylvano, and Selvagia), happiness is a temporary state that flows with fortune, which works through time. This is the unfathomable order of human existence, subject to something beyond it, outside it. Montemayor carefully represents loving in life as an ongoing and varied process, vital for its inconsistencies, not a literary process that begins and ends with its neo-Aristotelian knots tidily unravelled and laid flat. The moment in which the other characters appear in the narration, after suffering a disillusion, allows their point of view while in the *locus amoenus* to harmonize there with the one Sireno maintains throughout the book. The *Diana* and its characters are thus dominated by the past until it becomes so distant that it either loses meaning, freeing them from its clutches by fading their memories of it, or time itself brings a solution to them that joins the past satisfactorily to the present. Again, Sireno stands out as the exception.

The fact that Sireno's position of noble and guiltless suffering is depicted as unique falls neatly into the rest of Montemayor's works like a final puzzle piece. The result is a complete and generally consistent picture, not of perfect love, but of the perfect lovers' fate in time. Sireno's posture in the *Diana* is one of unyielding if increasingly problematic fidelity to the past and his ideals while all around him others are moving on, relinquishing the absolutism of their ideals to adjust to the present. His is the posture represented in the most effective of Montemayor's religious and secular poetry, his verse exposition of the *"Super flumina"* psalm, some of his pastoral and religious sonnets, his third eclogue, and his song "Ya no faltaba al corazón cansado" (Nothing remained for the tired heart). Sireno's inability to release his lament of the wronged one harmonizes perfectly with the privileged status allotted to innocent and willing suffering in all of Montemayor's works and those of the religious writers who inspired them. In the end, the *Diana* is his book, the story of one who wishes and deserves to be serene, but whose ideals make serenity impossible. Rather than sacrifice those ideals, he suffers, and in so doing, he is the guiltless victim whose life Montemayor, like the recogidos, chose to imitate.

Conclusion

"Oh mighty God!, where are you that you are not pained?"
(*"¡Oh alto Dios!, ¿dó estás que no te dueles?"*)
(*"Paráfrasis en el psalmo* Super flumina Babylonis*"*)

are you, my Sireno?"
(*¿Dó estás, Sireno mío?* Diana, *"Egloga tercera"*)

The vision of human life represented in Montemayor's religious writings illuminates an interpretation of the *Diana* that cannot be understood without them: they provide an immediate and rich context for Spain's first pastoral narration. It is a context of undeniable significance to the author and his readers, directly related to reformist Catholicism of the mid-sixteenth century, problematic as it is. The strong relationship between Montemayor's religiousness and his secular writings obtains even though he never directly links any of his characters' experiences to Catholicism, its rituals, or dogma; indeed, it may be that his silence about religiousness in the sphere of human activity speaks loudly of his alliance with that piety, which most tended to respect the differences between the human and the divine and the distance between the two.

Superficial religious interpretations of the *Diana* are bound to dissatisfy, for the spirituality of the work is much more subtle and profound than numbers, symbols, and words that function in a religious as well as secular lexicon (such as *fe,* [faith]). The overall structure of the book is deceivingly akin to a religious event, yet the shepherdesses and shepherds attaining entrance into Felicia's palace is not offered as any type of salvation, and the uneven happiness they achieve after their visit there would seem to prohibit the undertaking of any such comparisons. Regardless, there are extensive parallels between that procedure in the *Diana* and the process of earning grace as Montemayor describes it in his religious works. In neither context is the realization of just rewards ever actually represented. On the contrary, emphasis falls on the difficulties inherent in virtue, the testing ground for the merit of grace. Although this is an idealistic theme for its total attention to virtuous people, it is not unrealistic in itself.

As in his writings devoted to religious experience, Montemayor has accounted for both ideology and human reality in the *Diana*. From the combination emerges an interchange between the two replete with didacticism, but predominantly melancholy and therefore personal and sentimental. The *Diana* is the most personal of all Montemayor's works, with its rainbow of characters, each of whom tells a different version of one story, the fortune of constant love in time. In the pastoral narration, as in his religious writings, it is the first-person voice that sings the most moving song, because it is the melody of the author's own wondering and sad observations about love in life.

As indicated at the conclusion of the previous chapter, Sireno would seem to represent Montemayor's own conclusion: there is an order to things, the order of change itself, a way whose workings are beyond comprehension attainable through human experience. This is the essential tenet of recogimiento, which places responsibility for the ways in which events transpire in the hands of forces beyond the human. Montemayor's decision to cast his message in a literary mode that in itself implies resistance to change reveals how poignantly he lamented that message himself, even while accepting its truth. That acceptance is of great importance in the religious ideology Montemayor's writings support, for therein conformity to superhuman order, the very ways of God, is imperative. It is, as were so many of the virtues exalted by the Catholic reformists, a monastic practice recommended to the lay population: "Obedience says that there is no greater sanctity, no greater sacrifice than human conformity in all trials with the blessing of divine will" (La obediencia dice que no hay mayor santidad, ni mayor sacrificio, que conformarse el hombre en todos los trabajos con el beneplácito de la divina voluntad, *Guía*, 214). The *Diana* portrays, as much as do Montemayor's religious works and those of his sources for them, respect for hierarchical authority and ceremony. Like the recogidos, his lament surges forth through observation of human fallibility, leaving the divine untouched. In this context, the pastoral and the psalm were understandably the most eloquent forms in which Montemayor's conservative and disillusioned voice could express itself.

The sentimental theme of fidelity in the *Diana* is overshadowed by that of fortune, to which all else is subject. Its ways are those of God, unknowable and unavoidable. Although much lamented and occasionally praised, those ways are never challenged, in part because the characters' experiences have shown them that this would be futile, in part because Catholic reformism found extreme virtue in the acceptance of whatever life should bring, in the conforming of one's will to the realities of the present that Fray Luis de Granada recommends. "Who could escape what her or his fortune has allotted?" Selvagia asks (¿Quién podría huyr de lo que su fortuna le tiene solicitado?, LD, 45). Dórida likewise questions, "What shall we do, lovely lady, in the face of fortune's blows? What strong house can there be where one can be safe from the changes of time?" (¿Qué haremos, hermosa señora, a los golpes de la fortuna? ¿Qué casa fuerte avrá adonde la persona pueda estar segura de las mudanças del tiempo? LD, 125). Diana asks Sireno, "Could anyone keep you from leaving / if fate or fortune wanted you to go?" (¿Pudiera alguno hazer que no partieras / si el hado o la fortuna lo quería? LD, 27). Sireno says he would seek a solution to his problems "if time, fortune would let me" (si el tiempo, la fortuna me lo permitiesse, LD, 130). Love is ruled by fortune's superior power, as the assembled company sings at Felicia's palace:

> To fall from a favorable state
> is harsh and vexing pain,
> but love is not to blame;
> the fault lies with fortune
> that knows not how to make an exception of anyone.
>
> (Caer de un buen estado
> es una grave pena y importuna,
> mas no es amor culpado;
> la culpa es de fortuna
> que no sabe exceptar persona alguna.)
>
> (LD, 169)[1]

In Montemayor's earthly cosmos, fortune oversees everything that goes on and keeps a running account of each individual's accumulated happiness and pain, always ready to strike when the former gets out of balance. The notion is not only secular; Fray Luis de Granada says as much as well, admitting, "I don't know what kind of imbalance was this one, that nature gave troubles more power to give pain than pleasure to give hap-

---

1. The metaphor of falling cannot but remind one of Fernando de Rojas's tragicomedy *La Celestina,* and the general insecurity of life represented therein through the theme of the unexpected fall. See Stephen Gilman's introduction to the Severin edition, *La Celestina: Tragicomedia de Calisto y Melibea,* 18–23.

piness" (no sé qué género de desigualdad fue esta que más poderosos quiso naturaleza que fuesen los males para dar pena, que los placeres para dar alegría, *Guía*, 314). That same power is behind almost every event that occurs in Montemayor's book: Belisa describes her loss of happiness, "My misfortune resulted in fortune's being paid for the happiness that it had given me until then" (Mi desventura fué causa que la fortuna se pagasse del contento que hasta entonces me avía dado, LD, 158). Sireno's final conclusion is worth repeating: "Let no one tally an account without figuring in fortune, nor lay a foundation without considering the changes of the times" (Mas nadie haga cuenta sin la fortuna, ni fundamento sin considerar las mudanças de los tiempos, LD, 239). All-powerful, occasionally kind, but ever-vigilant, fortune is always aware of what is going on. Thus Sireno warns Sylvano and Selvagia to beware their own, hard-won, happiness, "I assure you that fortune is not neglecting to temper the happiness you are enjoying with your love" (yo te asseguro que la fortuna no se descuyde de templaros el contento que recebís con vuestros amores, LD, 239).

This is the power that runs Montemayor's universe, this is God, distant and exacting. Like the deity who keeps a running account of one's sins to be expiated in purgatory, fortune keeps track of every moment of happiness, for which payment will eventually be levied. This vision, quite distinct from humanistic optimism and emphasis on human potential on earth, is true to the world represented by the Catholic reformists, one worthy only of overcoming for its instability and disappointments: "How much change there is in the life of all of man, who is subject to all the vicissitudes of fortune, which never remains the same, rather is ever rolling from one state to another" (Cuánta [mudanza] la de todo el hombre que está subjeto á todos los vaivenes de la fortuna, la cual nunca permanesce un mismo ser, sino siempre rueda de un lugar en otro, LdO, 115).

The constantly moving nature of things may have its positive value, for once the individual undergoes a period of trial, things may change for the better: Polydora exclaims, "I always knew that my Belisa's sadness had to be turned into great happiness some time" (Siempre yo tuve creído que, en algún tiempo, la tristeza de mi Belisa se avía de bolver en grandísima alegría, LD, 249). It is this upward swing of fortune's turns that Arsileo celebrates, however fearfully, in the final books of the *Diana*, saying, "A calm usually follows the storm"; "Now love and fortune are turning"; "You tend, fortune, to move / with swift movement" (Venir suele bonança tras fortuna; Ya dan buelta el amor y la fortuna; Sueles, ventura, moverte / con ligero movimiento, LD, 233, 250, 255). He expresses his happiness as a settling of his accounts with fortune: "With what words can I extol the satisfaction fortune has brought me in exchange for so many and such unusual trials?" (¿Con qué palabras podré yo encarecer la satisfacción que la fortuna me a hecho de tantos y tan desusados trabajos?, LD, 256). Through the changes that the characters suffer, they also learn to expect the ups and downs of life, which therefore are not absolutely "gratuitous changes in circumstance,"[2] but rotations within the ways of the world, the details of which may be incomprehensible, but the overall system of which has a rhythm. To challenge that order would be to challenge the divinity itself. The ways of God and the ways of fortune are the same, worthy of fear, removed, but consoling for their omnipotence.[3]

Time is represented as the agent through which fortune makes its effects known, and it is the diachronic experience of the characters that allows them to learn from their trials by accepting time's dominion over life. Every character of the *Diana* feels time's effects: Selvagia, for example, mocks eternal love—that which would pretend to escape temporality—saying,

> Go along with time, with changes,
> go along with disorderly movements,
> you will see how free your heart becomes.
>
> (Tomáos allí con tiempos, con mudanças,
> tomáos con movimientos desvariados,
> vereys el coraçón quan libre queda.)
> (LD, 35)

She and Sireno are time's most eloquent victims, and she concludes from

---

2. Barbara Mujica, *Iberian Pastoral Characters*, 271.
3. In his depiction of fortune as a force with high as well as low points, however precarious, Montemayor differs from his compatriot and precursor Bernadim de Ribeiro, who represents fortune always taking successive turns for the worse. See Mujica's chapter on Ribeiro, *Iberian Pastoral Characters*, 43–110. In the same way, his vision differs from Fernando de Rojas's "axiological nihilism," in which fortune brings some sort of a fall to everyone (Gilman, introduction to Rojas's *Celestina*, 14). Unlike Rojas's characters, Montemayor's are all virtuous victims.

her experience what he concludes from his: "I am a woman and in me you will see, if I choose, how greatly one may love. But this does not keep me from supposing that all things may end, no matter how sure they may be, because the job of time and fortune is to proceed as swift in these movements as they have always been" (Yo muger soy y en mí verás si quiero, todo lo que se puede querer. Pero no me estorva esto imaginar que en todas las cosas podría aver fin por más firmes que sean porque oficio es del tiempo y de la fortuna andar en estos movimientos tan ligeros como ellos lo an sido siempre, LD, 70).

Montemayor's vivid concern with time and his immensely successful way of incorporating it into his pastoral narration is novelistic, according to Ian Watt, who maintains: "The novel's plot is also distinguished from most previous fiction by its use of past experience as the cause of present action.... The novel in general has interested itself much more than any other literary form in the development of its characters in the course of time."[4] Increased awareness of humanity's irrevocable movement along a temporal axis is a natural consequence of any self-examination, which inherently plots the present against the past. Whether the incorporation of chronological progression into prose is novelistic or not, Montemayor's emphasis on it is manifest not only in the events that transpire in his fiction and what his characters have to say about them, but also in the narrative structure defined in chapter 2.

Just as recogido authors tend to attribute human weaknesses and strengths to vices and virtues working through the individual, the characters of the *Diana* attribute the majority of events in their lives to fortune or some related force, external to themselves but made manifest through them. This tendency corresponds exactly to Montemayor's conception of the role of the divine as an external if omnipotent force in human life and destiny. The shepherds and shepherdesses perceive their futures as falling within the domain of a power greater than their desires, however pure and righteous they may be. Felismena says she will see Felis again "if time or fortune should provide the opportunity for my eyes to see him" (si el tiempo o la fortuna dieren lugar a que mis ojos le vean, LD, 94). Likewise, Sireno would be seeking a solution to his problem "if time, fortune would permit me to" (si el tiempo, la fortuna me lo permitiesse, LD, 130). They pass off

---

4. *The Rise of the Novel: Studies in Defoe, Richardson and Fielding*, 22.

events as the responsibility of a force which, although incapable of controlling their desires and emotions, directs them into circumstances they feel they do not deserve, thus leading them to take frequent recourse in the phrase "quiso mi ventura que" (my fortune had it that).[5] This corresponds to the tendency in Montemayor's religious works and those of the recogidos to define the forces acting on humanity as entities separate from human beings, such as the devil or separate virtues and vices. In this context, these external elements are the means through which the supernatural makes itself known in women and men, who can never experience the omnipotent directly or completely.

This posture in life, which focuses on events after they have happened and thereby presents the characters as victims, is alien to the modern reader's way of thinking and is typically disdained in the *Diana*. The attitude is nonetheless predominant in sixteenth-century literature, whose authors and precursors were generally sensitive to humanity's lack of autonomy from such forces, whether or not overtly identified as God or fortune. It may be a variant of the determinism that Johan Huizinga cites as characteristic of the late Middle Ages, consoling for its affirmation of power above and beyond humanity's confused existence.[6]

To what extent Montemayor's "fatalism" was typical of his day might deserve further consideration than it is typically given. The popularity of fifteenth-century literature during the sixteenth century, notably the *Celestina* by Fernando de Rojas and Jorge Manrique's "Coplas," was overwhelming. Montemayor's representation of the life experience is fundamentally akin to both of them; his repeated glosses of the "Coplas" have been mentioned. Rojas's book carries a message similar to that of the *Diana* about time and fortune in human life. His character Sempronio, for example, observes what the action of the *Celestina*'s plot reveals as well, "Evil and good, prosperity and adversity, glory and pain, all lose in time the force of their accelerated beginnings" (El mal y el bien, la prosperidad y adversidad, la gloria y pena, todo pierde con el tiempo la fuerza

---

5. See pp. 42, 125, 158 for a few examples. So consistently do the characters refer to their life experiences in these terms that they were probably conventional fillers rather than meaningful phrases. However, there are sufficient definitive references to both time and fortune beyond this superficial context to warrant special attention.

6. "The Forms of Thought and Practical Life." The troublesome power of fortune also concerned the humanists; Baldassarre Castiglione's passage acknowledging that power has been quoted (*supra* 170–71).

de su acelerado principio).[7] The most published authors of Montemayor's day insistently return to the same theme. Aside from Luis de Granada, also worthy of mention is Fray Antonio de Guevara, whose works, like those of Luis de Granada, were immensely popular during his day but are relatively neglected today. Guevara puts these words into the pen of Marcus Aurelius: "Our life is so fragile and fortune so absolute, that through that part where we were least watchful, right there entered all the danger upon us" (Es tan frágil nuestra vida y es tan absoluta la fortuna, que, por aquella parte por la cual estábamos sin recelo, por allí nos vino todo el peligro).[8]

In his preference to dwell on the *post factum* situation in which exemplary individuals find themselves, however, Montemayor imparts a tone to his works that is unique in the mid–1550's, consistently showing how bad things happen to good people. Cervantes, writing some fifty years later, has his virtuous characters express another variety of the same accepting posture, acknowledging the dominion of something greater than the human in the direction of human life; his characters up through *Los trabajos de Persiles y Sigismunda* (*The Trials of Persiles and Sigismunda*) consistently recognize the power of "fortune, which is nothing other than a firm disposition of heaven" (la fortuna, que no es otra cosa sino un firme disponer del cielo).[9] But whereas Cervantes captures his characters as they come upon situations requiring them to act, exercising what power they have, Montemayor chooses to consider them after the action is accomplished, from whence comes the lament, and the appropriateness for pastoral. Therefore, Cervantes was an unsuccessful author of pastoral literature, whereas Montemayor was a complete success. Likewise, Cervantes was able to write a piece of literature that engages the modern reader immediately, whereas Montemayor was not.

In spite of the many correspondences between Montemayor's religious works and his pastoral narration, the absolute focus on the human dilem-

---

7. *La Celestina*, 80. On fifteenth-century literature's success throughout the sixteenth century, see Keith Whinnom, "The Problem of the 'Best-seller' in Spanish Golden Age Literature," and Sara T. Nalle, "Literacy and Culture in Early Modern Castile."

8. *Reloj de príncipes y libro de Marco Aurelio*, 139. There are chapters dedicated to Guevara in Francisco Márquez Villanueva's *Espiritualidad y literatura en el siglo 16* (15–66) and Antonio Prieto's *La prosa española del siglo 16* (177–218).

9. *Los trabajos de Persiles y Sigismunda*, 474.

ma in the *Diana* allowed him to represent something therein that his religious writings, necessarily dealing with God in some way, did not; this focus itself was made possible by his religiousness, which disallowed intimate blends of the human and the divine. In his pastoral narration, in spite of the characters' awareness of their desire's subjection to the greater powers of time and fortune, the notion begins to dawn on them that the responsibility for life situations lies with women and men and their faults and virtues, not with powers outside them. During their numerous quarrels and their constant returning to their dissatisfying situations as if unbelieving of them or unwilling to accept them, the lovers stop looking beyond themselves for excuses to justify their situations and begin looking *at* themselves and each other for reasons to explain them. All of them suffer from the inconstancy of others and have those others to blame, and it is when they are actually expressing bitterness over another person's actions, not time or fortune's irrevocable control of things, that the humanity of the book shines: in Selvagia's spirited arguments with Sylvano and Sireno over men's and women's relative inconstancy, in Diana and Sireno's acerbic interchanges, in Felismena's pressing reminder to Felis that he owes her everything.

Nonetheless, Montemayor was too fond of the notion of a distant and powerful force above him and everyone else to abandon that divided universe consistently, for his is the cosmos in which God, however present, is also distant. In the world in which God's attendance is immediately and intimately evident on earth and in humanity, there is no way to describe life's imperfections without implicitly denigrating the deity; Montemayor never would have represented such a world. In his, God, like fortune, directs from the beyond with a mighty hand that is invisible but perceptible through events as they unfold. To question that control or to challenge it is never presented as a possibility. However, the distance perceived by Montemayor between earthly and heavenly activities facilitated his exclusive attention to human beings who, though ruled by forces beyond their control, live isolated from the obligation to realize the divine within them, an idealization that, like most, falls easily into repression. Unobliged to be miniatures of divine perfection, free from the restraining powers of Neoplatonic idealism, Montemayor's characters are human in their disappointments and their failures.

At some point, the depiction of human life had to be divorced from the overly positive as well as the overly negative effects of divine dominion in order to see itself clearly. It is reasonable to conclude that, in sixteenth-century Spain, the negotiation between human autonomy and superhuman power was taking place in texts like the *Diana*. Watt says, "The novel could only concentrate on personal relations once most writers and readers believed that individual human beings, and not collectivities such as the Church, or Transcendent actors, such as the Persons of the Trinity, were allotted the supreme role on the earthly stage."[10] Those forces, however, did not have to be denied for individual consciousness to be represented; conflict between individual experience and the ideal symbolized by such powers seems to have been sufficient to provoke the beginnings of psychological autonomy in literary characters.

The lovers in the *Diana* have attained the ideal in love once: their desire is pure, their intentions noble, and they have succeeded in the past. They inhabit a world, however, in which those intentions are thwarted and made impossible to bring to fruition. Recognizing this inspires the lovers to perceive a dramatic discrepancy between what they want and feel they deserve, which is a successful relationship, and what life brings them, which is trials much greater than the expected difficult rite of passage into happiness that characterizes all virtuous love. Theirs is a problem well beyond the dichotomy traditionally described in pastoral fiction between the neo-Aristotelian categories of poetry and history. The ideal, the world as it should be, is not the implied end toward which the characters are mechanically directed. It is incorporated into the psyches of the characters; it is what they want, and it is what they would get if life were a simple matter of receiving one's just reward, and if the narration were truly romance. But Montemayor's representation of life is no more characterized by clean and absolute resolution, the "happy ending," than life is itself. While readjusting their past expectations to their present situations, Montemayor's lovers are decidedly focused on themselves and fulfillment in sentimental relationships. The notion that their affection for another person might lead them to a higher ideal, the distinguishing theme of Neoplatonism, is never considered.[11]

Neoplatonism joined the divine with the human in harmony and unity;

---

10. *The Rise of the Novel*, 84.
11. Avalle-Arce, to the contrary, maintains that the characters display "concern with the latent ideal, with the very essence of things. . . . That world of perfect archetypes that Plato postulates, and that possesses an ideal reality" (NPE, 75).

it did not coincide with Montemayor's vision of either the human or the divine. It is a present-tense philosophy that looks outward from the self, to the other, to the divine in the other, and ultimately to the divinity itself. Montemayor's orientation is decidedly toward the other direction temporally—back in time—and the other direction psychologically—inward. His characters, accordingly, do not recollect a classical Golden Age of ease and bliss, for bliss did not interest him except as the remote end to the suffering in which he prefers to enmesh his characters and himself. Consequently, there is no Edenic paradise or Saturnic prosperity ever evoked in his works.

Montemayor certainly had contact with authors who could have led him to the Neoplatonic vision, had it been in his character to accept it. One would have been Raymundus de Sabunde, quoted twice, fleetingly, in his "Diálogo spiritual" ("Spiritual Dialogue"). Juan Boscán, for whom Montemayor declares repeated admiration, wrote poetry that speaks beautifully of God's presence on earth in the beloved:

> Of the world, the goodness, and of our time, the glory,
> was the birth of her for whom I live:
> emendation of all earthly things in error.
>   Declaration of nature the most vivid,
> it was to make a perfect tale of virtue,
> and was to join the heavens with the earth.
>
> (Del mundo, bien; de nuestros tiempos, gloria,
> fue nacer ésta por la cual yo bivo:
> enmienda fué de quanto aquí se yerra.
>   Fué declarar lo natural más bivo,
> fue de virtud hazer perfeta istoria,
> y fue juntar el cielo con la tierra.)
>   (vv. 9–14, Soneto 78)[12]

The beloved is never perceived as an intermediary between the human and the divine in Montemayor's writings; he does not even resort to the *donna angelicata* of the *dolce stil novo* to idealize the one for whom his lovers feel their pure affection. Indeed, the characters refer to their beloveds, who have, in most cases, betrayed them, as "that ungrateful and disloyal shepherdess" (aquella desgraciada y desleal pastora); "hard-hearted

---

12. *Obras*, 325.

wild beast" (fiera endurecida); "cruel, ferocious, inhuman" (cruel, fiera, inhumana); "the cruel enemy of my repose" (la cruel enemiga de mi descanso); "the traitor" (el traidor, LD, 37, 23, 67, 29, 47). In a system of beliefs that finds the purpose of love to be proof of the lover's worth, such phrases are logically the norm, for they underscore how much the lover is suffering on behalf of the ideal, pure love. There is, however, no room in such a vision of love for the positive and serene pulse of universal harmony perceived by the Neoplatonists. Indeed, Malcolm MacKenzie Ross posits an inherent discrepancy between Christianity itself and the Platonic cosmos: "The Christian is compelled, under the fixed star of the Incarnation, to believe in existence, in the act of existence. Therefore the Christian artist may not, like the Platonist and all his hybrid brood, oppose a shadow world of things to a real world of value. Rather . . . all things . . . participate proportionately in larger relationships and values which are moral and spiritual without ceasing to be actual, specific, concrete."[13]

This is not to say that the pastoral narrations are thematically or structurally antithetical to Neoplatonism. On the contrary, whenever nature is presented in terms of the Renaissance *topos* as the handmaiden of God, as Cervantes does, Neoplatonism is almost sure to follow.[14] In the *Galatea*, the shepherd Tirsi sings:

> Natural instinct that moves us
> to raise our thoughts so far
> that human vision scarcely can arrive there,
> stairway by which the one who dares, rises
> to the sweet regions of the holy heavens;
> . . . .
> Painter who within our souls portrays,
> with peaceful shadows and colors,
> now mortal, now immortal beauty;
> sun that dissipates all cloudy skies,
> pleasure to whom pains are a delight;
> mirror in which nature proves herself to be
> generous . . .

---

13. *Poetry and Dogma: The Transfiguration of Eucharistic Symbols in Seventeenth Century English Poetry,* 10.

14. Edward William Tayler's book *Nature and Art in Renaissance Literature* is illuminating on this theme.

(Instinto natural que nos conmueve
a levantar los pensamientos, tanto
que apenas llega allí la vista humana;
escala por do sube, el que se atreve,
a la dulce región del cielo sancto;
. . . .
Pintor que en nuestras ánimas retrata,
con apacibles sombras y colores,
ora mortal, ora inmortal belleza;
sol que todo ñublado desbarata,
gusto a quien son sabrosos los dolores;
espejo en quien se ve naturaleza
liberal . . .)
(LG, 2:70)

Nature in the *Diana* is the classical *locus amoenus*, the idealized natural environment that serves as a static backdrop for the poetic scene, in which the characters see their feelings reflected or at least absorbed. They find there no evidence of divine order on earth, rather a consoling and soft environmental blanket for their complaints. Although critics have developed an automatic tendency to interpret sixteenth-century pastoral as Neoplatonic because of the idealized natural environment depicted in it, that environment is not necessarily Neoplatonic. In the prose context, it is related to the idealization of scene concurrent with romance, and in the poetic context it derives ultimately from the classical poetic, not philosophical, tradition.[15] Montemayor's natural world provides a stable background for his characters' emotions, provoking the memories on which the shepherds and shepherdesses elaborate in the first narrative plane by reminding them of a specific past experience. Sireno's first sight of his homeland is "where he first had seen the beauty, grace, purity of the shepherdess Diana" (donde primero avía visto la hermosura, gracia, honestidad de la pastora Diana, LD, 10). The pastoral enclosure also serves to remind the characters of their absence from another time as well as from another place. Thus Selvagia curses her exile from her homeland as she gazes on the natural beauty around her, the separation moving her to cry, "Oh fortune, enemy of my glory, / how this wretched valley tires me!" (¡O

---

15. See Ernst Robert Curtius on the nature of the *locus amoenus* (*European Literature and the Latin Middle Ages*, 198).

fortuna, enemiga de mi gloria, / cómo me cansa este enfadoso valle!, LD, 65). It is difficult to classify as Neoplatonic the natural world that inspires a character to recognize her surroundings as beautiful but still leaves her unable to divorce her own anxiety from them.

The Neoplatonic vision is missing in the *Diana*, that doctrine which "broke the spell of the essential dichotomy that had been believed to exist between an imperfect, corruptible earth and the perfect, incorruptible heavens."[16] As should be apparent by now, Montemayor delighted in the irreconcilability of the divine and the human conditions, for it allowed him to believe that God's realm was untouched by the impurities he found dominating his own. In the *Diana*, as in his religious writings, his sorrowful gaze clearly falls on the human end of that spectrum, the divine being perceived as impersonally majestic and perfect. Consequently, the lovers of his pastoral narration do not look outward or upward because they are too busy looking inward. Their frequent complaints to heaven surge from their personal despair, in which they invoke divine attention, not necessarily assistance, as does the Psalmist crying out at injustices committed against him.

Montemayor is frequently taken to task for not gifting his characters with the strength of will to overcome their situations. Such a critical stance, however, discredits his choice to focus on the moment of disillusioned remembrance. Further, his characters are typically accused of refusing to be responsible for their problems and of not taking charge of their lives.[17] Emphasis would be more productively placed on his effective attention to those moments in life when one is indeed a victim, when action is impossible and inappropriate, when desire and purity of intention are worthless, and when that is all one cares to think about. It is a decidedly vital, not literary, posture. What is more, if his characters do not assume responsibility for their problems, it is because they indeed are not responsible for them. Their partners in courtship failed them by abandoning their promises of constancy. Those in whose cases the possibility for a solution exists (Felismena, Filemón, and Danteo) do pursue their desire, as did the other

---

16. Erwin Panofsky, "Artist, Scientist, Genius: Notes on the 'Renaissance-Dämmerung,'" 130.

17. Amadeu Solé-Leris, for example, finds in the *Diana* a "notion of ultimate irresponsibility," whereas Gaspar Gil Polo's *Diana enamorada* portrays an "affirmation of responsibility" ("The Theory of Love in the Two *Dianas:* A Contrast," 79).

characters before their beloveds turned on them. It is easy to overlook the fact that all the characters except Sylvano have known happiness in love as a result of their own willful pursuit of it, because those moments are recollections, not events in the narrative present. By the time the story begins, there is nothing most of them can do except remember their pasts, or forget them, which is recognized as something that will come with time. For the betrayed lovers among them to rise up against two inviolable events, marriage and death, with their personal desires would be folly (and heresy).

When the characters succumb to their destinies, as determined by the stars or other augurs from birth, as Felismena, Diana, and Filemón (LD, 98, 241, 261) or by the irrevocable forces of fortune and time, Montemayor is simply representing the power of a force greater than humanity to influence events in the lives of men and women. Whether their submission to fortune and time denies human free will or affirms divine power is a matter of debate. It must be noted, however, that Montemayor's religious works are completely orthodox in his affirmation of free will, even as the power of that free will is minimized by his insistence on its nothingness compared to the might of divine grace. This vision harmonizes perfectly with the tone and themes of the *Diana*.

What Montemayor captures, with great fidelity of kind if not of degree, is that moment of supreme disillusion when the ideal fails due to the fault of the other, the moment of victimization, which seems to endure endlessly when it arrives, tainting one's vision of the future and recollection of the past. Again, it is of paramount importance to recognize that the ideal to which Montemayor's characters aspire, before their disillusion and afterward, is a personal goal, limited to individual, earthly experience. It is their creator's own transmuted version of what he found to be correct in love behavior, deduced through experience and the manipulation of some prestigious sources. Therefore, Montemayor's love is allied to Hebreo's for Hebreo's own alliance with the medieval love tradition, which also exalted suffering and spiritual love.

Unlike Montemayor, Hebreo defines a love that can be eternal because it is ultimately independent of the beloved. In Neoplatonic devotion, the beautiful object of affection is merely an instrument, something to step on metaphorically, so as to transcend it. Montemayor rejected this approach and locked love instead within the suffering consciousness of the individual committed to contact with another living person on earth. Finding that path cut off, the lover turns back to introspection and review, as if engaged in a futile attempt to make right a wrong event that has irrevocably taken place. Human love, as represented by Montemayor, leads the lover back to the self, not to the other, and not to God. This is made clear by the several occasions when Sireno sees himself, not Diana, in his beloved's eyes. Diana speaks to her own eyes saying "You were the mirror in which he saw himself" (érades espejo en que se vía, LD, 24); Sireno repeats that she was "the mirror in which I saw myself" (el espejo a do me vía, LD, 70) and later repeats "It seems I am seeing / the eyes in which I saw myself" (Paréceme que estoy viendo / los ojos en que me vi, LD, 129).[18] Such movement ever toward the self, within the self, is deeply allied to the Spanish recogido experience in its initial stages, likewise dedicated to self-examination and critical review of the past. At its end, however, the mystic finally abandons the self in the other, a step not represented in any of Montemayor's works.

Neoplatonism made men and women responsible for living up to the divine image within themselves, and thereby discouraged scrutiny of humanity in strictly human terms. Just what positive and realistic effect such philosophical idealism had on the progression of literature from what it was to what it eventually became has yet to be determined; to hold humanity up to eternal ideals inevitably leads to disappointment and disallows representation of the fallibility that is part of the human condition and any literature proposing to depict it faithfully.[19] It seems likely that the eternal ideal had little place in the development of the mirror image in fiction, whether one recognizes the arrival at that point in literary history as a positive event or not, since the notion of timelessness did not take hold in the post-classical era. Of the classical concept of the eternal that exists beyond the temporal dimension, Watt says: "This premise is diametrically opposed to the outlook which has established itself since the Renaissance, and which views time, not only as a crucial dimension of the physical world, but as the shaping force of man's individual and collective history."[20] Significantly, Montemayor undercuts the eternal ideal of love in the *Diana*,

---

18. Approaching a similar theme, Ruth El Saffar speaks of Diana, who sees herself in a mirror Sireno holds up to her, concluding from Diana's point of view: "For the loved-one, the lover becomes secondary, a mere vehicle through whom her vision of herself can be sustained" ("Thematic Discontinuity in Montemayor's *Diana*," 187).

19. According to Marina Warner, for example, the attribution of divine qualities to women, via the cult of the Virgin Mary, had destructive and far-reaching consequences (*Alone of All Her Sex: The Myth and the Cult of the Virgin Mary*).

20. *The Rise of the Novel*, 21–22.

and recognizes instead the inevitable, synchronic flow of life. This representation was made possible by the ideology found in his religious works, which stress distinction between the human and the divine, not similarity.

For all his emphasis on immediate human states, such as frustrated attempts to reap the rewards of carrying out the mandates of virtuous desire, Montemayor may have brought more to literature than is typically imagined. Watt refers to Richardson's *Pamela* saying, "The complexities of the forces juxtaposed are largely responsible for the unique literary qualities which *Pamela* brought into fiction: they make possible a detailed presentation of a personal relationship enriched by a series of developing contrasts between the ideal and the real, the apparent and the actual, the spiritual and the physical." The *Diana*, with its emphasis on identical contrasts, did much the same thing centuries before.[21] Indeed, a chain of influence surely exists from Montemayor to Sidney to Richardson, whose Pamela was likely named after Sidney's, in which an expression of inner experience was fostered under the rubric of pastoral but subsequently reached well beyond it. Montemayor's shepherds and shepherdesses are key figures in this process, for they represent the human being striving for virtue and fulfillment on earth, not in a context of humanism, but of humanity.

It is inappropriate to label any of Montemayor's works as examples of Renaissance Neoplatonism. His own spiritual heritage—the Bible, Ausias March, Jorge Manrique, the recogidos—is too rich to deny and too present in his writings to successfully ignore. The characteristic that most allies him to the humanists, spiritual love, was the fundamental theme of the religious literature vividly present in Spanish culture during the years of the *Diana*'s creation and rapid acceptance. Montemayor's religious writings reveal a strong alliance to that tradition, one not only distinct from but actually critical of humanistic sources and practices such as extensive study and the perpetual engaging of the intellect. The interiorization or spiritualization of a problem that his works describe is a process in itself

---

21. Quotation is from *The Rise of the Novel*, 172. Watt's idea that Calvin (1509–1564) was the one responsible for reestablishing Augustine's "pattern of purposive spiritual introspection" in the sixteenth century (75) might be productively broadened to include Spanish literature published before Calvin's influence was widely felt, such as Osuna's *Tercer abecedario espiritual*, first published in 1527, and Granada's 1554 *Libro de la oración*. As has been mentioned, Spanish devotional treatises were widely read abroad.

intimately linked to the religiousness his works support, portraying the same pained sentimental disillusion before the ideal and the ideal's fate on earth that religious writers such as Luis de Granada lament.

The pastoral characters' love, like the love of Christ, is founded upon loss, loss of control in acceptance of a power greater than the individual, loss of the self, loss of the other, loss of the world, and even, in the case of happy love, loss of the beloved, for the loving moment must end, whether undone by human fallibility or ended by death. Love, like happiness, is represented as a transient state at best for the human lover, of God or of another human being. Given this focus, it is natural that Montemayor exalts neither the world, humans in it, nor love in itself. What he does exalt is the self, pained and pure, deserving and unreceiving. These are pure Christian values, and Christ on the cross hangs in heavy silence behind them. They stem from the deepest core of the Christian tradition, not from its happy marriage to the classics forged by the Italian humanists.

Representing the confrontation between timeless ideology and human beings—loving, fallible, and of a nature subject to time and change—Montemayor leads his reader not to heaven, but within herself or himself, through the same process of recollection he exalts in his religious works. It is a binary self-examination, recollecting in the sense of closing out all else but the feeling spirit, and recollecting what has been, remembering the past. It is a backward glance that enriched the future, the representation of life in literature. On the other hand, like human beings, Montemayor's characters are caught in the on-going processes of living, which, excepting the moments of birth and death, has little to do with the clear-cut starts and finishes of books. As Carolyn G. Heilbrun has put it, "'Endings' are for romance or for daydreams, but not for life."[22]

The *Diana* has long been faulted for its changes in perspective, its combination of disparate ideas and forms, its odd collection of different types of characters with their fond recollection of the past at the expense of the present, and especially for their failure to arrive at an ending that is neat in its total resolution with their expressed desires. It is truly remarkable that these are the very qualities of Montemayor's book most faithful to the experience of human life as every reader knows it to be.

---

22. *Writing a Woman's Life*, 130.

WORKS CITED

Works by Montemayor

Cancionero. Zaragoza, 1562.
El cancionero del poeta Jorge de Montemayor. Edited by Angel González Palencia. Madrid: Sociedad de Bibliófilos Españoles, 1932.
"Carta ao senhor Francisco de Sâ de Miranda." In *Poesias de Francisco de Sâ de Miranda,* edited by Carolina Michaëlis de Vasconcelos, 653–57. Halle: Max Niemeyer, 1885.
"Diálogo spiritual." Ms. cód. CXIII/1-41. Biblioteca Pública, Évora, Portugal.
"Epístola a Diego Ramírez Pagán." In *Floresta de varia poesía,* by Diego Ramírez Pagán, edited by Antonio Pérez Gómez, vol. 1, 122–37. Barcelona: Selecciones Bibliófilas, 1950.
"Exposición moral sobre el salmo 86." Edited by Francisco López Estrada. *Revista de Bibliografía Nacional* 5 (1944): 499–523.
"Glosa de diez coplas de Jorge Manrique hecha por Jorge de Montemayor . . ." In *Catálogo razonado y bibliográfico de los autores portugueses que escribieron en castellano,* edited by Domingo García Péres, 393–403. Madrid: Imprenta del Colegio Nacional, 1890.
"Glosa de diez coplas de Jorge Manrique hecha por Jorge de Montemayor . . . [facsimile]" In *Pliegos poéticos españoles de la Biblioteca Nacional de Lisboa,* 49–60. Madrid: Joyas Bibliográficas, 1975.
"Historia de Alcida y Silvano." Edited by Elizabeth Rhodes. *Dicenda: Revista de Filología Hispánica* 2 (1983): 201–36.
"Historia de los muy constantes y infelices amores de Píramo y Tisbe." In *Dos versiones de Píramo y Tisbe: Jorge de Montemayor y Pedro Sánchez de Viana,* edited by B. W. Ife, 3–66. Exeter: University of Exeter, 1974.
Obras. Amberes, 1554.
Las obras de Ausias March traducidas por Jorge de Montemayor. Edited by Francisco Carreres y de Calatayud. Biblioteca de Antiguos Libros

Hispánicos 8. Madrid: Consejo Superior de Investigaciones Científicas, 1947.

[Poema en contestación a Juan de Alcalá, "So palabras de loor"]. Manuscript 98-A-V of the Library at the Castle of Perelada, fols. 185v–86v.

Las obras de Ausias March traducidas por Jorge de Montemayor. In *Traducciones castellanas de Ausias March en la edad de oro,* edited by Martín de Riquer, 129–304. Barcelona: Instituto Español de Estudios Mediterráneos, 1946.

Las obras de Ausias March traducidas por Jorge de Montemayor. Edited by Martín de Riquer. Clásicos Universales Planeta 181. Barcelona: Editorial Planeta, 1990.

Segundo cancionero. Antwerp, 1558.

Segundo cancionero spiritual. Antwerp, 1558.

Los siete libros de la Diana. Edited by Francisco López Estrada. 4th ed. Clásicos Castellanos 127. Madrid: Espasa-Calpe, 1967.

"Three *Autos* of Jorge de Montmayor." Edited by Florence Whyte. *PMLA* 43 (1928): 953–89.

Other Works

Alonso, Dámaso. "Un poeta madrileñista, latinista y francesista en la mitad del siglo 16: Don Juan Hurtado de Mendoza." *Boletín de la Real Academia Española* 37 (1957): 213–98.

———. "Sobre Erasmo y Fray Luis de Granada." In *De los siglos oscuros al de oro: Notas y artículos de 700 años de letras españolas,* 218–25. 2d ed. Madrid: Editorial Gredos, 1971.

Alonso Cortés, Narciso. "Sobre Montemayor y 'La Diana.'" In *Artículos histórico-literarios,* 127–40. Valladolid: Imprenta Castellana, 1935.

Alpers, Paul. "Empson on Pastoral." *New Literary History* 10 (1978–1979): 101–23.

———. "Mode and Genre: The Example of Pastoral." Lecture at Boston University, February 19, 1987.

———. *The Singer of the Eclogues: A Study of Virgilian Pastoral.* Berkeley and Los Angeles: University of California Press, 1979.

———. "What is Pastoral?" *Critical Inquiry* 8 (1982): 437–60.

Amiel, Charles. "The Archives of the Portuguese Inquisition: A Brief Survey." Translated by Lawrence Scott Rainey. In *The Inquisition in Early*

Modern Europe: Studies on Sources and Methods, edited by Gustav Henningsen and John Tedeschi in association with Charles Amiel, 79–99. Dekalb: Northern Illinois University Press, 1986.

Andrés Martín, Melquíades. "Alumbrados, erasmistas, 'luteranos' y místicos, y su común dominador: El riesgo de una espiritualidad más 'intimista.'" In *Inquisición española y mentalidad inquisitorial.* Proceedings of the International Symposium on the Inquisition, New York, April 1983, 373–409. Barcelona: Editorial Ariel, 1984.

———. "Carácteres generales de la generación teológica humanista española (1500–1530)." In *Semana Española de Teología* (September 18–23, 1959), 261–74.

———. "Introducción general." In *Tercer abecedario espiritual,* by Francisco de Osuna, 3–117. BAC Normal 333. Madrid: Editorial Católica, 1972.

———. *Nueva visión de los 'alumbrados' de 1525.* Madrid: Fundación Universitaria Española, 1973.

———. *Los recogidos: Nueva visión de la mística española (1500–1700).* Monografías 13. Madrid: Fundación Universitaria Española, 1976.

———. *Reforma española y reforma luterana: afinidades y diferencias a la luz de los místicos españoles (1517–1536).* Conferencias 37. Madrid: Fundación Universitaria Española, 1975.

———. *La teología española en el siglo 16.* BAC Maior 13, 14. Madrid: Editorial Católica, 1976.

Antolín, Guillermo. "El traductor latino de las Coplas de Jorge Manrique." *Revue Hispanique* 14 (1906): 22–34.

Asensio, Eugenio. "El erasmismo y las corrientes espirituales afines." *Revista de Filología Española* 36 (1952): 31–99.

———. "Lourenço de Cáceres y su tratado *Dos trabalhos do Rei* (con una nota sobre Jorge de Montemayor plagiario)." *Ibérida* 4–6 (1960–1961): 56–78.

Aspe, María Paz. "El cambio de rumbo de la espiritualidad española a mediados del siglo 17." In *Inquisición española y mentalidad inquisitorial.* Proceedings of the International Symposium on the Inquisition, New York, April 1983, 424–33. Barcelona: Editorial Ariel, 1984.

Avalle-Arce, Juan Bautista. "El arco de los leales amadores en el *Amadís.*" *Nueva Revista de Filología Hispánica* 6 (1952): 149–55.

―――. *La novela pastoril española.* 2d ed. Madrid: Ediciones Istmo, 1974.
Bakhtin, Mikhail. *The Dialogic Imagination.* Translated by Caryl Emerson and Michael Holquist. Austin: University of Texas Press, 1981.
Barbosa Machado, Diogo. *Biblioteca lusitana histórica, crítica e cronológica.* 4 vols. Lisbon: I. Rodrígues, 1741.
Bataillon, Marcel. "El anónimo del soneto 'No me mueve, mi Dios, para quererte.'" *Nueva Revista de Filología Hispánica* 4 (1950): 254–69.
―――. "Chanson pieuse et poésie de devotion: Fr. Ambrosio Montesino." *Bulletin Hispanique* 27 (1925): 228–38.
―――. "De Savonarole à Louis de Grenade." *Revue de Littérature Comparée* 16 (1936): 23–39.
―――. *Erasmo y España: Estudios sobre la historia espiritual del siglo 16.* Translated by Antonio Alatorre. 2d ed. in Spanish. Mexico: Fondo de Cultura Económica, 1966.
―――. "Jeanne d'Autriche, Princesse de Portugal." In *Etudes sur le Portugal au temps de l'humanisme,* 262–83. Coimbra: Por ordem da Universidade, 1952.
―――. "¿Melancolía renacentista o melancolía judía?" In *Varia lección de clásicos españoles,* 39–54. Madrid: Editorial Gredos, 1964.
―――. "Une source de Gil Vicente et de Montemôr: La Méditation de Savonarole sur le *Miserere.*" *Bulletin des Etudes Portugaises* 3 (1936): 1–16.
―――. "Sur la diffusion des oeuvres de Savonarole en Espagne et au Portugal (1500–1560)." In *Mélanges de Philologie, d'Histoire et de Littérature offerts à M. Joseph Vianey,* 93–103. Paris: n.p., 1934.
Beltrán de Heredia, Vicente. *Las corrientes de espiritualidad entre los dominicos de Castilla durante la primera mitad del siglo 16.* Salamanca: Convento de San Esteban, 1941.
―――. *Historia de la reforma de la provincia de España (1450–1550).* Rome: Istituto Storico Domenicano, 1939.
Bernard of Clairvaux. *On the Song of Songs.* Translated by Kilian Walsh. Cistercian Fathers Series, nos. 4, 5. Kalamazoo: Cistercian Publications, 1981.
Bernheimer, Richard. *Wild Men in the Middle Ages: A Study in Art, Sentiment, and Demonology.* Cambridge: Harvard University Press, 1982.
Bilinkoff, Jodi. *The Avila of Saint Teresa. Religious Reform in a Sixteenth-Century City.* Ithaca and London: Cornell University Press, 1989.
Blecua, Alberto. "¿Signos viejos o signos nuevos? ("Fino amor" y "religio

amoris" en Gregorio Silvestre)." In *La literatura como signo*, 110–44. Madrid: Playor, 1982.
Boase, Roger. "Courtly Love in Spanish Literature: A Continuing Debate." *Journal of Hispanic Philology* 9 (1984): 67–73.
Boccaccio, Giovanni. *Decameron*. Edited by Cesare Segre. Testi 1. Milano: Mursia, 1966–1980.
Boscán Almugáver, Juan. *Obras*. Edited by Carlos Clavería. Barcelona: PPU, 1991.
Bromberg, Rachel. *Three Pastoral Novels*. New York: Postar Press, 1970.
Burke, Kenneth. *A Grammar of Motives*. Berkeley: University of California Press, 1969.
Bynum, Carolyn Walker. "The Body of Christ in the Later Middle Ages: A Reply to Leo Steinberg." In *Fragmentation and Redemption, Essays on Gender and the Human Body in Medieval Religion*, 79–118. New York: Zone Books, 1991.
———. *Holy Feast and Holy Fast: The Religious Significance of Food to Medieval Women*. Berkeley and Los Angeles: University of California Press, 1987.
———. *Jesus as Mother: Studies in the Spirituality of the High Middle Ages*. Publications of the Center for Medieval and Renaissance Studies, UCLA, 16. Berkeley and Los Angeles: University of California Press, 1982.
Caro Mallén de Soto, Ana. "Valor, agravio, y mujer." In vol. 268 of the *Biblioteca de Autores Españoles*, 179–212. Madrid: Atlas, 1975.
Carranza de Miranda, Bartolomé. *Comentarios sobre el Catechismo christiano*. Edited by José Ignacio Tellechea Idígoras. BAC Maior 1, 2. Madrid: Editorial Católica, 1982.
Carreño, Antonio. "La otra *Arcadia* de Lope de Vega: *Pastores de Belén*." In *Homenaje al Profesor Antonio Vilanova*, edited by Marta Cristina Carbonell, 137–55. Barcelona: Departamento de Filología Española, Universidad de Barcelona, 1989.
Cascardi, Anthony J. "Genre Definition and Multiplicity in *Don Quijote*." *Cervantes* 6 (1986): 39–49.
Castiglione, Baldassarre. *Il libro del cortegiano*. Edited by Ettore Bonora. 2d ed. Testi 15. Milan: Mursia, 1976.
Castro, Américo. "Lo hispánico y el erasmismo." *Revista de Filología Hispánica* 1 (1942): 1–66.
———. "Los prólogos al *Quijote*." In *Hacia Cervantes*, 275–80. 3d ed. Madrid: Taurus, 1967.

---. *La realidad histórica de España*. 4th ed. Mexico: Editorial Porrua, 1971.
Cátedra, Pedro M. "La biblioteca del caballero cristiano don Antonio de Rojas, ayo del príncipe don Carlos (1556)." *Modern Language Notes* 98 (1983): 226–49.
Cervantes Saavedra, Miguel de. "El coloquio de los perros." In vol. 2 of the *Novelas ejemplares*, edited by Harry Sieber, 297–359. 7th ed. Letras Hispánicas 107. Madrid: Cátedra, 1985.
---. *La Galatea*. Edited by Juan Bautista Avalle-Arce. Clásicos Castellanos 154, 155. Madrid: Espasa-Calpe, 1961.
---. *La Galatea*. Edited by Juan Bautista Avalle-Arce. Clásicos Castellanos, nueva serie 5. Madrid: Espasa-Calpe, 1987.
---. *El ingenioso hidalgo Don Quijote de la Mancha*. Edited by Luis Andrés Murillo. Clásicos Castalia 77–79. Madrid: Editorial Castalia, 1987.
---. *Los trabajos de Persiles y Sigismunda*. Edited by Juan Bautista Avalle-Arce. Clásicos Castalia 12. Madrid: Editorial Castalia, 1984.
Chevalier, Maxime. " 'La Diana' de Montemayor y su público en la España del siglo 16." In *Creación y público en la literatura española*, edited by J. F. Botrel and S. Salaün, 40–55. Madrid: Castalia, 1974.
---. *Lectura y lectores en la España del siglo 16 y 17*. Madrid: Ediciones Turner, 1976.
Correa, Gustavo. "El templo de *Diana* en la novela de Jorge de Montemayor." *Thesaurus* 16 (1961): 59–76.
Cortest, Luis. "Fray Alonso de Madrid, the *Arte para servir a Dios* and Sixteenth-century Religious Literature." *Bulletin of Hispanic Studies* 55 (1988): 369–82.
Covarrubias y Orozco, Sebastián de. *Tesoro de la lengua castellana o española*. Madrid, 1611.
Cravens, Sidney. *Feliciano de Silva y los antecedentes de la novela pastoril en sus libros de cabellerías*. Estudios de Hispanófila, no. 38. Chapel Hill: University of North Carolina Press, 1976.
Creel, Bryant L. "Aesthetics of Change in a Renaissance Pastoral: New Ideals of Moral Culture in Montemayor's *La Diana*." *Hispanófila* 33 (1990): 1–28.
---. "Reformist Dialectics and Poetic Adaptations of Psalm 137, *Super flumina Babylonis* in the Sixteenth Century." In *Camoniana Californiana*, edited by María de Lourdes Belchior and Enrique Martínez-López, 85–92. Santa Barbara: Jorge de Sena Center and Bandanna Books, 1986.

―――. *The Religious Poetry of Jorge de Montemayor.* London: Tamesis, 1981.
Cruickshank, D. W. "Literature and the Book Trade." *Modern Language Notes* 73 (1978): 799–824.
Cull, John. "Further Observations on Violence in the Pastoral Novel." In *El tema de la violencia en las literaturas hispánicas.* Proceedings of the Tenth Annual Conference on Hispanic Literatures at Indiana University of Pennsylvania, edited by J. Cruz Mendizábal, 58–68. Indiana: University Press of Pennsylvania, 1984.
Culler, Jonathan. "Poetics of the Lyric" and "Poetics of the Novel." In *Structuralist Poetics: Structuralism, Linguistics, and the Study of Literature*, 161–88, 189–238. 1975. Reprint. Ithaca: Cornell University Press, 1978.
Curtius, Ernst Robert. *European Literature and the Latin Middle Ages.* Translated by Willard R. Trask. 1953. Reprint. London: Routledge & Kegal Paul, 1979.
Damiani, Bruno. La Diana *of Montemayor as Social and Religious Teaching.* Lexington: University of Kentucky Press, 1983.
Darbord, Michel. "La Clara Diana a lo divino." In *Mélanges offerts à Marcel Bataillon. Bulletin Hispanique* 64*bis* (1962): 403–11.
―――. *La poésie religieuse espagnole des Rois Catholiques à Philippe II.* Paris: Centre de Recherches de l'Institut d'Études Hispaniques, 1965.
Darst, David H. "Renaissance Platonism and the Spanish Pastoral Novel." *Hispania* 52 (1969): 384–92.
Davis, Walter. *A Map of Arcadia: Sidney's Romance in Its Tradition.* In *Sidney's Arcadia*, 1–182. New Haven and London: Yale University Press, 1965.
de Armas, Frederick. "Las tres Dianas de Montemayor." In *Lingüística y educación.* Proceedings of the Fourth International Convention of the ALFAL, 186–94. Lima: Universidad Mayor de San Marcos, 1978.
Dedieu, Jean Pierre. "The Archives of the Holy Office of Toledo as a Source for Historical Anthropology." Translated by E. W. Monter. In *The Inquisition in Early Modern Europe: Studies on Sources and Methods*, edited by Gustav Henningsen and John Tedeschi in association with Charles Amiel, 158–89. Dekalb: Northern Illinois University Press, 1986.
Deyermond, Alan D. "El hombre salvaje en la novela sentimental." In

Actas del II Congreso Internacional de Hispanistas, edited by Jaime Sánchez Romeralo and Norbert Roulussen, 265–72. Nijwegen: Asociación Internacional de Hispanistas, 1967.

———. *The Middle Ages.* Vol. 1, *A Literary History of Spain,* director Royston O. Jones. London: Ernest Benn; New York: Barnes & Noble, 1971.

———. "Las relaciones genéricas de la ficción sentimental española." In *Symposium in honorem Profesor Martín de Riquer,* 75–92. Barcelona: Universitat de Barcelona, 1984.

Dias, José Sebastiao da Silva. *Correntes de sentimento religioso em Portugal (séculos 16 a 17).* 2 vols. Coimbra: Universidade, 1960.

Díez de Triana, Desiderio. "Introducción." In *Obra selecta de Fray Luis de Granada: Una suma de la vida cristiana,* xxvii–lxxvi. BAC Normal 20. Madrid: Editorial Católica, 1947.

DiSalvo, Anjelo J. "The Ascetical Meditative Literature of Renaissance Spain: An Alternative to Amadís, Elisa and Diana." *Hispania* 69 (1986): 466–75.

Dupont, Jean. "Un *pliego suelto* de 1552 intitulé: 'Cancionero de las obras de devoción de Jorge de Montemayor.'" *Bulletin Hispanique* 75 (1973): 40–72.

Egido, Aurora. "Teoría de la égloga en el Siglo de Oro." *Criticón* (Toulouse) 30 (1985): 43–77.

El Saffar, Ruth. *Beyond Fiction: The Recovery of the Feminine in the Works of Cervantes.* Berkeley and Los Angeles: University of California Press, 1984.

———. "Thematic Discontinuity in Montemayor's *Diana.*" *Modern Language Notes* 86 (1971): 182–98.

———. "The Truth of the Matter: The Place of Romance in the Works of Cervantes." In *Romance: Generic Transformation from Chrétien de Troyes to Cervantes,* edited by Kevin Brownlee and Marina S. Brownlee, 238–52. Hanover: University Press of New England, 1985.

Empson, William. *Some Versions of Pastoral.* 1935. Reprint. New York: New Directions, 1974.

Erasmus, Desiderius. *El Enquiridión o manual del caballero cristiano.* Translated by Alonso Fernández de Madrid. "Prólogo" by Marcel Bataillon, edited by Dámaso Alonso. *Revista de Filología Española,* Anejo 16. Madrid: S. Aguirre, 1932.

Estevá, María Dolores. "El 'Diálogo spiritual' de Jorge de Montemayor." In

1616: Sociedad de Literatura General y Comparada, 31–45. Anuario 1983. Madrid: Sociedad Española de Literatura General, 1985.

Ettin, Andrew. *Literature and the Pastoral*. New Haven: Yale University Press, 1984.

Ferguson, Margaret, Maureen Quinlan, and Nancy Vickers. "Introduction." In *Rewriting the Renaissance: The Discourses of Sexual Difference in Early Modern Europe*, xv–xxxi. Chicago: University of Chicago Press, 1986.

Fermo, Serafino de. *Las obras espirituales*. [Translated by Bonaventura de Morales.] Antwerp, 1556.

Ferry, Anne. *The "Inward" Language: Sonnets of Wyatt, Sidney, Shakespeare, Donne*. Chicago: University of Chicago Press, 1983.

Forcione, Alban K. *Cervantes, Aristotle, and the* Persiles. Princeton: Princeton University Press, 1970.

Fosalba Vela, Eugenia. *El* Abencerraje *pastoril: estudio y edición crítica*. Barcelona: Departamento de Filología Española, Universidad Autónoma de Barcelona, 1990.

Frye, Northrup. "Archetypal Criticism: Theory of Myths." In *Anatomy of Criticism: Four Essays*, 131–239. Princeton: Princeton University Press, 1973.

Gallego Morell, Antonio. *Garcilaso de la Vega y sus comentaristas*. 2d ed. Biblioteca Románica Hispánica, Textos 7. Madrid: Editorial Gredos, 1972.

García-Villoslada, Ricardo. "Pedro Guerrero, representante de la reforma española." In *Il Concilio de Trento e la riforma tridentina*. Proceedings of the International Convention of History, Trent, Sept. 2–6, 1963, vol. 1, 115–55. Rome: Herder, 1965.

Garcilaso de la Vega. *Obras*. Edited by Tomás Navarro Tomás. 1924. Reprint. Madrid: Espasa-Calpe, 1966.

Gil Polo, Gaspar. *Diana enamorada*. Edited by Francisco López Estrada. Clásicos Castalia 162. Madrid: Editorial Castalia, 1987.

Glaser, Edward. "Nuevos datos sobre la crítica de los libros de caballerías en los siglos 16 y 17." *Annuario de Estudios Medievales* 3 (1966): 393–410.

Googe, Barnabe. *Eclogues, Epitaphs and Sonnets*. Edited by Judith M. Kennedy. Toronto: University of Toronto Press, 1988.

González y Fernández-Corugedo, Santiago. "Ediciones de la poesía profana de Jorge de Montemayor." *Archivum* (Oviedo) 36 (1986): 414–20.

Grant, W. Leonard. *Neo-Latin Literature and the Pastoral.* Chapel Hill: University of North Carolina Press, 1965.

Green, Otis. "Se acicalaron los auditorios: An Aspect of the Spanish Literary Baroque." *Hispanic Review* 27 (1959): 413–22.

Groult, Pierre. *Literatura espiritual española: Edad Media y Renacimiento.* Translated by Rodrigo A. Molina. Biblioteca de Hispanismo 4. Madrid: Fundación Universitaria Española, 1980.

———. *Los místicos de los paises bajos y la literatura espiritual española del siglo 16.* Translated by Rodrigo A. Molina. Madrid: Fundación Universitaria Española, 1976.

Guevara, Fray Antonio de. *Reloj de príncipes y libro de Marco Aurelio.* Edited by Angel Rosenblat. Madrid: Igno, 1936.

Hahn, Juergen. *The Origins of the Baroque Concept of Peregrinatio.* University of North Carolina Studies in the Romance Languages and Literatures 131. Chapel Hill: University of North Carolina Press, 1973.

Harrison, Thomas P. "Bartholomew Yong, Translator." *Modern Language Review* 21 (1926): 129–39.

———. "Concerning 'Two Gentlemen of Verona' and Montemayor's *Diana.*" *Modern Language Notes* 41 (1926): 251–52.

———. *Diana de Monte mayor done out of Spanish by Thomas Wilson (1596)* New York: British Museum, 1921.

———. "*The Faerie Queene* and the *Diana.*" *Philological Quarterly* 9 (1930): 51–56.

———. "Shakespeare and Montemayor's Diana." *Texas Studies in English* 6 (1926): 72–120.

———. "A Source of Sidney's *Arcadia.*" *Texas Studies in English* 6 (1926): 53–71.

Hazañas y la Rua, Joaquín, ed. *Obras de Gutierre de Cetina.* 2 vols. Seville: Francisco de P. Díaz, 1895.

Heilbrun, Carolyn G. *Writing a Woman's Life.* New York and London: W. W. Norton, 1988.

Huerga, Alvaró. "Fray Luis de Granada en Escalaceli. Nuevos datos para el conocimiento histórico y espiritual de su vida." *Hispania* (Revista Española de Historia) 9; 10 (1949; 1950): 434–80; 297–335.

———. *Fray Luis de Granada: Una vida al servicio de la Iglesia.* BAC Normal 496. Madrid: Editorial Católica, 1988.

———. *Predicadores, alumbrados e Inquisición en el siglo 16.* Madrid: Fundación Universitaria Española, 1973.
———. *Savonarola, reformador y profeta.* BAC Normal 397. Madrid: Editorial Católica, 1978.
Huizinga, Johan. "The Forms of Thought and Practical Life." In *The Waning of the Middle Ages,* translated by F. Hopman, 225–42. 1949. Reprint. New York: Anchor Books, 1954.
Hurtado de Mendoza, Juan. *Alvorada trovada.* Edited by Antonio Pérez Gómez. Textos Literarios Rarísimos. Cieza: El Aire de la Almena, 1956.
Ife, B. W. *Reading and Fiction in Golden-Age Spain: A Platonist Critique and Some Picaresque Replies.* Cambridge and New York: Cambridge University Press, 1985.
La Iglesia en la España de los siglos 15 y 16. Vol. 3, Parts 1 and 2 of *La Historia de la Iglesia en España,* directed by Ricardo García-Villoslada. BAC Maior 18, 21. Madrid: Editorial Católica, 1979–1980.
Ignacis de Loyola, San. *Ejercicios espirituales.* In *Obras completas,* edited by Ignacio Iparraguirre and Cándido de Dalmases, 207–90. 4th ed. BAC Normal 86. Madrid: Editorial Católica, 1982.
Ilie, Paul. "Grotesque Elements in the Pastoral Novel." In *Homenaje a William L. Fichter,* edited by A. David Kossoff and José Amor y Vázquez, 319–24. Madrid: Editorial Castalia, 1971.
Jehenson, Myriam Yvonne. *The Golden World of the Pastoral: A Comparative Study of Sidney's* New Arcadia *and d'Urfé's* L'Astrée. Ravenna: Longo Editore, 1981.
Johannes Climacus. *Escala espiritual.* Translated by Fray Luis de Granada. In vol. 3 of *Obras de Fray Luis de Granada,* 281–379. Vol. 11 of the *Biblioteca de Autores Españoles.* Madrid: Atlas, 1849.
———. *Libro llamado Escala Espiritual . . .* Valencia, 1553.
———. *Sant Juan Climaco que trata de las tablas y escalera spiritual . . .* Toledo, 1504.
———. *Scala paradisi.* Cologne, 1540.
———. *Scala spiritualis.* Toledo, 1505.
Johnson, Carroll B. "Montemayor's *Diana*: A Novel Pastoral." *Bulletin of Hispanic Studies* 48 (1971): 20–35.
Jones, Joseph R. "'Human Time' in *La Diana.*" *Romance Notes* 10 (1968): 139–46.

Jones, Royston O. *Siglo de oro: Prosa y poesía*. Vol. 2 of *Historia de la literatura española*. 4th ed. Barcelona: Editorial Ariel, 1979.
Juan Buenaventura, San. [*Estimulo de amor, que cõpuso el seraphico doctor sant Juan Buenaventura, de la orden de los Frayles Menores*] [Baeça, 1551].
Juan de Ávila, San. *Avisos y reglas cristianas sobre aquel verso de David: Audi, filia*. Edited by Luis Sala Balust. Espirituales Españoles, Textos 10. Barcelona: Juan Flors, 1963.
Kalstone, David. "The Transformation of Arcadia: Sannazaro and Sir Philip Sidney." *Comparative Literature* 15 (1963): 234–49.
Kamen, Henry. *Inquisition and Society in Spain in the Sixteenth and Seventeenth Centuries*. Bloomington: Indiana University Press, 1985.
———. *Spain: 1469–1714. A Society of Conflict*. Essex: Longman Inc., 1983.
———. "Toleration and Dissent in Sixteenth-Century Spain: The Alternative Tradition." *Sixteenth Century Journal* 19 (1988): 3–23.
Kennedy, Judith M. *A Critical Edition of Yong's Translation of George de Montemayor's* Diana *and Gil Polo's* Enamoured Diana. Oxford and New York: Clarendon Press, 1968.
King, Willard F. *Prosa novelística y academias literarias en el siglo 17. Boletín de la Real Academia Española*. Anejo 10. Madrid: Real Academia Española, 1963.
Lascelles, Mary. "Shakespeare's Pastoral Comedy." In *More Talking of Shakespeare*, edited by John Garrett, 70–85. New York: Longmans, Green, 1959.
Lawrance, J. N. H. "The Spread of Lay Literacy in Late Medieval Castile." *Bulletin of Hispanic Studies* 62 (1985): 79–94.
Lea, Charles Henry. *A History of Auricular Confession and Indulgences in the Latin Church*. 2 vols. Philadelphia: Lea Brothers & Co., 1896.
Leone Hebreo [Jehuda Abarbanel]. *Dialoghi d'amore*. Edited by Carl Gebhardt. Heidelburg: Carl Winters Universitätsbuchhandlung, 1929.
———. *Diálogos de amor*. Edited by José María Reyes Cano. Translated by Carlos Mazo del Castillo. Barcelona: PPU, 1986.
———. *The Philosophy of Love*. Translated by F. Friedeberg-Seely and Jean H. Barnes. Introduction by Cecil Roth. London: The Socino Press, 1937.
Lewis, C. S. *The Allegory of Love. A Study in Medieval Tradition*. 1937. Reprint. Oxford and New York: Oxford University Press, 1977.

Lindenbaum, Peter. *Changing Landscapes: Anti-Pastoral Sentiment in the English Renaissance.* Athens: University of Georgia Press, 1986.

Literature Among the Discourses: The Spanish Golden Age. Edited by Wlad Godzich and Nicholas Spadaccini. Minneapolis: University of Minnesota Press, 1986.

López Estrada, Francisco. *El Abencerraje y la hermosa Jarifa: Cuatro textos y su estudio.* Madrid: Publicaciones de la Revista de Archivos, Bibliotecas y Museos, 1957.

———. *Los libros de pastores en la literatura española.* Estudios y Ensayos 213. Madrid: Editorial Gredos, 1974.

———. *Notas sobre la espiritualidad española de los siglos de oro. Estudio del Tratado llamado El Deseoso.* Publicaciones de la Universidad de Sevilla. Anales de la Universidad Hispalense. Serie Filosofía y Letras. Núm 12 (1972).

———. *Siglos de oro: Renacimiento.* Vol. 2 of the *Historia y crítica de la literatura española,* directed by Francisco Rico. Barcelona: Editorial Crítica, 1980.

López Toro, José. "El poeta sevillano Juan de Alcalá." *Archivo Hispalense* 14 (1951): 9–28.

Luis de Granada, Fray, [trans.] *Contemptus mundi. Cōpuesto por el famoso maestro en sancta theologia Juã gerson . . .* Burgos: n.d.

———. *Guía de pecadores* [1556]. Edited by Matías Martínez Burgos. Clásicos Castellanos 97. Madrid: Espasa-Calpe, 1966.

———. *Guía de pecadores* [1567]. Edited by José María Balcells. Autores Hispánicos 119. Barcelona: Editorial Planeta, 1986.

———. *Introducción del símbolo de la fe.* Edited by José María Balcells. Libros Clásicos 158. Barcelona: Bruguera, 1984.

———. *Libro de la oración y meditación.* Vol. 2 of the *Obras de Fray Luis de Granada,* edited by Fray Justo Cuervo. Madrid: Imprenta de la Viuda e Hija de Gómez Fuentenebro, 1906.

Luis de León, Fray. *De los nombres de Cristo.* Edited by Cristóbal Cuevas García. Letras Hispánicas 59. Madrid: Cátedra, 1984.

———. *The Original Poems.* Edited by Edward Sarmiento. 1953. Reprint. Manchester: University Press, 1972.

Macpherson, Ian. "Secret Language in the *Cancioneros:* Some Courtly Codes." *Bulletin of Hispanic Studies* 62 (1985): 51–63.

Malkiel, Yakov, and Charlotte Stern. "The Etymology of Spanish *Villan-*

cico 'Carol'; Certain Literary Implications of this Etymology." *Bulletin of Hispanic Studies* 61 (1984): 137–50.

Malón de Chaide, Fray Pedro. *La conversión de la Magdalena*. Edited by P. Félix García. 3d ed. 3 vols. Madrid: Espasa-Calpe, 1959.

March, Ausias. *Poesies*. Edited by Pere Bohigas. 5 vols. Col.lecció A 71–73; 77; 86. Barcelona: Editorial Barcino, 1952–1959.

Márquez, Antonio. *Los alumbrados, orígines y filosofía (1525–1559)*. 2d ed. Madrid: Taurus, 1980.

Márquez Villanueva, Francisco. *Espiritualidad y literatura en el siglo 16*. Madrid: Alfaguara, 1968.

———. "Los joyeles de Felismena." *Revue de Littérature Comparée* 52 (1978): 267–78.

Martínez de Bujanda, Jesús. *Index des livres interdits*. 11 vols. Sherbrooke, Canada: Centre d'Études de la Renaissance, 1982–1987.

———. "Introducción." In *Lumbre del alma*, by Juan de Cazalla, 1–47. Serie A, Textos 22. Madrid: Universidad Pontífica de Salamanca, Fundación Universitaria Española, 1974.

Martins, Mario. "Uma obra inédita de Jorge de Montemayor." *Broteria* 43 (1946): 399–408.

Martz, Louis Lohr. *The Poetry of Meditation: A Study in English Religious Literature of the Seventeenth Century*. New Haven: Yale University Press, 1954.

Maylender, Michele. *Storia delle Accademie d'Italia*. 4 vols. Bologna: Licinio Cappelli, 1929.

Mele, Eugenio, and Narciso Alonso Cortés. *Sobre los amores de Gutierre de Cetina y su famoso madrigal*. Valladolid: Imprenta Provincial, 1930.

Menéndez Pelayo, Marcelino. *Historia de las ideas estéticas en España*. Vols. 1–5 of the *Edición nacional de las obras completas de Menéndez Pelayo*. 3rd ed. Madrid: Consejo Superior de Investigaciones Científicas, 1962.

———. "La novela pastoril." In *Orígenes de la novela*, edited by Enrique Sánchez Reyes, 185–346. Vol. 14 of the *Edición nacional de las obras completas de Menéndez Pelayo*. Madrid: Consejo Superior de Investigaciones Científicas, 1961.

Montalvo, Garcí Rodríguez de. *Amadís de Gaula*. Edited by Edwin B. Place. 4 vols. Madrid: Consejo Superior de Investigaciones Científicas, 1959–1969.

Montesino, Fray Ambrosio de. *Cancionero.* Valencia: Cieza, 1964.
Moreno Báez, Enrique, ed. "Prólogo." In *Los siete libros de la Diana,* by Jorge de Montemayor, IX–LV. 2d ed. Madrid: Editora Nacional, 1981.
Mujica, Barbara. "Antiutopian Elements in the Spanish Pastoral Novel." *Kentucky Romance Quarterly* 26 (1979): 263–82.

———. *Iberian Pastoral Characters.* Scripta Humanistica. Potomac, Md.: Porrua Turranzas, 1986.

———. "Violence in the Pastoral Novel from Sannazaro to Cervantes." *Hispano-Italic Studies* 1 (1976): 39–55.

Müller-Bochat, Eberhard. "Técnicas literarias y métodos de meditación en la poesía sagrada del siglo de oro." In *Actas del tercer Congreso Internacional de Hispanistas,* 611–17. Mexico: Asociación Internacional de Hispanistas, 1970.
Nalle, Sara T. "Literacy and Culture in Early Modern Castile." *Past and Present. A Journal of Historical Studies* 125 (1989): 65–96.
Navarro Gómez, José. "El autor de la versión del *Abencerraje* contenido en la *Diana,* ¿era Montemayor?" *Revista de Literatura* 39 (1978): 101–4.
Nelson, John Charles. *Renaissance Theory of Love: The Context of Giordano Bruno's Eroici Furori.* New York: Columbia University Press, 1958.
Nieto, José C. "El carácter no místico de los alumbrados de Toledo, 1509(?)–1524." In *Inquisición española y mentalidad inquisitorial.* Proceedings of the International Symposium on the Inquisition, New York, April 1983, 410–23. Barcelona: Editorial Ariel, 1984.
O'Donoghue, Bernard. *The Courtly Love Tradition.* Manchester: Manchester University Press, 1982.
Oliveira e Silva, John de. "Recurrent Onomastic Textures in the *Diana* of Jorge de Montemayor and the *Arcadia* of Sir Philip Sidney." *Studies in Philology* 79 (1982): 30–40.

———. "Sir Philip Sidney and the Castilian Tongue." *Comparative Literature* 34 (1982): 130–45.

Ortega Costa, Milagros. *Proceso de la Inquisición contra María de Cazalla.* Documentos Históricos 8. Madrid: Fundación Universitaria Española, 1978.
Osuna, Francisco de. *Tercer abecedario espiritual.* Edited by Melquíades Andrés Martín. BAC Normal 333. Madrid: Editorial Católica, 1972.

———. *The Third Spiritual Alphabet.* Translated and edited by Mary E.

Giles. Preface by Kieran Kavanaugh. New York: The Paulist Press, 1981.
Panofsky, Erwin. "Artist, Scientist, Genius: Notes on the 'Renaissance-Dämmerung'." In *The Renaissance: Six Essays*, 123–84. New York: Harper & Row, 1962.
Parker, Alexander A. *The Philosophy of Love in Spanish Literature, 1480–1680*. Edited by Terence O'Reilly. Edinburg: Edinburg University Press, 1985.
Patterson, Anabel. *Pastoral Ideology: Virgil to Valéry*. Berkeley and Los Angeles: University of California Press, 1987.
Pérez, Joseph. "Des Alumbrados aux Chuetes." *Bulletin Hispanique* 76 (1974): 503–29.
Perry, T. Anthony. *Erotic Spirituality: The Integrative Tradition from Leone Hebreo to John Donne*. Tuscaloosa: University of Alabama Press, 1980.
Pinta Llorente, Miguel de la. "Los alumbrados de Sevilla." In *Aspectos históricos del sentimiento religioso en España*, 83–117. Madrid: Consejo Superior de Investigaciones Científicas, 1961.
Pinto, Virgilio. "La censura: sistemas de control e instrumentos de acción." In *Inquisición española y mentalidad inquisitorial*. Proceedings of the International Symposium on the Inquisition, New York, April 1983, 269–87. Barcelona: Editorial Ariel, 1984.
Pliegos poéticos españoles de la Biblioteca Nacional de Lisboa. Madrid: Joyas Bibliográficas, 1975.
Ponce, Fray Bartolomé. *Primera parte de la Clara Diana a lo divino, repartida en siete libros . . . . Dirigida al prudente lector*. Zaragoza, 1599.
Ponce de la Fuente, Constantino. *Confissión de vn pecador delãte de Iesu Christo . . .* Évora, 1554.
Pozo, Cándido. *Catolicismo y protestantismo como sistemas teológicos*. Conferencias 22. Madrid: Fundación Universitaria Española, 1974.
Prieto, Antonio. *La prosa española del siglo 16*. Vol. I. Madrid: Ediciones Cátedra, 1986.
Rahner, Hugo. *Saint Ignatius Loyola: Letters to Women*. Translated by Kathleen Pond and S. A. H. Weetman. 2d ed. New York: Herder and Herder, 1960.
Randall, Dale B. J. "*The Troublesome and Hard Adventures in Love:* An

English Addition to the Bibliography of *Diana*." *Bulletin of Hispanic Studies* 38 (1961): 154-58.
Raymundus de Sabunde. *Theologia naturalis*. Venice, 1581.
Rennert, Hugo A. *The Spanish Pastoral Romances*. 1912. Reprint. New York: Biblo and Tannen, 1968.
Resina Rodrigues, María Idalina. *Fray Luis de Granada y la literatura de espiritualidad en Portugal (1554-1632)*. Serie C, Monografías 20. Madrid: Fundación Universitaria Española, 1988.
Rhodes, Elizabeth. "*La Galatea* and Cervantes' 'Tercia Realidad.'" *Cervantes*. Special Issue (1988): 17-28.
———. "Introducción a la 'Historia de Alcida y Silvano' de Jorge de Montemayor." *Dicenda: Cuadernos de Filología Hispánica* 2 (1983): 121-34.
———. Review of La Diana *of Montemayor as Social and Religious Teaching* by Bruno Damiani. *Modern Language Notes* 101 (1986): 432-34.
———. "Sixteenth-century Pastoral Books, Narrative Structure, and *La Galatea* of Cervantes." *Bulletin of Hispanic Studies* 66 (1989): 351-60.
———. "Skirting the Men: Gender Roles in Sixteenth-century Pastoral Books." *Journal of Hispanic Philology* 11 (1988): 131-49.
———. "Spain's Misfired Canon: The Case of Fray Luis de Granada's *Libro de la oración*." *Journal of Hispanic Philology* 15(1990): 3-28.
Ricciardelli, Michele. *Notas sobre* La Diana *de Montemayor y* La Arcadia *de Sannazaro*. Montevideo: Publicaciones Lingüísticas y Literarias del Instituto de Estudios Superiores de Montevideo, 1965.
———. "La novela pastoril española en relación con la *Arcadia* de Sannazaro." *Hispanófila* 28 (1966-1967): 1-7.
Rico, Francisco. *El pequeño mundo del hombre: varia fortuna de una idea en la cultura española*. 2d ed. Madrid: Alianza Editorial, 1986.
———. "Prólogo." In *Las novelas a Marcia Leonarda*, by Lope de Vega y Carpio, 7-20. Clásicos 142. Madrid: Alianza, 1968.
Riguer, Martín de. *Història de la literatura catalana*. Vol. 2. 2d ed. Barcelona: Editorial Ariel, 1990.
Riley, Edwin C. "'Romance' y novela en Cervantes." In *Cervantes, su obra y su mundo*. Proceedings of the First International Convention on Cervantes, 5-13. Madrid: EDI-6, 1981.
Robb, Nesca A. *Neoplatonism of the Italian Renaissance*. London: G. Allen & Unwin, 1935. Reprint. New York: Octagon Books, 1968.

Robinson, Lillian S. "Treason Our Text: Feminist Challenges to the Literary Canon." In *The New Feminist Criticism: Essays on Women, Literature and Theory*, edited by Elaine Showalter, 105–21. 1985. Reprint. London: Virago Press, 1986.
Rodríguez, Isaías. "Autores espirituales españoles (1500–1572)." In *Repertorio de historia de las ciencias eclesiásticas en España*, vol. 3, *Siglos 12–16*, 407–655. Salamanca: Instituto de Historia de la Teología Española, 1971.
Rodríguez-Moñino, Antonio. "El cancionero de Pedro del Pozo." *Boletín de la Real Academia Española* 29 (1949): 453–509.
———. *Manual bibliográfico de cancioneros y romanceros impresos durante el siglo 17*. 2 vols. Madrid: Editorial Castalia, 1977.
Rojas, Fernando de. *La Celestina: Tragicomedia de Calisto y Melibea*. Edited by Dorothy Severin. Introduction by Stephen Gilman. 4th ed. Clásicos 200. Madrid: Alianza Editorial, 1976.
Ros, Fidel de. "Los místicos del norte y Fray Luis de Granada." *Archivo Ibero-americano*. 2a época. 25; 26–28 (1947): 5–30; 145–65.
Rosand, David. "Giorgione, Venice and the Pastoral Vision." In *Places of Delight: The Pastoral Landscape*, 20–81. New York: Clarkson N. Potter, 1988.
Ross, Malcolm MacKenzie. *Poetry and Dogma: The Transfiguration of Eucharistic Symbols in Seventeenth Century English Poetry*. New Brunswick: Rutgers University Press, 1954.
Sâ de Miranda, Francisco de. *Poesias*. Edited by Carolina Michaëlis de Vasconcelos. Halle: Max Niemeyer, 1885.
Sainz Rodríguez, Pedro. *Antología de la literatura espiritual española (Edad Media, Siglo 16)*. Colección Espirituales Españoles, Serie A, Textos, vols. 28–30. Madrid: Universidad Pontífica de Salamanca y Fundación Universitaria Española, 1980–1984.
———. *La siembra mística del Cardenal Cisneros y las reformas en la Iglesia*. Colección Espirituales Españoles, Serie C, Monografías vol. 8. Madrid: Universidad Pontífica de Salamanca y Fundación Universitaria Española, 1979.
Sala Balust, Luis. "La espiritualidad española en la primera mitad del siglo 16." In *Cuadernos de Historia: El tránsito de la Edad Media al Renacimiento*, 167–87. Anexos de la revista *Hispania* del Instituto "Zorita" del CSIC, 1. Madrid: Consejo Superior de Investigaciones Científicas, 1967.

―――. "Introducción." In *Avisos y reglas cristianas sobre aquel verso de David: Audi filia*, by Juan de Ávila, 3–80. Espirituales Españoles, Serie A, Textos 10. Barcelona: Juan Flors, 1963.

Saldoni, Baltasar. *Diccionario biográfico-bibliográfico de efemérides de músicos españoles*. 2 vols. Barcelona: I. Torres, 1890.

Sánchez Arce, Nellie E. *Las glosas a las "Coplas" de Jorge Manrique*. Madrid: Sancha, 1956.

Sánchez de Lima, Miguel. *El arte poética en romance castellano*. Edited by Rafael de Balbín Lucas. Biblioteca de Antiguos Libros Hispánicos, Serie A, Vol. 3. Madrid: Consejo Superior de Investigaciones Científicas, 1944.

Sannazaro, Jacopo. *Arcadia*. Intro. Francisco López Estrada. Valencia: Cieza, 1966. [Facsimile edition of the 1547 Spanish translation.]

San Pedro, Diego de. *Cárcel de amor*. Vol. 2 of the *Obras completas*, edited by Keith Whinnom. Clásicos Castalia 40. Madrid: Castalia, 1971.

Scholes, Robert. *Protocols of Reading*. New Haven and London: Yale University Press, 1989.

―――. "Towards a Poetics of Fiction: An Approach through Genre." *Novel* 2 (1969): 101–11.

Selke, Angela. "El iluminismo de los conversos y la Inquisición. Cristianismo interior de los alumbrados: resentimiento y sublimación." In *La Inquisición española. Nueva visión, nuevos horizontes*. Proceedings of the First International Symposium on the Spanish Inquisition, Cuenca, Sept. 1978, edited by Joaquín Pérez Villanueva, 617–36. Madrid: Siglo XXI, 1980.

Sicroff, Albert A. *Los estatutos de limpieza de sangre: Controversias entre los siglos 15 y 17*. Madrid: Taurus, 1985.

Sidney, Sir Philip. *The Countess of Pembroke's Arcadia (The Old Arcadia)*. Edited by Jean Robertson. Oxford and New York: Oxford University Press, 1973.

Smith, Hilary. *Preaching in the Spanish Golden Age: A Study of Some Preachers of the Reign of Philip III*. Oxford and New York: Oxford University Press, 1978.

Smith, Juston. "Judaism." In *The Religions of Man*, 254–300. 1958. Reprint. New York: Harper & Row, 1965.

Solé-Leris, Amadeu. *The Spanish Pastoral Novel*. TWAS 575. Boston: Twayne Publishers, 1980.

———. "The Theory of Love in the Two *Dianas:* A Contrast." *Bulletin of Hispanic Studies* 36 (1959): 65-79.

Soria Olmedo, Andrés. *Los* Dialoghi d'amore *de León Hebreo: Aspectos literarios y culturales.* Granada: Universidad de Granada, 1984.

Soufas, Teresa Scott. *Melancholy and the Secular Mind in Spanish Golden Age Literature.* Columbia and London: University of Missouri Press, 1990.

Subirats, Jean. "La 'Diana' de Montemayor, roman à clef?" In *Etudes Ibériques et Latino-Américaines,* Fourth Convention of French Hispanists, 105-19. Paris: Presses Universitaires de France, 1968.

Surtz, Ronald E. *The Guitar of God: Gender, Power, and Authority in the Visionary World of Mother Juana de la Cruz (1481-1534).* Philadelphia: University of Pennsylvania Press, 1990.

Swietlicki, Catherine. *Spanish Christian Cabala: The Works of Luis de León, Santa Teresa de Jesús, and San Juan de la Cruz.* Columbia and London: University of Missouri Press, 1986.

Tayler, Edward William. *Nature and Art in Renaissance Literature.* New York: Columbia University Press, 1964.

Tellechea Idigoras, José Ignacio. *El catecismo del Arzobispo Carranza.* Madrid: Fundación Universitaria Española, 1972.

Teresa of Avila, Saint. *Libro de la vida.* In *Obras completas,* edited by Efrén de la Madre de Dios and Otger Steggink, 3-232. 8th ed. BAC Normal 212. Madrid: Editorial Católica, 1986.

———. *Moradas del castillo interior.* In *Obras completas,* edited by Efrén de la Madre de Dios and Otger Steggink, 469-583. 8th ed. BAC Normal 212. Madrid: Editorial Católica, 1986.

Tillier, Jane. "Passion Poetry in the *Cancioneros.*" *Bulletin of Hispanic Studies* 62 (1985): 65-78.

Timoneda, Joan. *El Patrañuelo.* Edited by José Romera Castillo. Letras Hispánicas 94. Madrid: Ediciones Cátedra, 1978.

Todorov, Tzvetan. *The Fantastic: A Structural Approach to a Literary Genre.* Translated by Richard Howard. 1973. Reprint. Ithaca: Cornell University Press, 1975.

Tompkins, Jane P. "Sentimental Power: *Uncle Tom's Cabin* and the Politics of Literary History." In *The New Feminist Criticism: Essays on Women, Literature and Theory,* edited by Elaine Showalter, 81-104. 1985. Reprint. London: Virago Press, 1986.

Torquemada, Antonio de. *Jardín de flores curiosas.* Edited by Giovanni Allegra. Clásicos Castalia 129. Madrid: Editorial Castalia, 1982.

Trasmiera, Francisco de. *Vida y excelencias de la ... Virgen.* Valladolid, 1547.

Underhill, Evelyn. *Mysticism: A Study in the Nature and Development of Man's Spiritual Consciousness.* 1955. Reprint. New York: Meridian, 1974.

Várvaro, Alberto. *Literatura románica de la Edad Media: Estructuras y formas.* Translated by Lola Badía and Carlos Alvar. Barcelona: Editorial Ariel, 1983.

Vasconcelos, Carolina Michaëlis de. *A Infanta D. Maria de Portugal (1521–1577) e as suas damas.* Lisbon: Biblioteca Nacional, 1983.

Vega y Carpio, Lope de. *Arcadia.* Edited by Edwin S. Morby. Clásicos Castalia 63. Madrid: Castalia, 1975.

———. *Poesía selecta.* Edited by Antonio Carreño. Letras Hispánicas 187. Madrid: Cátedra, 1984.

Vicente, Gil. *Tragicomedia de Don Duardos.* Edited by Dámaso Alonso. Madrid: Consejo Superior de Investigaciones Científicas, 1942.

Vives, Juan Luis. *Instrucción de la mujer cristiana.* Colección Austral 138. Buenos Aires: Espasa-Calpe Argentina, 1940.

Wallis, Rutherford Theopilus. *Neoplatonism.* New York: Charles Scribner's, 1972.

Walsh, John K. *El Coloquio de la Memoria, la Voluntad y el Entendimiento (Biblioteca Universitaria de Salamanca ms. 1.763) y otras manifestaciones del tema en la literatura española.* Pliegos Hispánicos 3. New York: Lorenzo Clemente, 1986.

Wardropper, Bruce, ed. "The *Diana* of Montemayor: Revaluation and Interpretation." *Studies in Philology* 48 (1951): 126–44.

———. "'Don Quixote': Story or History?" *Modern Philology* 63 (1965): 1–11.

———. "Fictional Prose, History and Drama: Pedro de Urdemalas." In *Essays on Narrative Fiction in the Iberian Peninsula in Honor of Frank Pierce,* edited by R. B. Tate, 212–27. Oxford: Dolphin Book Co., 1982.

———. *Historia de la poesía lírica a lo divino en la cristiandad occidental.* Madrid: Revista de Occidente, 1958.

———. "La poesía religiosa del Siglo de Oro." *Edad de Oro* 4 (1985): 195–209.

———, ed. *Cancionero espiritual (Valladolid 1549)*. Valencia: Editorial Castalia, 1954.
Warner, Marina. *Alone of All Her Sex: The Myth and the Cult of the Virgin Mary.* 1976. Reprint. New York: Vintage Books, 1983.
Watt, Ian. *The Rise of the Novel: Studies in Defoe, Richardson and Fielding.* Berkeley: University of California Press, 1957.
Weber, Alison. *Teresa of Avila and the Rhetoric of Femininity.* Princeton: Princeton University Press, 1990.
Weiner, Andrew D. *Sir Philip Sidney and the Poetics of Protestantism: A Study of Contexts.* Minneapolis: University of Minnesota Press, 1978.
Weitz, Margaret Collins. "François de Belleforest's *La Pyrénée*: The First French Pastoral Novel." *Renaissance Quarterly* 31 (1978): 322–30.
Whinnom, Keith. "Hacia una interpretación y apreciación de las canciones del *Cancionero general* de 1511." *Filología* 13 (1968–69): 361–81.
———. "El origen de las composiciones religiosas del Siglo de Oro: Mendoza, Montesino y Román." *Revista de Filología Española* 46 (1963): 263–85.
———. *La poesía amatoria de la época de los Reyes Católicos.* Durham Modern Languages Series, Hispanic Monographs 2. Durham: Duke University Press, 1981.
———. "The Problem of the 'Best-seller' in Spanish Golden-Age Literature." *Bulletin of Hispanic Studies* 57 (1980): 189–98.
———. "The Supposed Sources of Inspiration of Spanish Fifteenth-century Narrative Religious Verse." *Symposium* 17 (1963): 268–91.
Williams, John D. "The Savage in Sixteenth-century Spanish Prose Fiction." *Kentucky Foreign Language Quarterly* 3 (1956): 4–46.
Wilson, Edward. "Spanish and English Religious Poetry of the Seventeenth Century." *Journal of Ecclesiastical History* 9 (1958): 38–53.
Wind, Edgar. *Pagan Mysteries in the Renaissance.* London: Faber and Faber, 1958.
Young, R. V. *Richard Crashaw and the Spanish Golden Age.* Yale Studies in English 191. New Haven: Yale University Press, 1982.
Zayas y Sotomayor, María de. *Parte segunda del Sarao y entretenimiento honesto [Desengaños amorosos].* Edited by Alicia Yllera. Letras Hispánicas 179. Madrid: Ediciones Cátedra, 1983.
Zimmerman, T. C. "Confession and Autobiography in the Early Renaissance." In *Renaissance Studies in Honor of Hans Baron*, edited by Anthony Molho and John A. Tedeschi, 119–40. University, Ill.: University Press, 1971.

INDEX

Affective piety: 15, 92; isolation for, 102; symbols of, 115
Alba, duke of: on Portuguese religious affairs, 45
"Alcalá, Juan de." *See* "Juan de Alcalá"
Allegory: in pastoral literature, 112-14; in the *Diana*, 131
Alpers, Paul: analysis of pastoral mode by, 111
Alumbrados (illuminists): 1524 Franciscan decree against, 55, 56
Alvaro de Zamora, Fray: importance of, to reform, 50
Andrés Martín, Melquíades, 4; on origin of recogimiento, 55
Anti-Semitism: in Montemayor's works, 38
Arcadia (Vega y Carpio), 14
Arcadia (Sidney), 64, 122-24
Arcadia (Sannazaro), 112
Audi, filia (Juan de Ávila): publication of, 61; *Index*, appearance in, 61
Augustine: *Confessions*, 31
Aurelius, Marcus, 222
Auto de fe: 1558, 27
Avalle-Arce, Juan Bautista: on transformation of the pastoral, 122, 139, 158, 174, 190
Ávila, San Juan de. *See* Juan de Ávila, San

Bataillon, Marcel: *Erasmo y España*, 5, 26, 57, 64, 70, 77
Belleforest, François, 21
Beltrán de Heredia, Vincente, 47
Bembo, Pietro: *The Courtier*, 177
Blecula, Alberto, 14
Bonaventure, Saint, 117
Borja, Francisco de: as Catholic reformer, 26; influence of, on Princess Juana, 26; canonization of, 27; flight from Spain of, 27
Boscán Almugáver, Juan: as precursor to Montemayor, 35; *Soneto 78*, 225
Burke, Kenneth: theory of representative anecdote by, 111
Bynum, Carolyn Walker: on medieval female piety, 86

Cancionero (Montesino), 38

Cancionero espiritual (Pozo), 28
Cancionero (songbook) lyrics: in Montemayor's poetry, 10
Cano, Melchor: as censor of Luis de Granada, 60; as Bartolomé Carranza's convictor, 62; as censor of Carranza's *Catechismo*, 73
Cárcel de amor (San Pedro), 114, 148n9
Carranza de Miranda, Bartolomé, 68; persecution of, by Inquisition, 32, 33, 62; *Comentariós sobre el catechismo christiano*, 62, 73; as recogido, 72-73; on union with the divine, 96
Carreño, Antonio, 14
Cascardi, Anthony: on stability, 204
Castidad: definition of, 172
Castiglione, Baldassare: *Il libro del cortegiano*, 170
Castro, Américo: on development of pastoral character, 135, 137
Catholicism. *See* Religion
Cervantes, Miguel de: *El coloquio de los perros*, 109-10; puncturing of the pastoral myth by, 109-10; the *Galatea*, 112, 120, 129, 226-27; *Don Quijote*, 192-93; criticism of Montemayor, 192-93; *Los trabajos de Persiles y Sigismunda*, 222
Cetina, Gutierre de, 49
Chaide, Fray Malónde: as critic of the *Diana*, 20
Characters, pastoral: definition of, 110; representative nature of, 110-38
Charitas (essence of love): in Catholic ideology, 83; elimination of, in Montemayor's work, 182
Cisneros, Francisco Jiminez de: as leader of Spanish Catholic reform, 38, 51-54; patrons of, 50; as founder of University of Alcalá, 51; publication of treatises by, 63; as target of the *Index*, 63
Clara Diana a lo divino (Ponce), 20
Climacus, St. John, 67, 98; canonization of, 47; *Scala paradisi*, 47, 90-91, 165
Comentariós sobre el catechismo christiano (Carranza de Miranda), 62, 73
Confessions (Augustine), 31
Contemptus mundi: translation of, by Luis de Granada, 80-81

Conversion: by decree, 22; and statutes of pure blood, 35
Conversos, 27–28, 57; converts from Judaism, 22; majority of illuminists, 57
"Coplas," gloss of, 28, 79, 342
"Coplas que fizo a la muerte de su padre" (Manrique), 25, 69
Cortest, Luis: on bias toward Erasmism, 14–15
Council of Trent, 62
Courtier, The (Bembo), 177
Creel, Bryant L.: on the *Diana* as erotic-sentimental literature, 11
Crema, Fray Baptista de, 72
Cruz, Fray Luis de la. *See* Luis de la Cruz, Fray.
Cruz, San Juan de la. *See* Juan de la Cruz, San

De los nombres de Cristo (Luis de León), 30
Dialoghi d'amore (Leone Hebreo), 174–87
"Diálogo Spiritual," 28–29, 67; and dedication to King João, 25; rejection of humanism in, 54; as prose exposition of Catholic doctrine, 89–91; form of, 92, 165, 225
Diana, the: popularity of, 1, 139, 140, 222; relationship of, to Montemayor's religious writings, 3–4, 215–32; rejection of humanism in, 3, 5; as pastoral narration, 3, 128, 139, 208; relationship of, to the modern novel, 8; as culmination, 34; influence of culture on, 45, 142, 173; influence of religion on, 50, 109–38, 165, 215; recogido influence in, 77, 116–26, 136, 137, 138, 167, 216, 220, 230, 231; idealization in, 120–21, 135, 227, 229; as ideological instruction, 121; prose and verse in, 126–27; time in, 126–28, 130–31, 136, 192, 219, 220, 227, 232; structure of, 126–38, 140, 141; narrative planes in, 128–38; the *Galatea* as imitation of, 129; point of view in, 129, 216; allegory in, 131; *locus amoenus* in, 168, 169, 189, 193, 196, 198, 199, 200, 202, 204, 205, 213, 227; dream sleep in, 189, 190; disillusion in, 206, 212, 213; male/female interchange in, 212; rejection of Neoplatonism in, 224–32
—characters: relationships of, 10–12, 132–33, 134, 172; typical of pastorals, 110; motivation of, 116; shifting identities of, 133; introduction of, 141; Montemayor as Sireno, 142; Selvagia's story, 143–46; Felismena's story, 148–53, 205; Belisa's story, 154, 175; Felicia's story, 161–63; abulia of, 169; Sylvano's story, 170; Sireno's story, 174; Jarifa's story, 188; Arsileo's story, 193–94; Diana's story, 195–96; Amarilida's story, 200
—themes, 5–6; love, 10–12, 40, 113, 115, 116, 118, 120, 126, 127, 132, 133, 163, 165, 169, 174, 175, 182, 183, 217, 219, 224, 229–32; sentimentality, 10–11, 216–17, 232; spirituality, 18, 113; betrayal, 38, 120, 173, 176, 191, 208, 228–29; suffering, 113, 125, 131, 168, 169, 213, 214, 222, 225, 226, 227, 229; destiny, 135–38, 156, 190, 217–19, 221, 222, 223, 228–29; nobility, 178, 214; virtue, 203, 209
Diana enamorada (Gil Polo), 121
Dias, José Sebastiao da Silva: on history of reformation, 50
"Dios puso en hombre su nombre," 28
DiSalvo, Anjelo J., 13
Dominicans: reformists among, 46; spirituality of, 47
Don Quijote (Cervantes), 144, 192–93
Dupont, Jean, 29

Eclogues (Virgil), 112
Ejercicios espirituales (Loyola), 53
El arte poética en romance castellano (Sanchez de Lima), 24
El coloquio de los perros (Cervantes), 109–10
Enchiridion (Erasmus), 70, 168; the devil in, 88
Encina, Juan de, 30
Enrique de Portugal, Cardinal, 26
"Epistola a Sâ": Montemayor to Francisco de Sâ de Miranda, 23
Erasmism: critical bias toward, 14, 15; as perceived by reformers, 59
Erasmists, 5, 85; motto of, 65
Erasmo y España (Bataillon), 5, 57
Erasmus, Desiderius (of Rotterdam): *Enchiridion*, 70
Espinosa, Pedro: on Montemayor's military career, 24
Ettin, Andrew: on feminism and pastoral literature, 17
Experentia fallax (flawed human experience), 73; in love, 181–82

Felipe II (of Spain), 25
Feminism: and pastoral literature, 17–19
Fuego de amor (fire of love): in mystical literature, 31

Galatea, the (Cervantes), 21; as pastoral,

112; love in, 120; as imitation of the *Diana*, 129; Neoplatonism in, 226–27
Gil Polo, Gaspar de: *Diana enamorada*, 121
Godzich, Wlad: *Literature Among Discourses: The Spanish Golden Age*, 6
Golden Age literature: approaches to, 6, 8; role of devotional writing in, 7; modern understanding of, 8; sentimentality in, 9; connection of, to British metaphysical poetry, 15–16; influence of medieval themes on, 28, 184; love in, 169, 184
Googe, Barnabe, 21, 151n11
Granada, Fray Luis de. *See* Luis de Granada, Fray
Guevara, Fray Antonio de, 222

Hazañas y la Rua, Joaquín: on Montemayor's death, 24
Hebreo, Leone. *See* Leone Hebreo, Jehunda Abarbanell
Heilbrun, Carolyn G.: on endings, 232
Herrera, Fernando de: formula for pastoral by, 110
Historia de Alcida y Silvano, 31
Historia y crítica de la literatura española (López Estrada), 7
Humanism: in the Renaissance, 3; rejection of, in the *Diana*, 3, 5; overemphasis of, 5, 8; and classicism, 6; rejection of, in Montemayor's works, 30, 54; ideology of, 35, 72, 183; adherents of, 72
Humility, 124; symbols of, 115
Hurtado de Mendoza, Juan, 46

Il libro del cortegiano (Castiglione), 170
Illuminism, 53, 59, 85
Index (of prohibited works), 25, 27, 62, 63; and Fernando de Valdés, 27, 32, 57; Montemayor's works in, 32–33
Inquisition, the, 13, 33, 37, 49, 52; threat to conversos by, 22; Fernando de Valdés's role in, 27, 32, 57; persecution of authors by, 27–28, 32–33, 62, 63; censorship of Montemayor by, 32–33; evaluation of piety by, 60
Isabel, Empress, 45
Isabel la Católica, Queen, 23

Jerome, Saint, 117
Jesuit order, 27; admission of Princess Juana to, 25
Jew(s): identification of Montemayor as, 22, 23; forced conversion of, 22, 35; exile of, 179n41
João III, King (Portugal), 25

John, Saint. *See* Climacus, St. John
Jones, Royston: *A Literary History of Spain*, 7
Juana, Princess: Jesuit vows of, 25; as protectress of reformers, 25; as Montemayor's employer, 25–26; as "Mateo Sanchez," 26; and *auto de fe*, 27
"Juan de Alcalá": on Montemayor as Jew, 22
Juan de Ávila, San: as converso, 57; *Audi, filia*, 61; and the Inquisition, 61; on salvation, 87, 88; on recogido meditation, 117
Juan de la Cruz, San, 8, 73

"La pasión de Cristo," 31, 83
León, Fray Luis de. *See* Luis de León, Fray
Leone Hebreo, Jehunda Abarbanell: *Dialoghi d'amore*, 174–87; as exiled Jew, 179n41; on nature of beauty, 184–85; on eternal love, 229–30
Liber creaturarum or *Theologia naturalis* (Raymundus de Sabunde), 72
Libro de la oración (Luis de Granada), 118; suffering in, 47–49; recogimiento in, 57, 70–73, 86–87
Literary History of Spain, A (Jones), 7
Literature Among Discourses: The Spanish Golden Age (Godzich and Spadaccini), 6
Locus amoenus: in pastoral literature, 110, 112, 114, 117, 122, 123, 132, 133; in the *Diana*, 168, 169, 189, 193, 196, 198, 199, 200, 202, 204, 205, 213, 227
Lombard, Peter, 91; *Sententiae*, 47, 92
Lope de Vega y Carpio. *See* Vega y Carpio, Lope de
López Estrada, Francisco, 54; *Historia y crítica de la literatura española*, 7; on secular spirituality, 13–14; on waters of forgetfulness, 190
Los siete libros de la Diana. *See Diana*, the
Los trabajos de Persiles y Sigismuna (Cervantes), 222
Love: in the *Diana*, 10–12, 40, 113, 115, 116, 118, 120, 126, 127, 132, 133, 163, 165, 169, 174, 175, 182, 183, 217, 219, 224, 229–32; as transcendence, 11; betrayal of, 11–12; Montemayor's fascination with, 24; suffering as objective of, 87; in the *Galatea*, 120; in pastoral literature, 120, 121, 125, 126; in Golden Age literature, 169, 184; Racine on, 202; eternal love, 229–30
Loyola, San Ignacio de: *Ejercicios espirituales*, 53
Luis de Granada, Fray, 1, 15, 67, 68, 74, 167; as leading reformist, 27, 46; *Libro de*

la oración, 47–49, 57, 70–73, 86–87, 118; connection of, to Montemayor, 50; censoring of, by Cano, 60; on God's presence, 80–81; translation of *Contemptus mundi*, 80–81; on recogido meditation, 117
Luis de la Cruz, Fray, 74
Luis de León, Fray, 8, 184; *De los nombres de Cristo*, 30
Luther, Martin, 53, 59
Lutheranism, 54, 59

Manrique, Jorge, 34; "Coplas que fizo a la muerte de su padre," 25, 69
March, Ausias, 33, 231
María, Princess (Portugal), 25, 26
Martins, Mario, 54
Mártires, Bartolomeu dos, Archibishop (Portugal), 46
"Missus est angelus," exposition on, 39
Modal theory: as base of pastoral, 5
Montemayor, Jorge de: origins of, 21–22, 24; conversion of, 21, 171n31; death of, 24; as soldier, 24; as courtier, 25, 26, 49; and the Inquisition, 27, 32–33, 118; as reformist, 28; aspirations to nobility of, 35, 36–37; precursors of, 54; influence of religion on, 91
—works: intentions in, 1; idealization in, 12; influence of religion, 8, 26, 29, 30–31, 33, 34, 42, 46, 49, 82, 107, 215–16; themes of, 9, 28, 31, 33, 40, 41, 89, 103, 118, 186–88; "Epístola a Sâ," 23; "Diálogo spiritual," 25, 28–29, 54, 67, 89–92, 165, 225; *Obras*, 26, 29, 118; "Dios puso en hombre su nombre," 28; gloss of "Coplas," 28, 79, 342; rejection of humanism in, 30, 54; cancionero lyrics in, 31; *Historia de Alcida y Silvano*, 31; "La pasión de Cristo," 31, 83; *Segundo cancionero*, 31, 141–42; *Segundo cancionero spiritual*, 31–32, 89, 106; sentimentality in, 32; connection of religious and secular, 34, 35, 108–9, 113–14, 215–32; anti-Semitism in, 38; exposition on "Missus est angelus," 39; didactic posture of, 39–44; "Regimiento de principes," 40; *Super flumina Babylonis*, 68, 69, 104; free will in, 79–80. *See Diana, the*
Montesino, Fray Ambrosio de: *Cancionero*, 38
Moradas de castillo interior (Santa Teresa), 73

Naharro, Torres, 30
Nebrija, Antonio de, 58

Neoplatonism: rejection of, in the *Diana*, 5, 174–87, 224–32; ideology of, 35, 167, 174, 184; adherents of, 72, 99, 225; Hebreo's vision of, 175–87; in the *Galatea*, 226–27
Nobility: in Montemayor's characters, 11; aspirations to nobility of Montemayor, 35, 36–37; in pastoral literature, 115, 178, 214; in the *Diana*, 122–24, 170, 171

Obras, 26, 29, 118
Orpheus, 171, 172
Osuna, Francisco de: as recogido leader, 52; *Tercer abecedario espiritual*, 52, 73, 98

Pacheco, Fray Miguel, 27
Parker, Alexander, 13
Passion, the: poetry of, 38; in recogimiento, 85–88
Paston, Edward, 21
Pastoral literature: critical approaches to, 9, 16; spirituality in, 15, 123, 124, 126; and the Peace Movement (1960s), 16; feminist theories on, 17–19; recogido meditation in, 17–18, 115, 116, 117, 118; popularity of, 18, 116, 124, 125; importance of the past to, 108, 118; religious influences on, 108–9; subjective experience in, 108–9, 112–13, 114; universality of, 109, 111; versions of, 110; *locus amoenus* in, 110, 112, 114, 117, 122, 123, 132, 133; psychic reality in, 110–13; characters in, 110–26, 116–38; motivation of characters in, 110–38; representative anecdote in, 111; allegory in, 112–14; violence in, 112, 114; Montemayor's adaptations of, 113; sentimentality in, 113, 212–22; heroic ideal in, 113, 114, 122–23; unmet need for resolution in, 114–15; nobility in, 115, 122–24, 170, 171; humility in, 115, 124; connection of religious literature to, 117; love in, 120, 121, 125, 126; English pastoral literature, 124; influence of recogido piety, 125, 131–32; tradition of verse in, 127; religious themes in, 131–32; advance of character portrayal in, 135; influence of Catholic reformism on, 137
Pastores de Belén (Vega y Carpio), 14
"Pastor que con tus silbos amorosos" (Vega y Carpio), 30
Plato, 5, 184, 185
Point of view: in the *Diana*, 129, 216
Ponce, Fray Bartolomé: *Clara Diana a lo divino*, 20; on Montemayor's writing, 24, 36; on idleness, 119

Index 259

Ponce de la Fuente, Constantino, 27–28
Pozo, Pedro del: *Cancionero espiritual,* 28
"Problem of the Best-Seller in Golden-Age Spanish Literature, The" (Whinnom), 4
Protocols of Reading (Scholes), 46

Racine: on love/hatred, 202
Raymundus de Sabunde: *Theologia naturalis* or *Liber creaturarum,* 72; as Neoplatonist, 225
Recogerse: definition of, 68
Recogido meditation: in pastoral literature, 17–18, 115, 116, 117, 118; Juan de Ávila on, 117; Luis de Granada on, 117
Recogido piety: history of, 2, 4, 50; influence of, in the *Diana,* 77, 116–26, 136, 137, 138, 167, 216, 220, 230, 231; and pain, 85; relationship with God in, 86, 99; the devil in, 88; influence of, on Montemayor's works, 116–26; influence of, in pastoral literature, 125, 131–32; and human condition, 147
Recogimiento: practice of, 2, 4, 53, 64–65, 68; adherents of, 50, 72–73, 74; origin of, 55, 61; in Granada's works, 57, 70–73, 86–87; philosophy of, 73, 75, 76; vision of, 76; happiness through death in, 209
Reform, Spanish Catholic, 32, 45, 50; influence of, on secular literature, 3; role of recogidos in, 4; proponents of, 27, 55; influence from other countries on, 51; and pre-reform, 51; Cisneros and, 51–53; role of faith in, 51, 70–71; tenets of, 52, 59, 64, 67, 69, 106, 186; and counter-reformation, 61; Socrates and, 77; Montemayor's views on, 90, 103, 163. *See also* Erasmism; Illuminism; Recogimiento
Reform, Tridentine, 52
"Regimiento de principes," 40
Religion: importance of, in Golden Age culture, 2, 4; influence of, on Montemayor's works, 8, 26, 29, 30–31, 33, 34, 42, 46, 49, 82, 107, 215–16; influence of, on secular literature, 12–16, 18; influence of, on the *Diana,* 50, 109–38, 165, 215; influence of, on pastoral literature, 108–9
Rembrandt [Harmenszoon van Rijn]: pastoral portrait by, 21
Rennert, Hugh: on sentimentality in literature, 9
Ross, Malcolm MacKenzie, 226

Sala Balust, Luis, 4; on history of reform, 50; on Juan de Ávila, 61
Saldoni, Baltasar: on Montemayor's birth, 21

Sanchez de Lima, Miguel: *El arte poética en romance castellano,* 24
Sannazaro, Jacopo de: *Arcadia,* 112
San Pedro, Diego de: *Cárcel de amor,* 114, 148*n*9
Savonarola, Girolamo, 64, 84
Scala paradisi (Climacus), 47, 90–91, 165
Scholes, Robert: reading theories of, 1, 2; *Protocols of Reading,* 46
Segundo cancionero, 31, 141–42
Segundo cancionero spiritual, 31–32, 89, 106
Sententiae (Lombard), 47, 92
Sentimentality: in Golden Age literature, 9; in Montemayor's works, 11, 32; in the *Diana,* 10–11, 216–17, 232; in Spanish religiousness, 52; in pastoral literature, 113, 121–22
Sessa, duke of, 36, 175
Shakespeare, William, 21
Sidney, Sir Philip, 21; *Arcadia,* 64, 122–24
works of, 64
Silva, Juan de, 25
Silvestre, Gregorio, 33, 35
Socrates, 77
Soneto 78 (Boscán Almugáver), 225
Spadaccini, Nicholas: *Literature Among Discourses: The Spanish Golden Age,* 6
Spirituality: López Estrada on, 13–14; in pastoral literature, 15, 123, 124, 126; in the *Diana,* 18, 113
Statutes of pure blood, 35. *See also* Conversion; Conversos; Jew(s)
Suffering: as objective of love, 87; in the *Diana,* 113, 125, 131, 168, 169, 213, 214, 222, 225, 226, 227, 229
Summa theologica (Saint Thomas), 62
Super flumina Babylonis (interpretation of Ps. 137), 68, 69, 104
Symbols: of humility, 115; of recogido asceticism, 115

Taylor, Edward William: on pastoral as meditation, 17–18
Tercer abecedario espiritual (Osuna), 52, 73, 98
Teresa de Jesús, Santa, 8, 52; *Moradas de castillo interior,* 73
Theocritus, 5
Theologia naturalis or *Liber creaturarum* (Raymundus de Sabunde), 72
Thomas, Saint: *Summa theologica,* 62
Time: in pastoral literature, 108, 118; in the

Diana, 126–28, 130–31, 136, 192, 219, 220, 227, 232
Trattati d'amore (treatises), 177
Troublesome and Hard Adventures in Love, The (anonymous), 21
University of Alcalá de Henares: as center of theological study, 92
Urfé, Honoré d', 64

Valdés, Fernando de (Inquisitor General): and *Index*, 27, 32, 57
Válvaro, Alberto, 74
Vasconcelos, Michaëlis de, 26
Vega y Carpio, Lope de: *Arcadia*, 14; *Pastores de Belén*, 14; "Pastor que con tus silbos amorosos," 30

Vincente, Gil, 30
Virgil, 25; *Eclogues*, 112

Wardropper, Bruce, 28; sexuality in *Diana*, 152
Watt, Ian: on patterns in literature, 139
Weiner, Andrew: on modern perspectives, 64
Whinnom, Keith, 8; "The Problem of the Best-Seller in Golden-Age Spanish Literature," 4
Wilson, Edward, 52
Wilson, Thomas, 21

Zamora, Fray Alvaro de. *See* Alvaro de Zamora, Fray